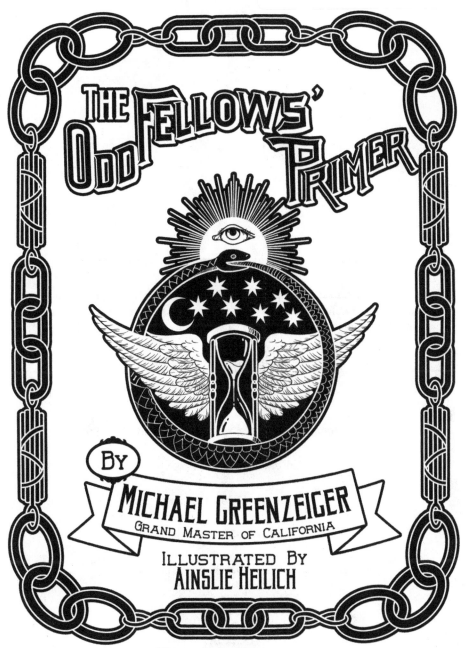

# The Odd Fellows' Primer

By

## MICHAEL GREENZEIGER
GRAND MASTER OF CALIFORNIA

ILLUSTRATED BY
AINSLIE HEILICH

FIRST EDITION

First Edition: August 2021

First Printing

Illustrations copyright © 2021 by Ainslie Heilich

Edited by Scott Moye

Layout by Lisa Connery

ISBN 978-0-578-93857-8 (hardcover)

ISBN 978-0-578-93860-8 (paperback)

Published by the Heart in Hand Institute

Tuscola, IL

LADDER AND RECORD OF

# ODD FELLOW ACHIEVEMENTS

Sovereign Grand Master: _____

Sovereign Grand
Lodge Officer: _____

Grand Representative: _____

### Enter the Sovereign Grand Lodge

Grand Master: _____

Grand Lodge Officer: _____

District Deputy
Grand Master: _____

### Enter the Grand Lodge

Noble Grand: _____

Lodge Officer: _____

Third Degree: _____

Second Degree: _____

First Degree: _____

Initiatory Degree: _____

Name: _____ Lodge: _____

# DEDICATION

To the incomparable James L. Ridgely (1807–1881) who built
the edifice of American Odd Fellowship, having served as
Grand Secretary from 1840 to 1881 and having made unparalleled
contributions to the laws, ritual, and literature of the Order

# AUTHOR ACKNOWLEDGEMENTS

To Erik Meyer-Curley and James Goode who first invited me to join the Odd Fellows; to Desmond Reeves Jr., PGP and Ronald Pynn Jr., PGP who taught me what Odd Fellowship is all about and supported me in becoming a leader in the lodge; to Gerard Gilmore Jr., PGM who placed his trust in me as Grand Herald of Massachusetts and brought me into the world of Grand Lodges; and to B. Scott McInnes who gave me my very first copy of the **Improved Odd Fellows Manual**, thank you all for starting me on the journey to write this book.

To Donald Lang, PGM, who made me feel welcome in the Jurisdiction of California and has given me advice of inestimable value on my path to becoming Grand Master; to Dr. Mel Astrahan, PGM, who placed his confidence in me as Grand Instructor of California; to Dave Reed, PGM, who sponsored me as Grand Master of California; to Barry Prock, PGM, who has always reminded me to keep the "Good of the Order" in mind and advised me on countless matters, large and small; and to James Jepsen Jr., PGM, and Greg Schomaker, PGM who were a pleasure to work with during my terms as Grand Warden and Deputy Grand Master; to Jimmy Humphrey, PSGM, who believed in me and guided me as I began to work with Sovereign Grand Lodge, thank you all for helping me to continue to grow in my service to the Order in California and beyond.

To the excellent slate of appointed officers I am looking forward to sharing my travels with: Grand Marshal Sasha St. John, Grand Conductor Jack Fullmer, Grand Color Bearer Joseph Benton, Grand Guardian Martha Galvan, Grand Herald Matthew

Finklestein, and Grand Instructor Rick Bragge, thank you for supporting me as I assume the demanding office of Grand Master.

To James Moody, who was installed as my first Grand Color Bearer but unexpectedly passed away a week after the installation, I'm glad I got the chance to know you and I appreciate your many contributions to the Order. You will be deeply missed.

To Rev. A. B. Grosh, who wrote the **Improved Odd Fellows Manual** and bequeathed me a template for this project; to Toby Hanson, PGM and Sovereign Grand Musician, Michael Duminiak, Vanessa O'Connor, and Sergio Paredes, who went above and beyond the call of duty to provide indispensable input on the subject matter addressed herein; and to Mario Guzman, Harrison Moore, Debra LaVergne, Wilbert Lemuel, Ron Mills, Ron Myres, and Billy Sanderson, who contributed helpful feedback on my manuscript, thank you for making this work possible.

To Linnea Bredenberg, Grand Chaplain, who is my partner in Odd Fellowship as much as she is my partner in life; to Angelina and Joel Greenzeiger, my beloved daughter and son, who bring joy to my world each and every day; to my parents, Mark Froimowitz and Marilyn Berman, and to my sister Lisa Druskat, thank you for your love and support in everything that I do.

# ILLUSTRATOR ACKNOWLEDGEMENTS

Firstly, I would like to thank the early 18th-century Odd Fellows who created our symbolic visual language and the 19th-century artisans who created the images that adorn our halls today.

Secondly, to all the great members I have met along my journey as a member and have been mentors and supporters of whatever pie in the sky project I come up with. Jim Turner, PGM (IL), for being instrumental in getting my home lodge reinstituted. Dan Davis, PGM (IL), Fran Davis, Gene Curfman, PGM (IL), and Nancy Curfman, PGMatriarch-LEA (IL), for their loyal dedication to being my lodge parents to ensure my lodge has the foundation for the long haul. And to my lodge Brothers and Sisters, Tuscola #316, for their dedication to forging the way forward as Odd Fellows. To Scott Moye for his resilience in the face of every obstacle this organization has thrown at him. To Toby Hanson, PGM (WA), Sovereign Grand Musician, for always having the right words and approach to the most difficult of situations. To Wayne Geurts, PGM (ON), for being a calm force to move things forward in the storm.

Finally, I thank my family for their undying love and support for me and all my artistic endeavors.

# FOREWORD

Odd Fellowship has played an important role in our North American history. For over 200 years our Three Link Symbol has helped to spread the message of "Friendship, Love and Truth," which we believe is the ultimate destiny of all mankind.

Throughout the annals of time, the tenets of our order have been "to visit the sick, relieve the distressed, bury the dead, and educate the orphan." We have reached out and helped many of our members, our families, and our friends. We are a community of devoted members who seek to build a better world in which to live. We've influenced many lives in the past, and as people read this manual and join our order, we will continue to touch many more in the years to come.

Our order has grown and changed over the centuries, and we've passed our traditions down from mouth to ear, each generation of Odd Fellows passing them on to the next. As a result, many of our cherished ideas have never been recorded. Therefore, Brother Greenzeiger has developed a manual to help us all, especially new members entering the Order. He has taken our history, rituals, structure, and everyday operations, and explained every detail in a way that is easy to understand. This book clarifies many things which might otherwise be unclear, from how to live the principles of Odd Fellowship, to how to perform each role within a lodge. I truly believe that it will be a great help for all members, both old and new.

I commend Brother Greenzeiger for taking on this project for his Grand Master year and for helping all of us to better understand the principles and practices of Odd Fellowship.

Odd Fellowship must grow with the times, but the principles of our community remain the same. If our commitments to our Odd Fellows family, our community, and all the people of the world stand strong, our order will continue to thrive, and serve as a beacon of hope for future generations.

> E. Wesley Nelson
> Sovereign Grand Master
> Independent Order of Odd Fellows

# INTRODUCTORY

When I first joined an Odd Fellows Lodge in 2005, I didn't know what I was signing up for. I had friends in the lodge, and they were badly in need of more members to keep the lodge going. I was willing to help. My initiation was a blur of sounds, colors, and a lot of speeches I couldn't completely digest. I figured that once I started attending meetings, the meanings would become more apparent. The brothers and sisters were friendly, welcoming, and more than happy to teach me how to participate in the meeting. However, no one ever told me why I should care about the business going on or the myriad of intricate rituals involved in working a lodge. I didn't understand the big picture of what Odd Fellowship was about and how it was relevant to me. Just doing the work wasn't enough for me. I wanted to know what it meant and why we were doing it.

I might never have found the answer, or at least not for many years, if I hadn't had the good fortune to be pulled aside by one of the oldest members in the lodge and handed a book. It had a purple cloth cover with embossed gold printing, faded from age. Inside, I found all manner of answers to questions I hadn't even known enough to ask. What was described were all the fundamentals of Odd Fellowship. The book was laid out neatly into a series of chapters. They touched on what the degrees meant, how an Odd Fellow should conduct themselves, and why the mission of Odd Fellowship was so vitally important in the world. Also contained was practical advice on how a lodge functions and the roles of the different officers and committees.

There was one problem, however. The descriptions were of the Independent Order of Odd Fellows in the 19th century.

Back then, there were six degrees instead of the present four and many other differences as well. The core principles and goals into which I had been initiated were laid out and still recognizable from the later incarnation. With careful study and contemplation, I was able to understand what was still considered relevant today and perhaps also what should still be considered relevant. This book was the *Improved Odd Fellows Manual*, by Rev. A. B. Grosh, and it was published in 1871.

Since then, I have made it a habit to read every Odd Fellows historical text I could get my hands on. There was an entire class of Odd Fellows literature devoted to serving as an introductory manual. The more well-known titles were by names such as Ross, Donaldson, and Bristol, in addition to the good Reverend. There was even one by Ridgely himself.

As a Grand Lodge officer in two different **jurisdictions**, and having visited lodges in several others, I have had the opportunity to see Odd Fellowship from a broader perspective. I have always been fascinated with the little differences in the way the Ritual is performed and how different customs and practices form in different regions. These coalesce to create a living web spanning the world, but tied together at the center through the core tradition and laws. An Odd Fellow may still visit any other lodge within the Independent Order and be enveloped in the familiar, even if some of the customs may be foreign.

All of this tangled and beautiful diversity is in danger of being lost to the sands of time, however, if we do not take steps to set it down for posterity. That is what this book sets out to do. It is for the new member with unanswered questions or for the experienced member who always wondered if there was something more profound. I have done my best to set out Odd Fellowship as I have seen it practiced. I have sought to capture all the complexity of its practices, the unbroken thread of its symbolic meanings, and the dynamism of the brothers and sisters themselves. They elevate Odd Fellowship from being mere words on a page to a living, breathing force for good in the world. I wish for every new brother and sister who crosses our threshold to gain a full knowledge and benefit of their heritage as Odd Fellows.

This book is not a replacement for your Noble Grand, Grand Master, or the laws and customs of your particular jurisdiction. These should always be given priority and adhered to. Should your local practices differ from those contained herein, I would be most interested in hearing about them. Please do not hesitate to contact me and share your experiences with the traditions of Odd Fellowship for possible inclusion in a future edition. Odd Fellowship is as broad as it is deep.

This book may contain terminology unfamiliar to the modern reader. I have indicated such terms in **bold**, and any such term is defined in the Glossary section at the end.

Odd Fellowship, as it exists in the 21st century, is a story yet to be written. Indeed, it will be authored through the contributions of brothers and sisters spanning the globe. Let us be ever mindful of our past, and the continuity of our history as the Order marches forward through time. The world needs us and our work, and we have the power to rise and meet the challenges of our day, that the links of Odd Fellowship may carry on unbroken.

SUNNYVALE, CALIFORNIA, JULY 2020

# TABLE OF CONTENTS

# EMBELLISHMENTS

*All unattributed illustrations are by Ainslie Heilich*

Patriarchs Militant - The Sovereign Grand Lodge IOOF
Current Patriarchs Militant Uniform - CE Ward
Junior Odd Fellows - The Sovereign Grand Lodge IOOF
Theta Rho - The Sovereign Grand Lodge IOOF
Youth Group - The Sovereign Grand Lodge IOOF
AMOS - Ancient Mystic Order of Samaritans
Muscovites - Imperial Order of Muscovites
LOTO - Ladies of the Orient

*Conclusion*
Carry the Light of Odd Fellowship

# CHAPTER I

## ON THE NATURE AND
## ORIGINS OF ODD FELLOWSHIP

### *OUR NAME*

When asking the meaning of the name Odd Fellows, one will often hear that when the Order was founded, it was odd for people to help each other and that those who did were called "Odd Fellows." Others will report that, as with some other fraternal orders, Odd Fellowship descended from a medieval craft guild. The explanation is that Odd Fellowship descended from a craft guild of men who worked at odd jobs. This is probably not entirely correct either, however. It is likely that Odd Fellowship was not tied to any particular craft. Perhaps the best way to understand what Odd Fellowship means is to look at the individual words themselves. During its founding, "odd"

"Three Men Working Together"

frequently referred to items that did not match and "fellow" to a person who belonged to a particular professional association or partnership. Therefore, Odd Fellowship is an assortment of individuals from more than one profession or walk of life. No further embellishment is needed beyond the fundamental fact that an Odd Fellow is a person who unites with others across the boundaries of demographic or social class in order to form a far greater whole.

## *OUR ORIGINS*

As with the name, the origins of Odd Fellowship are also much debated and shrouded in mystery. Like many other fraternal organizations, it seems an effort was made to bestow the organization with the earliest possible origins. Thus, stories are told that Odd Fellowship was founded in Ancient Rome during the reign of Nero.[1] Titus is said to have coined the name and granted the Odd Fellows a **dispensation** in return for their loyalty to him.[2] More ambitious tales tell that Odd Fellowship originated among the ancient Israelites, where Moses and Aaron propagated it.[3] Not to be outdone, others yet report that the first Odd Fellow was, in fact, Adam himself.[4]

In truth, though, no known records of the Order exist prior to 1748, from which we have a fragmentary set of rules and **minutes** from Aristarcus Lodge #9 of the Order of Odd Fellows.[5] This is generally regarded as the first clear evidence of Odd Fellowship, though no extant copy remains. James Spry tells us that he copied it from an ancient vellum leaf he was

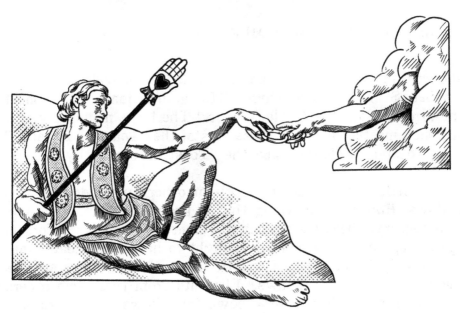

"Adam as the First Odd Fellow"

"Meeting Night of the Club of Odd Fellows"

shown. This was clearly not the first lodge, as evidenced by the number. Still, it met at three different locations in London at the direction of "the Noble Master." The lodge met in taverns, and each meeting included three toasts, the "Toast of Loyalty," the "Toast of Fidelity," and the "Toast of Sympathy."

Little more is known of this or other early lodges of Odd Fellows. However, one thing that is known is that by the late 18th century, there were many different Odd Fellows orders in operation, some of which are thought to have consolidated into two principal orders: the Patriotic Order of Oddfellows and the Ancient Order of Oddfellows.[6] Elements from these two orders and potentially other lesser-known Oddfellows orders are said to have merged at some point during the late 18th century to

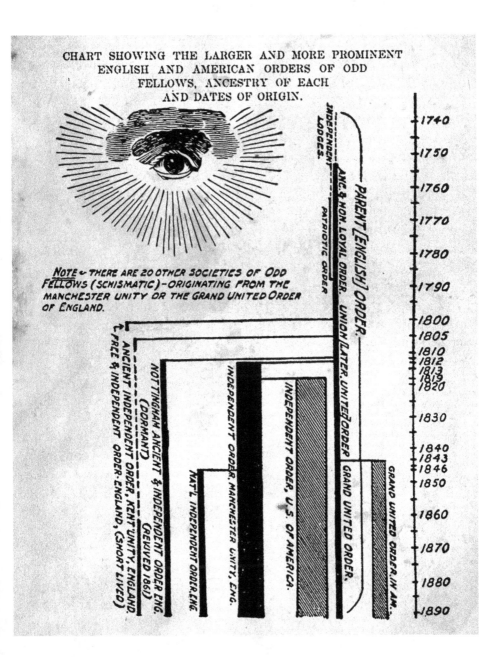

CHART SHOWING THE LARGER AND MORE PROMINENT
ENGLISH AND AMERICAN ORDERS OF ODD
FELLOWS, ANCESTRY OF EACH
AND DATES OF ORIGIN.

NOTE ~ THERE ARE 20 OTHER SOCIETIES OF ODD
FELLOWS (SCHISMATIC) ~ ORIGINATING FROM THE
MANCHESTER UNITY OR THE GRAND UNITED ORDER
OF ENGLAND.

form the Grand United Order of Oddfellows, also known as the "Union Order." However, there is no clear extant record of this.[7]

In 1813, sources report that a group of members who were displeased with how the Order was being run split off to form the Independent Order of Oddfellows Manchester Unity, based in Manchester, England.[8] They were very effective organizationally and rapidly spread, including to the United States in the early 19th century. While there were other early American lodges in various locations, the most famous was Washington Lodge No. 1, founded by Thomas Wildey and four other Oddfellows from England, John Welch, John Duncan, John Cheatham, and Richard Rushworth, on April 26th, 1819, in the Seven Stars Tavern of Baltimore, Maryland.[9] They successfully received a **charter** for their lodge from the Manchester Unity in 1820.[10] They proceeded to form the Grand Lodge of the United States in 1825,[11] receiving a charter for that body from the Manchester Unity in 1826.[12] The Grand Lodge of the United States was successful in issuing charters to other existing and new lodges around the country.

By 1842, the lodges in the United States and England had drifted far apart enough from each other that the Grand Lodge of the United States opted to declare its own independence from England.[13] Differences in the **Ritual** were a significant factor, as the English lodges had made significant modifications that were not considered acceptable by the American lodges. This was followed by a formal schism in 1843,[14] at which time the

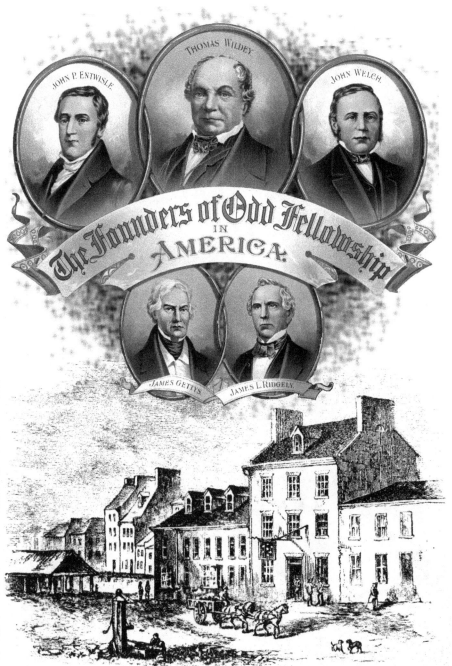

Seven Stars Tavern, Baltimore, MD

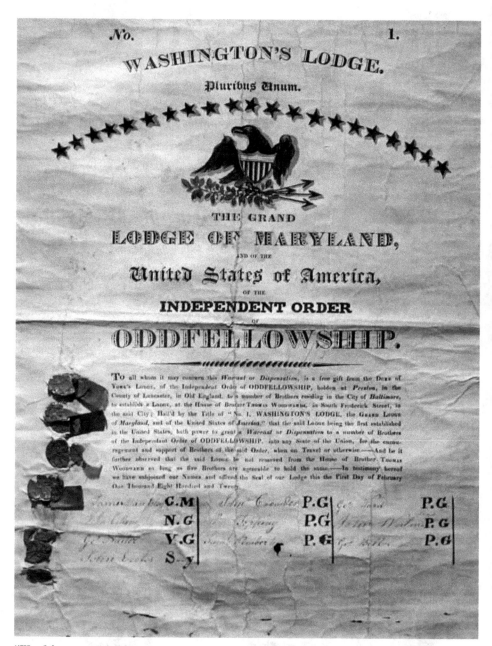

"Washington #1 Charter, seen hanging in the Sovereign Grand Lodge offices"

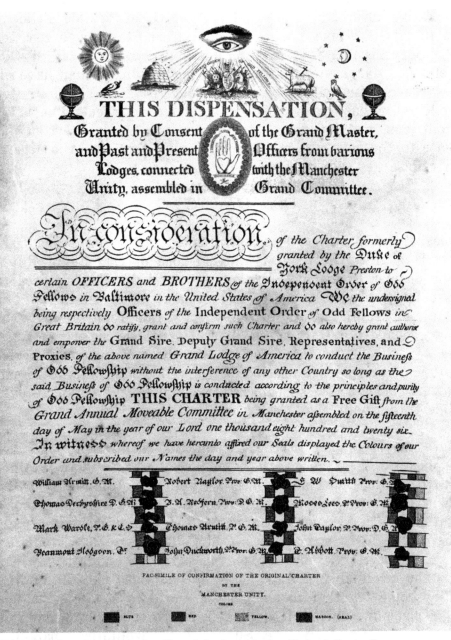

"Dispensation forming the Grand Lodge of the United States"

lodges under the Grand Lodge of the United States began operating under the name Independent Order of Odd Fellows. In 1879, the Grand Lodge of the United States was renamed the Sovereign Grand Lodge.[15] The Independent Order of Odd Fellows, Manchester Unity, and Grand United Order have all been successful in spreading internationally. As a result, Odd Fellowship has reached every populated continent. The laws, traditions, and rituals of the Order are different from one place to the next and have evolved with time, but the general principles and objects remain the same.

## OUR OBJECTS

One of the questions frequently asked by members and non-members alike is "What is the purpose of Odd Fellowship?" The answer given may determine if an individual chooses to associate with the Order or to continue said membership. The inquiring public wants to know why Odd Fellows do what they do and what it means. There is no one right or wrong answer to be given for questions like these because the precise nature of every lodge and indeed every Odd Fellow is different. Nevertheless, a few fundamental principles have persisted over time throughout the Order's long and storied history.

As is taught in the Ritual, Odd Fellowship provides a place to meet as brothers and sisters on equal footing. Furthermore, Odd Fellows meet without social masks, allowing them to know each as their most authentic self. A person's station in life does not matter in the <u>lodge room</u> and nor should their petty likes and dislikes. Odd Fellows are bound together as children of one common parent and thus obligated to help and support each other through the trials and travails of life. They come together to elevate the world as a whole, making it a place in which all human beings are bound together in brotherly and sisterly love. Such a world would be a paradise, and all may do their part to bring it about merely by exercising the principles of Friendship, Love, and Truth in interactions within the lodge room and in the world outside.

## OUR PRINCIPLES

Odd Fellowship enacts its objects through the application of certain principles, chief amongst them being the **Three Links** of Friendship, Love, and Truth. The first Link of Friendship refers not to a shallow or superficial form of acquaintance whereby one may see the same individuals regularly and perhaps engage in pleasantries or polite discussion. Rather, it refers to a deep and abiding friendship which links soul to soul. A true friend is someone who can be relied on for support when it matters, even if doing so is not of any direct benefit to themselves. They will even sacrifice their comfort or advantage to help because of the deeply shared tie. This type of friend is not easily acquired. Nevertheless, it is what

all should be striving towards with brothers and sisters in the Order, particularly if the Odd Fellow has attained the **Degree of Friendship**. Anything less is not what is being referred to when speaking of the principle of Friendship.

The second Link is Love, specifically what is referred to as "brotherly love." This is not related to romantic love and is only similar to familial love by analogy. It refers to the selfless love a person has for their fellow creatures beyond that which would typically be expected for their relationship or lack thereof. This love should prompt a brother or sister to look beyond their relations in life and the Order and to extend themselves in service to all of humankind. It is very unusual in this world to see that sort of selfless dedication to the care and betterment of all humanity, as opposed to a specific family, nationality, or group. This focus on serving all humankind puts Odd Fellowship in relatively rare company. A brother or sister who has achieved the **Degree of Love** is expected to aspire to this form of higher love even if they cannot always achieve it.

Truth is the third Link and is often referred to as the "cardinal" or "imperial" virtue of the Order. Thus, it relates to the **Third Degree**, which is the highest degree that can be achieved in an Odd Fellows Lodge. The nature of Truth is two-fold. On one hand, one must work to know what is true about themselves and their world. Without knowledge of self, one cannot understand one's own motivations or how one can best contribute one's unique gifts and abilities to the world at large. Without knowledge of one's

brothers and sisters, one cannot effectively work together for greater acts of good which are possible when united as a lodge or as a fraternity. Without knowledge of the world, one cannot understand the nature of humanity's challenges, and certainly not what the best remedy will be.

On the other hand, one must also promote the spread of the truth through one's own words and deeds. If a brother or sister fails to speak the truth or act with integrity, they harm others and detract from the purpose of Odd Fellowship in the world. The misguided brother or sister also ultimately harms themselves and their own ability to be effective, because they will soon develop a reputation as one who cannot be trusted. Truth is not a finite resource in the world to be hoarded for personal gain. Rather, truth begets truth. The more one shares knowledge of the truth with others, the more it becomes available to all. A brother or sister of the **Degree of Truth** should always do their best to seek out, understand, and ultimately share the truth. They should ensure their actions also reflect what they understand to be true.

Ultimately, the Three Links of Odd Fellowship provide a ladder by which a brother or sister may climb to the pinnacle of virtue. Through this, they may better the world. Each rung in this ladder forms the secure basis needed to construct the next level of the structure. Only by having close relationships of Friendship can one put oneself in a position to serve humanity through Love. Only through an outpouring of Love can one attain the selfless devotion needed to discover and share Truth

with all. By seeking out and achieving these virtues in sequence, one furthers the mission of Odd Fellowship, namely, to elevate humankind, and to ultimately transform the world into the paradise so devoutly wished for.

## OUR NATURE

Beyond the core purposes of Odd Fellowship, there are infinite possibilities for how a lodge can operate. One may think of it as a platform for holding whatever social, fraternal, or service activities fit its members' desires and interests – so long as those activities are in harmony with Odd Fellowship's fundamental principles. Lodges have been successful in many different ways: through shared meals and parties, through sharing in hobbies and activities, through serving the local community in whatever capacity, through raising money to give to good causes, through practicing and performing the Ritual of the Order, through studying the deeper meanings of Odd Fellowship and its rituals, or through engaging with its history. What is essential is that each lodge finds a way that works for its members and their community and adds to the overall vibrancy of the Order worldwide.

There are some who seek to uncover hidden mysteries within the realm of Odd Fellowship. Similarly, many aspirants delve for an esoteric or even occult meaning within the other great fraternal orders of the 18th and 19th centuries. This quest will often take the form of seeking relationships between the symbols and rituals of Odd Fellowship and Renaissance or Enlightenment-era mysticism, such as Kabbalah, Alchemy, Astrology, or Tarot. The progenitors of Odd Fellowship and similar traditions, in most cases, did not have a background in these lesser-known aspects of Western spiritual philosophy and made no special effort to incorporate their teachings. Instead, where comparisons may be drawn, they are likely the result of the common heritage of symbols and ideas circulating within Europe and the surrounding environs. While this search may provide intellectual fulfillment and personal meaning, the erstwhile traveler should be reminded that the map is not the territory.

On the whole, mysticism attempts to put into words certain ineffable aspects of the human experience. Attachment to a particular set of words or symbols as being objectively indicative of a higher truth is generally a mistake. It ignores the dazzling diversity of expressions of the contents of the human mind and soul.

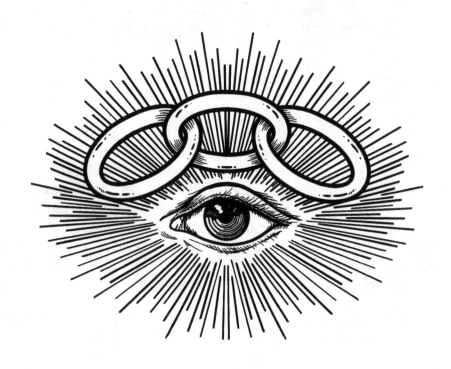

# CHAPTER II

## ON THE GOVERNING PRINCIPLES

## OF THE ORDER

### *OUR STRUCTURE*

Like most other fraternal organizations, the Independent Order of Odd Fellows has a lodge structure at its heart. Individual members belong to lodges that meet in a particular location at a set day and time. These lodges are grouped together to form Grand Lodges that are responsible for Odd Fellowship in an entire state, province, or country. Grand Lodges are typically subdivided into geographical districts for administrative purposes. Sovereign Grand Lodge is the highest authority for Odd Fellowship worldwide for those lodges <u>chartered</u> within the Independent Order. At every level of this hierarchy, Odd Fellowship follows certain structural and organizational principles.

Lodge organizations are a deliberative body, meaning that the members assemble to make decisions using parliamentary procedure. As such, they follow certain democratic principles. Each member in a lodge gets a vote in most lodge business, such as admitting new individuals to membership, approving expenditures, and electing officers. They are also permitted to speak on any business matter at hand subject to the rules of order which govern how the body conducts its business. To exercise their rights as a member, they must be in **good standing**, which means paid up to date for any dues, fines, or assessments and not under **suspension** from membership.

The majority of the work of a lodge should not be done in a meeting of the entire lodge but rather in smaller committees composed of a subset of members who typically meet separately to conduct their business. Additionally, particular roles within the lodge of an executive, administrative, or ceremonial nature are delegated to specific individuals who are elected or appointed for a term of office, often one year. One important aspect of the lodge system is that different members should be given the opportunity to serve in various capacities, particularly the leadership positions. Taking a turn as the leader of the lodge is an essential part of the personal development of an Odd Fellow, so it should be made available to as many different members as possible so long as they are worthy and well qualified.

While the **desk officer** positions of Secretary, Financial Secretary, and Treasurer do often remain with the same individuals from year to year, there also exist the **line offices**. These offices are a series of steps leading up through Noble Grand, which are designed to be switched every year as the members advance. Traditionally, the line offices consist of the Outside Guardian, Inside Guardian, Left Scene Supporter, Right Scene Supporter, Conductor, Warden, Vice Grand, Noble Grand, and Junior Past Grand. During the times when lodges were far larger than today, often consisting of hundreds or thousands of members, it was challenging to get into **line** and these offices were considered quite prestigious. The average member would never have an opportunity to serve in these offices. Today, in most lodges, there is ample opportunity to do so. In fact, occupying the highest lodge office of Noble Grand can and should be thought of as an important rite of passage. The leadership experience and confidence that a successful term as Noble Grand bestows cannot be underestimated in its importance to helping with members' personal and professional development.

It may be observed that the first six positions in the line are appointed, and the remainder are the result of election. The line in no way implies that the lodge's right to elect whomever they wish should be abrogated by this tradition. Instead, it remains the lodge's duty and responsibility to reject any member for election if he or she is unfit for office.

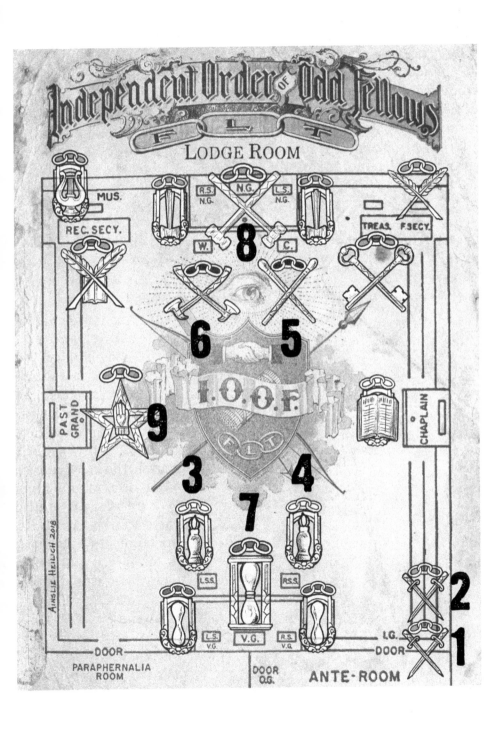

The advantage of this system of anticipated offices is two-fold. Firstly, it gives the candidate for Noble Grand or Vice Grand the opportunity to experience the other ritual offices of the lodge in preparation for their term, so that they are fully conversant in the lodge's operation by the time they assume office. Secondly, it allows for a measure of predictability in who will assume the office of Noble Grand, enabling them to thoroughly think through and prepare the program for their year in the **principal chair**.

## OF SECRECY

Secrecy is an important manner in which an Odd Fellows lodge differs from other types of organizations. At first glance, this may seem to put Odd Fellows more in the category of secret societies than of civic or charitable organizations. That would be

a superficial assessment of the nature of secrecy in the lodge. A secret society is secret because its aims are accomplished more easily without the public having knowledge of those aims, efforts, or even the existence of the group in question. By contrast, Odd Fellowship proudly proclaims its existence, its aims, and its works to any who would listen.

Rather, the secrecy practiced within Odd Fellowship is of two main types. First, there is the secrecy surrounding what transpires in the meetings of the lodge. This is the same type of secrecy that exists within a family's private home. The matters discussed or transacted are hidden from public view because they are the personal business of that family. It may include disagreements or the foibles of individual family members and thus should be kept within the family. Also, as with a family, the checkbook is not a public record except as required by law for taxes or other filings with the government.

Even more critical is the secrecy surrounding the **Ritual**, particularly the work of initiation which transpires within the lodge. The efficacy of the initiatic work is greatly enhanced through the element of surprise and drama which surrounds it. Suppose a candidate knows what to expect before embarking on their initiation. In that case, the dramatic scenes portrayed for them will not penetrate as deeply into their emotional core. They will remain within the more shallow, rationalistic layers of the mind. If the candidates are surprised, they will be caught off guard and primed to absorb the lessons being taught more fully.

# CHAPTER III
## ON THE BENEFITS OF MEMBERSHIP

### *OF HISTORICAL BENEFITS*

People have many different reasons for joining an organization. The reasons why so many have flocked to Odd Fellowship in ages past have varied considerably over time. Before the advent of modern entertainments such as television and the Internet, Odd Fellowship provided an opportunity for an individual to get together with others of like mind for socialization and enjoying shared food and drink. This was a major focus during the "convivial" period of Odd Fellowship in the 18th century.

In times when less governmental assistance was available to assist the needy, Odd Fellowship also provided aid to members who became sick or injured and needed care or help in supporting

their families while they recovered. If a member met with an untimely death, the lodge would pay a __death benefit__ to the family to assist in funeral costs or other needs. Lodges also made a special effort to care for widows and orphans from the families of Odd Fellows. If a member was traveling to look for work or otherwise, they would often contact a lodge in whatever city they visited. The lodge would often provide them with food, shelter, and potentially useful local contacts, simply based on their possession of a __dues card__ and the password. This archaic version of a social network was a significant factor in the 19th century until governments began taking over aspects of this role in the mid 20th century.

"Inside Conductor"

*The venerable Warden visits the widow and orphans.*

During the "Golden Age of Fraternalism" in the late 19th through early 20th centuries, the high drama of initiation and ritual was of keen interest to the majority of members. Production values of degree work were typically of a very high standard, comparable to attending the theater. Besides providing entertainment, the degrees were used to guide the individual on a path of self-improvement and teach valuable life lessons. Men and women who participated felt closer to each other based on having certain shared experiences in common which most of the rest of the world had not experienced.

## OF PRESENT BENEFITS

The benefits of belonging to the Order today are similar to those from the past. However, the possibilities are now even more endless. The need for more in-person social contact is more significant than it has ever been due to the loneliness of largely online interactions and friendships today. Online relationships, particularly those fostered by social networking apps and websites are often very superficial. They don't include the depth of sitting with a fellow member after a meeting to talk about philosophy, life, or even the local sports team. One may ascertain that a lodge is doing well in this regard if the members linger long after the meeting to share refreshments and enjoy each other's company.

For younger members, in particular, Odd Fellowship can be a great boon for learning valuable professional skills. Many members have begun to attend meetings, but are afraid to speak in front of even a small group. Gradually becoming more active in the lodge, the member may start speaking up on issues of interest to them and, over time, can gain comfort and confidence with public speaking. With time, they may find themselves speaking before dozens or hundreds of their peers at Grand Lodge and feel perfectly comfortable doing it.

The types of professional skills that may be attained in the Order go far beyond public speaking. Odd Fellows who are active in their lodges, particularly those who "go through the

chairs" to help lead their lodge, gain other valuable experience. One may learn how to organize others to work towards a common goal by chairing a committee or learn how to run a meeting and keep it on track by serving in the **principal chair**. In a broad sense, Odd Fellowship teaches members highly sought-after soft skills, which include interpersonal relationship building and communication with a diverse group of individuals holding widely varied opinions. While these may sound elementary to some, they are increasingly hard to come by in this world of increasing isolation and remote relationships. The relevance of the skills attained through in-depth participation in Odd Fellowship extends to virtually every career and calling in life.

At all times in history, there is a substantial benefit to belonging to a community, and the present day is certainly no exception. Human beings were not meant to face the world single-handedly, but a community can be increasingly hard to find. Upon joining an Odd Fellows lodge, one discovers that one now belongs to an interconnected network of communities spread worldwide and tied together by common beliefs, principles, and experiences.

From time to time, adversity rears its ugly head, and one of us is forced to seek help from beyond our immediate four walls. In these times of need, it is essential that one has already built a community to support and sustain one. This is a far better approach than laying the track while the train is already barrelling down it. Part of this preparation lies in helping others in their own time of need.

# CHAPTER IV

## ON INITIATION

### *OF ITS PURPOSE*

Initiation is a key factor separating fraternal organizations from others of a primarily civic or social nature. Initiation is a set of shared experiences gained through participation in a rite of passage, or ceremony, which communicates the fundamental tenets of the organization.

This consistent point of origination ensures that all who join a lodge have a profound, shared experience. It helps to bring Odd Fellows together in the same way that members of the same profession are often bound by their everyday experiences. A person may learn much from reading books or even from talking to other members, but initiation interfaces with the individual's psyche on an even deeper level: that of lived experience.

AN INITIATORY SCENE IN AN ODD FELLOW'S LODGE.
Published by Dr. E. Willis, Member of the Scarlet Degree, Harvard, Mass.

The lessons learned in the Order may not be fully expressed verbally because they rely on personal experience, which is the greatest of all teachers. How valuable it is that we may benefit from these lessons without living through the difficult real-life experiences they represent!

The lodge may be thought of as a sealed laboratory where experiences may be simulated through artificial means so that we can learn without experiencing real danger or trauma. When conducted with care and appreciated with the proper spirit, the wisdom attained may be comparable to that gained through the more usual means.

## OF ITS CONTENT

The specifics of the initiations undergone in the Odd Fellows should not be communicated to the general public so as not to lessen its effect on those who have not yet experienced it.

"Alchemical Alembic Distilling Odd Fellowship"

Nevertheless, it is perfectly reasonable to speak of initiation generally for those who wish to better understand what they may later choose to undergo. Initiation into an Odd Fellows Lodge is composed of four degrees, which are received in sequence.

The first of these is the **Initiatory Degree** by which the applicant becomes a member. This is the most important initiation within Odd Fellowship and communicates the fundamentals of what it means to be an Odd Fellow. It begins by illustrating the most fundamental problem of life, shared by all regardless of their wealth, power, or station, and then explains the remedy to this predicament. This explanation is given through the voice of age and experience, passing on vital knowledge to the next generation. The candidate for membership is invited to pledge to work together with peers in the Order to relieve suffering and build a better world. They are instructed in certain **signs** and

passwords by which a member may know another so the circle of trust may be maintained and extended. Finally, as they re-enter the world, they are given basic instruction in the Order's purpose to broaden their understanding of Odd Fellowship.

After the Initiatory Degree, three additional degrees are conferred by an Odd Fellows lodge. These pertain to and more fully explain the three principles of Friendship, Love, and Truth in sequence. At one time, these degrees were communicated with a period of time between them, allowing the candidates to fully digest and integrate the degree's lessons into their lives. The sequence of degrees constituted a gradual process of drawing closer to the Order. The new member would take up new responsibilities and a more profound connection to their brothers and sisters. More recently, candidates are often pushed

through these degrees as rapidly as possible, including through **one-day classes** where all the degrees are conferred in a single day. While this can be a useful tool for a lodge that may be on the brink of extinction to rapidly rebuild its numbers, it is far from ideal for helping those new members grow in their lives and in their relationship with their lodge and the Order.

Recently, there is a movement of lodges who seek to restore the **Three Degrees** to their former role as an experience worth having for their own sake, and as a means for the betterment of our members. Requirements may differ in each lodge or **jurisdiction** to suit the membership in that area. The underlying idea is that the candidate should have the time and space to grapple with the principle of that degree. Attaining the degree may include attending meetings, or participating in

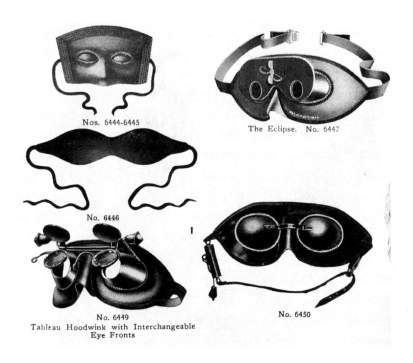

Nos. 6444-6445

The Eclipse. No. 6447

No. 6446

No. 6449
Tableau Hoodwink with Interchangeable
Eye Fronts

No. 6450

social gatherings, service projects, and educational programs of the lodge or district. Memorizing the signs, passwords, and meanings of the current degree is also compulsory. The last requirement, in particular, is strongly traditional and has a designated place in the **Ritual** of the Order to this very day.

When candidates are permitted to earn the degrees, it can be shown that they not only understand them more but also value and appreciate them more. Over time, this translates to a more informed and dedicated group of more fully conversant members who can discuss the meaning of Odd Fellowship. If done correctly, it can also lead to a greater connection between lodge members. There is no right or wrong way for earning the Three Degrees so long as they follow the Order's regulations and principles. Lodge programs of this nature may vary considerably from one locale to the next.

The **First Degree** or **Degree of Friendship** retells the Biblical story of David and Jonathan, setting it forth as an

exemplar of the virtue of Friendship. When those who may not be natural allies band together for the common good, great things may be achieved worldwide. A recipient of the First Degree should look to see how they may build relationships with their brothers and sisters in Odd Fellowship to carry forth this degree's lessons. It can be a challenge to reach beyond oneself to honestly give one's soul to another. Nevertheless, the rewards for those who successfully achieve this are inestimable.

The **Second Degree** or **Degree of Love** is drawn from the New Testament parable of the Good Samaritan, an exemplar of the virtue of Brotherly Love. It shows that there is yet another level of giving beyond that of mere friendship, a giving of one's self that demands nothing in return. When one chooses to love those who are not of the same tribe or family, the good one can accomplish sets one apart from ordinary men and women. A Second Degree recipient should look to what good

they can achieve in the world, taking the deeds themselves as their own reward.

The **Third Degree** or **Degree of Truth** alludes to the highest virtue embodied in a lodge of Odd Fellows. As it is not the mere truth of facts and figures, but rather the eternal and

ineffable truth of the human condition, it cannot be conveyed through simple story-telling as in the previous degrees. Instead, the candidate is introduced to a series of symbols that betoken the inner nature of what must be grappled with as men, women, and Odd Fellows. Be not misled. These are not simple ideograms to be apprehended through a single explanation. They require thought and meditation to fully plumb their depths.

# CHAPTER V

## ON SEEKING MEMBERSHIP

### OF PRELIMINARIES

The first task in seeking to become an Odd Fellow is finding the right lodge to join. One may be constrained in this endeavor should there be only a single lodge in one's vicinity or, worse still, no lodge at all. In the former case, the choice is clear, but one may have to take matters more fully into one's hands in the latter. If sufficient, other prospective members may be gathered to **institute** a new lodge, that may be the best solution. Failing that, one may make arrangements with a more distant lodge to become initiated while one labors over time to build up the local membership base for a new body to be **chartered**. Many of the benefits of Odd Fellowship accrue without a **local lodge**. Still, to gain full benefits, a local lodge is required.

"Who goes there?"

In the best case, where there are multiple lodges available, one may benefit from a careful investigation of each lodge's nature and composition. Lodges are like individuals in that each is unique with its own strengths and foibles. It is essential to find a body that is compatible with one's own nature and preferences. Lodges may also vary in their overall quality. The best lodges are those which are knowledgeable, active, and dedicated to the principles of Odd Fellowship. Some may also be more or less open to new ideas and innovations and more willing to take newer members under their wing and allow them to grow in the Order. It can sometimes be desirable to join a higher-quality lodge, even if it is a bit further from one's residence, as one's **primary lodge** significantly impacts one's overall experience in Odd Fellowship.

## *OF THE APPLICATION PROCESS*

Once one has determined what lodge one wishes to pursue membership in, the next step is to identify a **sponsor** and fill in an application. The sponsor is an existing lodge member who will vouch for the applicant seeking to unite with the lodge. It is not necessary to have a sponsor who knows the candidate for membership in advance. Still, one needs to get to know them sufficiently that the sponsor feels confident enough to stake their good name to the aspirant's character and sincerity. Finding a sponsor can often be as simple as contacting the Noble Grand, Secretary, or other representatives of the lodge and meeting with them, perhaps over food or drink, to make their acquaintance.

The **sponsor** will typically provide the candidate with an application and help them to fill it out correctly. The application requires basic contact information such as address

and telephone number, and some additional information about the applicant, including date of birth. There are also spaces to list the sponsor and the name of the lodge to which one is applying. The specific contents of the application may vary from one **jurisdiction** to the next. Along with the written application, the candidate must also remit a designated application fee before their application can be considered.

The candidate is required to subscribe to a belief in a Supreme Being. This is an ancient requirement for membership and perhaps existed to establish a signpost to indicate that a prospective member could be trusted with the valuable secrets of the Order. At the time, these secret methods by which one Odd Fellow may identify another were highly valuable. These methods could be used to gain material support and benefits from lodges all over the world. It was not intended that candidates be excluded from participation based on belonging to a particular religion. The stated belief in a Supreme Being is sufficient. It is not appropriate for a candidate to be asked to describe the specifics of their belief. There are Odd Fellows from all major world religions and some whose belief in a Supreme Being is primarily philosophical or abstract.

The sponsor brings the completed application to a meeting of their lodge, where it is read before the assembled membership. An **Interviewing Committee**, typically of three individuals, is appointed to meet with the candidate. The purpose of the interview is two-fold: to ascertain whether the candidate would be a suitable addition to the lodge and to better inform the candidate as to whether the lodge is right for them. It should ideally be a back-and-forth, with the candidate getting a chance to have their questions answered as well. The topics asked about usually include necessary information about the candidate as well as why they want to join the lodge. Some lodges even ask about what ideas the candidate may have for events or programs the lodge might wish to hold in the future. Traditionally, the candidates are also asked whether they believe in a Supreme Being, whether they are in good health, and whether they drink alcohol. The latter two questions' purpose was tied to the fact that the lodge would have to pay **sick benefits** to the new member should they become sick or injured. These are customarily still asked, though they are no longer as relevant. In former times, the interview was often held at the candidate's home so that the committee could assess their lifestyle more fully. Today, it is generally held in a neutral location such as the lodge hall or a coffee shop or restaurant.

The Interviewing Committee reports back to the lodge during a meeting. After hearing the report, the lodge members immediately vote via a ball ballot. White balls and black balls or cubes indicate whether the member thinks the candidate would or would not be suitable to join the lodge, respectively. Originally a single black ball or cube was sufficient to deny the candidate membership, but more recently, the requirement has become a simple majority of white balls to elect. The entire ballot occurs anonymously, to ensure that every member is allowed to vote their conscience without fear of judgment or reprisal. The candidate is notified of the election results by the lodge's Secretary and is often contacted by their sponsor. If elected, the candidate will be invited to take the **Initiatory Degree** as early as practicable. If the candidate is not selected, they must wait at least six months to re-apply and are not permitted to apply to any other lodge. Their application fee is refunded if they are not elected to membership.

The candidate's sponsor or the lodge Secretary will generally be the one to notify the candidate of the time and place for initiation. In some jurisdictions, this is permitted to be the same meeting at which the candidate is elected. However, in others, it must be on a separate and subsequent occasion. Initiation into the lodge is a serious matter and a significant ceremony in the candidate's life. Traditionally, it is regarded as a solemn occasion, and dress for the candidate and other participants is formal. In recent years this can vary considerably from one lodge to the next. The candidate is best advised to ask their sponsor how they should dress for their initiation.

## OF THE VARIOUS TYPES OF APPLICATION

When first applying to the Order, the candidate applies to join the lodge "by initiation" and receives the Initiatory Degree. There are other methods of joining a lodge which become relevant when a member wishes to change their primary lodge affiliation or assume membership in a **secondary lodge**. The process of switching **home lodges** is to fill out a membership application "by **transfer**," which is submitted to the new lodge for consideration with the transfer fee, which should be specified in the lodge's **by-laws**.

A member may only apply to transfer to another lodge if not under **charges** and having paid dues at least ninety days in advance. This application follows the standard procedure, including interviewing and balloting, except that no initiation is needed. If elected, the Secretary of the new lodge notifies the original lodge, sends the transfer fee, and requests a **transfer**

**certificate.** The Secretary of the original lodge provides the transfer certificate, fully signed and **sealed** in return, which does not require a vote of the lodge.

Once the new lodge receives the transfer certificate, the member may present themselves at a subsequent meeting and sign the lodge's **members' register**, completing the transfer. This may be handled formally, often with the lodge Warden **escorting** the candidate to the Secretary's desk with suitable musical accompaniment if possible while the brothers and sister present arise and applaud the new arrival. Following the transfer, the Secretary of the new lodge must send the "certification" from the transfer certificate back to the original lodge to confirm that the transfer occurred, after which the original lodge should remit any dues paid in advance of the date shown.

**Deposit of card** is a lesser-known but equally valid method for uniting with a lodge. In this scenario, a member intends to switch their primary lodge affiliation but has not selected a new lodge to make their home. The first step is to request a **withdrawal card** from the original lodge, which serves as proof of the member's status as an Odd Fellow. It must be granted if the member is in **good standing** and has paid dues in advance sufficient to cover the one-year period for which the card is valid.

The member must also pay any prescribed fees for the card, depending on the laws and regulations of their jurisdiction. It is to be signed by the Noble Grand of the lodge and attested by the Secretary. The withdrawing member should also be given the **Annual Traveling Password** to assist in seeking out a new lodge, which need not be in the same jurisdiction as the original lodge.

Although this is not used as frequently in the current era, at one time, it was quite commonplace indeed. It was used particularly by members who intended to move to a

"Withdrawal Certificate"

new locale in search of work or other opportunities but did not yet know where they would settle. Upon arriving in the new place, the withdrawal card entitled them to select a local lodge, prove their identity as an Odd Fellow, and resume participation in the Order through the new affiliation. After due **examination** and interview, the new lodge has the same right to accept or reject the candidate through the voting process as in any other application.

Suppose more than one year should transpire from the card's issuance. In that case, continuity of membership in the Order is lost. However, the card still serves as proof of the individual's rank and status within Odd Fellowship and permits reuniting with the Order through deposit of card.

So long as any outstanding indebtedness to the lodge has been discharged, Odd Fellows who have resigned or been **suspended** from membership due to nonpayment of dues may be **reinstated** upon application and lodge vote. In the case of a resignation, the member presents evidence of the resignation to the lodge they seek reinstatement in as an accompaniment to the standard application.

In the case of a suspension for nonpayment, the brother or sister must pay the full amount owed except in jurisdictions where a lesser amount, such as one full year of dues, has been established. If the lodge votes not to readmit the suspended Odd Fellow even after the **arrearage** has been resolved, they will provide a **dismissal certificate**, which may be presented at any other lodge with an application for reinstatement. The application fee is to be returned should the member not be granted admission, as in any other form of the application process. A lodge may only vote on a reinstatement at a regular meeting.

## OF CATEGORIES OF MEMBERSHIP

Although an Odd Fellow in good standing has the right to visit or attend any lodge within the Order, if they wish to possess the full rights of membership such as voting and holding office, they must apply to join the new lodge as an **associate member.** The application process is the same as in other forms of admission, with proof of good standing in the home lodge being provided in the form of an **official card or certificate.**

Though the member is already an Odd Fellow, the new lodge still retains the full right to accept or reject the member. In practice, however, it is relatively uncommon for a lodge to reject an Odd Fellow from uniting with them. The member must maintain their good standing status within the original lodge to be a member in good standing of the new lodge. A member is prohibited from being an associate member of more than three lodges within a single jurisdiction.

For those who have chosen to make Odd Fellowship a priority and wish to extend their membership indefinitely, **life membership** may be an option, depending on the jurisdiction. Sovereign Grand Lodge gives Grand Lodges the power to establish life membership programs. However, the details of this may vary from one jurisdiction to the next. In jurisdictions that allow this, the membership category must be permitted by all local lodges.

In all cases, applying for life membership requires payment of one year's dues in advance plus the life membership fee, which can be tailored to the member's present age by Grand Lodge. For example, a jurisdiction may require a payment equal to twenty years' dues. This fee, together with all necessary documentation, is submitted to Grand Lodge, which maintains records of life members within the jurisdiction. These funds are to be invested by Grand Lodge, the proceeds being applied to pay the member's dues.

When the member dies, the principal is to be disposed of in accordance with the laws of the jurisdiction, which may include payment to the members' estate. Should a life member wish to transfer to another lodge within or outside the original jurisdiction, the proceeds from the invested life membership fee are redirected to the new home lodge's coffers, but in no case will the principal be transferred to a new jurisdiction if there be one. Younger members of the Order, in particular, should seriously consider opting for life membership if within their means, as it could result in substantial savings on their cost of membership over time.

The additional class of **non-contributing membership** is an option for members who have been contributing members of their lodges for a minimum of forty years or who are over the age of seventy-five and have belonged to the Order for at least ten years. This program is intended for long-standing members who have difficulty affording their dues due to personal financial circumstances. Granting this status requires a vote of the local lodge after consideration of the particulars of the application. If granted, the member is no longer obligated to pay dues. The local lodge is also exempt from any **per capita** fee for the member. The non-contributing member may still be eligible for paid benefits, depending on the established laws of the jurisdiction.

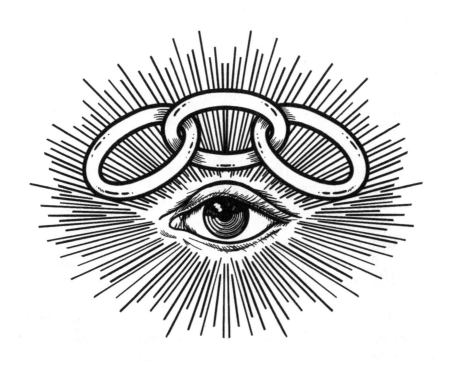

# CHAPTER VI
## ON THE CONDUCT AND
## VOCATION OF A MEMBER

### *CONCERNING FELLOW MEMBERS*

Odd Fellows are pledged to treat each other as brothers and sisters. Consequently, they should have concern for the welfare of their fellows, as one should for their own birth or chosen family. As with all families, this does not necessarily mean one must agree or get along all the time. Instead, there is a deep and abiding commitment to support and help each other through the trials and adversities of life. If a brother or sister is sick and wants to be visited, one should make every effort to visit them. If they are suffering from financial difficulties and one can discreetly assist them, they should do so. If one can direct them towards a useful job or other opportunity, one should do that as well. Perhaps the most helpful way to support brothers and sisters, however, is simply by being there to talk to when they need a friend.

Further, the beneficence of Odd Fellows should also extend to the children or other immediate family members of other Order members when possible. This may bring more satisfaction to the brother or sister than if they are helped directly. One might assist their child by gifting them with toys or other items that their own children have outgrown. For older children, one might help them to secure educational opportunities or internships. If an Odd Fellow should help the families of their living brethren, how much more so should they bestow whatever aid they can upon the orphans or surviving spouses of departed brothers and sisters, in keeping with traditional practices of Odd Fellowship.

This duty to fellow members extends not only to what one should do but also to what one should not. An Odd Fellow must guard their tongue to ensure that they do not speak ill of other Odd Fellows, even if they feel that the criticism is justified. Rumors and gossip have a poisonous effect on relationships, and one should refrain from these assiduously. So far as one can, one should speak politely and with respect to brothers and sisters. One should also give them the benefit

of the doubt and assume they are doing their best to do the right thing unless presented with clear proof to the contrary. Maintaining peace between all Odd Fellows is beneficial to all and constitutes part of the fraternal duties of Odd Fellowship.

## IN THE WORLD AT LARGE

The immediate tendency upon joining Odd Fellowship may be to jump in completely. For those who wish to avail themselves, there are often meetings or events available almost every night of the week. While this may be good for the lodge and gratifying to the individual, one should not neglect to consider the effect this may have on others in one's life. The first duty should always be to fulfill an Odd Fellow's responsibilities to their birth or chosen family. That includes spending quality time or having family dinners with spouses, children, or other family members. It also includes undertaking a fair share of chores around the house. If one behaves correctly, Odd Fellowship should be regarded by one's family as a benefit to their lives and not a detriment.

Odd Fellows should strive to act properly and justly in every aspect of life, not only in relation to brothers and sisters in the Order. As human beings, even Odd Fellows will undoubtedly fall short on occasion. It may be helpful to bear in mind the obligations of Odd Fellowship when confronted with the moral and ethical choices inherent in life. If others know one is an Odd Fellow, they will judge the entire fraternity by one's actions. An Odd Fellow must act uprightly so that the general public may perceive that good faith and virtue are the peculiar characteristics of a true Odd Fellow. If Odd Fellows set an excellent example in all words and deeds, it is only natural that men and women of good character will want to unite with the Order.

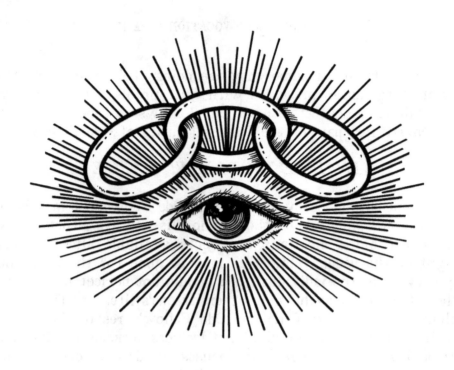

# CHAPTER VII
## ON MEETINGS AND CEREMONIES

### *OF REGULAR MEETINGS*

Lodges meet regularly at prescribed intervals to do the basic work of Odd Fellowship. This includes lofty matters such as voting on and initiating new members, determining what service work to do, and allocating money to charitable causes. Lodges also discuss mundane functions such as paying the bills, keeping the building in good repair, and deciding what social event to hold next. In ages past, lodge meetings were held quite frequently, such as once a week or more, but at present, they are more likely to meet twice a month, or even just once a month for regular business.

For newer members or others who may not remember all the procedural details involved in **working into a lodge,**

it is best to arrive slightly before the start of the meeting. Socializing and catching up with other members before or after the meeting is part of the fraternal experience, so coming a bit early can be beneficial for this as well. Some lodges also hold dinners in conjunction with their meetings.

Suppose a member does not remember the **term password** or any of the **Secret Work** necessary to prove oneself to be an Odd Fellow. In that case, they should approach the Noble Grand for a reminder of any of those items. No member should transmit the knowledge of these to other lodge members except for the Noble Grand of the lodge. They should not be given to visitors except by that visitor's own Noble Grand.

The Outside Guardian's station is outside of the **lodge room**, in the **anteroom**, and that officer is to remain there and ensure that no one unauthorized approaches the lodge room. The Outside Guardian does not enter the lodge room except as requested by the Noble Grand. To avoid a regular lodge member missing out on meetings, it may be desirable to find a member from another lodge who is willing to become an **associate member** of the lodge and serve as Outside Guardian.

The meetings open and close in ceremonial form as prescribed in the **Ritual** of the Order. The Warden should have laid out the **regalia** for the officers in advance as well as prepared the rest of the lodge room. This is done by placing the Bible or other holy books on the Chaplain's station, putting out the **gavels** for the Noble Grand and Vice Grand, and ensuring all lodge furniture

is in the proper position. The flag of the country the lodge is meeting in is required to be posted in advance in the hall or alternatively carried in ceremonially during the opening of the lodge. It is also required that the lodge **charter** be displayed in the lodge room or within the lodge's anteroom to hold a legal meeting. The one exception to this requirement is when the Grand Master has issued a valid **dispensation** in conjunction with meeting in an alternative location.

During the opening, the term and **degree passwords** must be given by the members and visitors present to ensure that all are qualified to be present in the lodge. It is typically taken up by the Warden, beginning with the Noble Grand and then proceeding to all the other members present. When there are many members or visitors present, the Noble Grand may ask the Conductor to assist in taking up the passwords. In this case, the Warden and Conductor meet in the center of the **floor** after the Warden receives the passwords from the Noble Grand. The Warden transmits the passwords to the Conductor.

Each officer then takes up the passwords from their half of the room. They meet up again in the center of the floor to report back to the Noble Grand. When receiving the passwords, it is traditional for the Warden or Conductor to shake hands with the member giving the passwords. Some lodges ask all members to rise while the password is being taken up and to be seated after giving it. This assists the Warden or Conductor in knowing who has not yet been tested.

Originally, lodges would conduct business in the highest degree, which today is the **Third Degree**. Nowadays, most lodge business is conducted in the **Initiatory Degree** so that all members may participate regardless of what degree they have attained. Voting on or conferring degrees continues to require being open in the degree in question, so lodges do open or re-open in those degrees from time to time. To ensure that members get a chance to use the **signs** and passwords of all the degrees and remember them, a Noble Grand can open in those degrees for practice purposes. This may be done even if no business demands them, so long as all wishing to attend the meeting have attained that degree.

Customs involving the **escort** and posting of the flag are to be in accordance with the laws and customs of the country in which the lodge meets. The flag is carried in by Color Bearer or Warden if there is no Color Bearer. Other members may be called upon by the Noble Grand to escort the Color Bearer. Once the flag has been secured, the Noble Grand calls upon the lodge to recite the Pledge of Allegiance, sing the National Anthem, or salute the flag in whatever other way is customary. When the flag is posted before opening, the Noble Grand will generally still call for the Pledge or Anthem at the point in the opening when the flag would typically be carried in.

The Noble Grand will ask each lodge officer to recite their duties. They each rise when addressed and remain standing through the completion of the officer duties, and are seated when the Noble Grand seats the lodge after the **Opening**

**Prayer.** Every officer has a **charge** to recite except for the Chaplain and the Acting Past Grand. The charges serve to remind each officer of their particular duties and help educate new brothers and sisters about how the lodge functions. They set the tone for the meeting to come by recommitting everyone to their unique role.

The tone of the meeting to come is further enhanced by the **Opening Ode**, which the Noble Grand calls up the entire lodge before singing. The odes are frequently omitted in many lodges because of the hustle and bustle of modern life, but this may be a mistake. Joining all the brothers and sisters together in song serves as a blueprint for the harmony that should characterize lodge meetings. Even when a lodge comes together with distinct voices and opinions, they should blend into a single work of music, as is done in the Opening Ode. If the lodge cannot secure a pianist to act as a Musician, other types of musical accompaniment may be considered or pre-recorded music played over a speaker system. Having musical accompaniment adds significantly to the quality and enjoyment of the odes. However, if this is not possible, some lodges have the practice of reciting the odes in unison, which is also a laudable approach.

Directly following the Opening Ode is the Opening Prayer. This, too, serves to get all the lodge members on the same page. It includes a reminder of why all are coming together as Odd Fellows and what the organization's values are. This is very important because there should indeed be a focus on those grand principles that tend to make people social and humane. The prayer concludes with a recitation of the Lord's Prayer, which should be familiar to brothers and sisters from a variety of Christian religious denominations. Interestingly, this prayer was not included initially, but adding it on became such a widespread practice in the 19th century that it was added as optional and later became a required part of the Ritual.

If an **alarm** at the **inner door** occurs during the opening ceremony, the Inside Guardian should open the **wicket** and

inform the brother or sister that they must wait until the opening is completed before gaining admittance. Once the lodge is declared open, and the **Order of Business** has begun, the Inside Guardian should re-open the wicket and proceed normally to question and admit the newcomer.

The Order of Business for a lodge meeting is considered to be suggestive, a helpful aid rather than a strict procedure to be enforced. The **Noble Grand** has the prerogative to skip items, return to items already addressed, and generally approach the lodge's business in any order desired. The Order

*Order of Business*
1. *Roll call of Officers*
2. *Introduction of Visitors*
3. *Reading of the Records*

of Business should never be used as a tool to prevent members from bringing business before the lodge or otherwise interfere with the will of the lodge. All of the items in the Order of Business exist for a reason. However, some of the reasons are now somewhat opaque, as they may have served a specific purpose historically, which is no longer as relevant today. The Noble Grand bangs the gavel between each of the sections of the Order of Business.

The "Roll call of officers" is read by the Recording Secretary and includes all the lodge's installed officers, whether elected or appointed. The Warden stands and responds with "present" or "absent" as the names are read. Simultaneously, the officer whose name was announced also rises and remains standing until the completion of the roll call, at the end of which the Noble Grand seats the officers. In situations requiring greater expediency, the Noble Grand may call for a silent roll call, in which case the Recording Secretary notes down those present and absent in the **minutes** without going through the formal process.

The "Introduction of visiting brothers and sisters" serves two purposes. Firstly it aids the Recording Secretary in making a record of what Odd Fellows from other lodges visited the lodge. Secondly, it allows the members present to learn the names and **primary lodges** of any visitors present.

The "Reading of the records of the last session" consists of the Recording Secretary or another member appointed for this purpose reading aloud the minutes from the previous meeting. In cases where the minutes from an antecedent meeting had not yet been read, either due to haste or because they were not available, it may be necessary to read the minutes from more than one meeting. After each set of minutes is read, the Noble Grand calls for the lodge members present to report any errors or omissions. If none are reported, the Noble Grand asks that the minutes be approved "as read." If changes were requested, then the approval is "as amended." This approval does not require a vote because it is generally done by **unanimous consent**, meaning that it is approved if no one objects. Should a single member object, it cannot be approved in this manner and requires a full vote.

"Members reported sick or in distress" is vital to the meeting from a historical perspective. In earlier times, lodges played a significant role in supporting members who were sick, injured, or otherwise prevented from caring for themselves and their families. This was the portion of the meeting in which the needs of a brother or sister could be brought to the lodge's attention. In addition to the Visiting Committee, the lodge would also sometimes provide watchers who would stay by the infirm member's bedside. This would give some much-needed rest to the family members who would otherwise be occupied with caring for them. It brought cheer to the infirm member to have the opportunity to interact with a brother or sister and to know that they had the support and protection of the lodge. More recently, these ancient practices have become less relevant, with modern healthcare and changing trends in how newer generations view visiting and privacy. Some lodges continue to send visitors to cheer up members convalescing in hospitals, nursing homes, or private residences. Others simply send cards, flowers, fruit baskets, and the like. Regardless of what form this concern for fellow brothers and sisters takes, it remains an integral part of being an Odd Fellow and should be a facet of any well-functioning lodge.

The "Report of the visiting committee" is to be delivered directly after "Members reported sick or in distress" and was initially given by a committee appointed by the Noble Grand for the term. During the present day, the formal committee is rarely used by lodges. Instead, in this section of the Order of Business, members often take the opportunity to report any sick members they may have personally visited and how the member was doing.

"Bills read and referred" allow the members to hear all bills which have been submitted to the lodge for payment. It is fundamental to the lodge system that members are informed about and have a say in decisions of the lodge, including disbursement of funds. The bills are typically read by the Secretary and are then passed to the Finance Committee for examination. Some lodges prefer to give the bills to the Finance Committee before the opening of the lodge so that they have ample time to review them without distracting from the rest of the meeting. Other lodges have the Warden carry the bills around the lodge room to the Finance Committee members for examination and signature while the meeting continues. In either case, the Finance Committee examines, signs, and reports on the bills before the lodge votes to pay them.

"Communications read and disposed of" consists of the Secretary or another designated brother or sister reading aloud correspondences received by the lodge since the previous meeting. It is not required to read all correspondences, merely those from the District Deputy Grand Master, Grand Master, Grand Lodge, Sovereign Grand Master, or Sovereign Grand Lodge. It may also be desirable to read other correspondences, such as those from other members, from the city or town, or from charitable organizations the lodge has donated to or partnered with. However, it is generally not a good idea to read solicitations or other items that would not be of general interest to the membership, as this would only serve to bore the members and prolong the meeting unnecessarily. In some cases, the Secretary will merely announce the general topic of a correspondence and make it available on the desk for those members interested in pursuing it after the meeting. This can also expedite the meeting and ensure it remains focused on the important work of Odd Fellowship.

The "Reading of applications for membership" is the lodge's first step in beginning to process a new application that has been received by the Recording Secretary. It may not be read until a **sponsor** has signed it and the applicant has paid the application fee stipulated by the lodge's **by-laws**. Directly following the reading, the **Interviewing Committee** for the application is assigned. The Noble Grand appoints two brothers or sisters to the committee, and the Vice Grand appoints a third. In cases where multiple applications are read together, it is entirely permissible and often desirable for the same committee to interview more than one candidate.

The "Reports of interviewing committees" are delivered after the designated Interviewing Committee has had the opportunity to interview the candidate. The committee chair addresses the lodge and renders a recommendation to elect or reject the candidate. It is also good practice for the committee to give some specific feedback on why they have issued that particular recommendation and to provide a little bit of information about the candidate so that the lodge may be well-informed prior to voting. The **chairperson** may also call on committee members to provide further input to this end.

"Balloting on applications for membership" is required to occur directly after the Interviewing Committee has given their report so that the information received by the lodge members will be fresh in their minds during voting. The voting procedure is fairly complicated for the officers involved in overseeing it, particularly the Warden, who is responsible for carrying the ballot box to the Noble Grand and Vice Grand and supervising it in the center of the room while the members vote. After being given a chance to ensure that the ballot box is empty and that there are sufficient white balls and black balls or cubes, the Noble Grand and Vice Grand must ballot from their stations because those stations must be occupied at all times. Furthermore, the two should have a clear view of the ballot box in the center of the floor to ensure that all members vote once and only once. In some jurisdictions, the Warden votes immediately after the Noble Grand and Vice Grand, after placing the ballot box on a pedestal in the center of the floor. In others, the Warden votes last, once all the other lodge members have voted. All lodge members must vote. No one may enter or leave the lodge room while balloting is underway.

"Applications and balloting for degrees" is another portion of the meeting which is rarely used in lodges today. However, it once had an essential purpose in lodges. As noted earlier, in olden times, the degrees were most commonly conferred with a substantial lapse of time intervening so that the candidates could fully absorb the lessons of each degree before moving on to the next. A separate vote was required to allow the candidate to pass on to each subsequent degree and gain further knowledge of the Order. The basic voting procedure was the same as for balloting on a new member. Naturally, only those brothers or sisters who had attained the degree being voted on could cast a vote to bestow it on another. The lodge was opened in the degree in question to allow the vote to take place.

The Ritual also now allows for lodges to vote for conferring all **Three Degrees** upon a candidate at the same they vote to admit that candidate to membership, but only if all members voting are Third Degree. If members who have not attained the Third Degree vote, then the only degree which may be conferred without a further vote is the Initiatory. This law of the Order is clearly stated in the Ritual. Nevertheless, it is one of the most common mistakes made by even very experienced Odd Fellows in conducting lodge business.

The "Report of committee on finance" is delivered by the chairperson or other designated committee member once the committee has reviewed and, if appropriate, signed off on each bill individually. They are tasked with identifying whether the expense has been pre-approved by the lodge or otherwise falls into the category of expenses that the lodge should pay. This is particularly critical for reimbursements or other payments to lodge members, ensuring that no lodge member may embezzle money or engage in any other type of financial impropriety. After hearing the report, a **motion** is made to pay the bills, either by the chairperson of the committee or by another lodge member. Once the bills have been approved, they may be paid.

"Initiation or conferring of degrees" is the portion of the meeting during which initiation or degree work would normally occur. This is a regular part of the Order of Business dating back to a time when new members were so frequent, and degree work such a popular activity, that many lodges would hold them during most meeting nights. Initiation and degree work no longer happens as often. This portion of the meeting is now also used to announce when future initiations and degrees will be held nearby. If such work is to be held during the meeting and the slate of officers for the degree is different from the officers currently occupying the various stations, the Noble Grand may call a **recess.** This is the easiest way to get all the officers to their respective stations for the degree. The lodge is then called back to order by whomever has assumed the Noble Grand's station for the degree. It is important to remember that when a lodge puts on an initiation or degree, no lodge officer may be displaced from their role in the degree by another member without their consent.

"Reports of committees" is the opportunity for any standing or special **committees** of the lodge to give their reports. Typically, the chairperson is the one to report, but any committee member may deliver the report if called upon. Committees play a major role in any well-functioning and active lodge. This portion of the meeting allows the lodge to understand the work committees have been engaged in and accept or reject any recommendations the committee brings before the entire body. The lodge as a whole always has the power to override any decision of a committee if desired.

Officially, "Unfinished business" refers to any matter which was taken up but not completed at the previous meeting. This could include topics discussed but not yet acted on or items that were postponed to the current meeting. This concept exists for the purpose of privileging items of business that did not get completed so that business cannot be put off indefinitely without an explicit vote.

"New business" allows all lodge members to bring up new matters that the lodge has not previously discussed. Under normal circumstances, it is not a correct practice to bring up a new item for discussion without formulating it as a motion, which also requires a second before reaching the floor. Once the motion is on the floor, the discussion and disposition of the motion is in accordance with the rules of order adopted by the lodge.

"Receipts and disbursements" consists of the Financial Secretary or Treasurer reporting on the total income, total expenditures, and final operating account balance for the lodge. This helps keep lodge members informed as to the financial condition of the lodge.

"Good of the Order" is the final part of the meeting before closing, and it has served a wide variety of purposes over the years. Its original purpose appears to have been to provide the lodge members with a forum to give feedback on how the meeting itself had gone, how the lodge has been doing overall, or other similar matters. It has also been used for thanking individuals or making announcements that may be of interest to the lodge members, such as upcoming events at the lodge or at other nearby lodges. Visiting dignitaries or other guests who are called upon to speak are generally called to speak during this portion of the meeting. In recent years, lodges have also begun using this time for other purposes such as presenting educational materials or even telling jokes. This is the final part of the meeting prior to closing the lodge.

The **Closing Ode** is the symmetric counterpoint to the Opening Ode. Similarly, it serves to once more unite the lodge together in harmony. It should encourage the members to put aside any differences that may have arisen in the meeting and restore the unity of the lodge family. As with the Opening Ode, it is ideal to have a pianist or other Musician, but recorded music may also be put to good purpose. Many lodges sing the odes with no accompaniment at all. Also, parallel to the opening is the **closing prayer** in which it is acknowledged that the deeds performed during the meeting may have been for good or for ill. Although Odd Fellows aspire to act rightly, even the most righteous do occasionally err. It is profoundly hoped that the balance of actions taken will always accrue towards the good.

Following the closing prayer, the Vice Grand leads the lodge in a recitation of the **Valediction**. This is a brief statement of the values and beliefs endemic to Odd Fellowship. It is recited as the members prepare to depart from the lodge and go their separate ways as a reminder that the work performed in daily life is as important as the work done in the lodge. Although the wording appears to be archaic, many brothers and sisters are surprised to learn that the Valediction is of modern origin, albeit significantly derived from the Past

# I AM AN ODD FELLOW

I BELIEVE IN THE FATHERHOOD OF GOD
AND THE BROTHERHOOD OF MAN;
I BELIEVE IN FRIENDSHIP, LOVE AND TRUTH
AS THE BASIC GUIDES TO
THE ULTIMATE DESTINY OF ALL MANKIND;
I BELIEVE MY HOME, CHURCH OR TEMPLE,
MY LODGE AND MY COMMUNITY
DESERVE MY BEST WORK, MY MODEST PRIDE,
MY EARNEST FAITH AND MY DEEPEST LOYALTY,
AS I PERFORM MY DUTY
"TO VISIT THE SICK, RELIEVE THE DISTRESSED,
BURY THE DEAD AND EDUCATE THE ORPHAN"
AND AS I WORK WITH OTHERS
TO BUILD A BETTER WORLD BECAUSE,
IN SPIRIT AND IN TRUTH, I AM, AND MUST ALWAYS BE,
GRATEFUL TO MY CREATOR, FAITHFUL TO MY COUNTRY
AND FRATERNAL TO MY FELLOW MAN;

# I AM AN ODD FELLOW

"Valediction"

Grand's Charge of the Initiatory Degree. It was written by Past Sovereign Grand Master D. D. Monroe and added to the Ritual in 1968.[16] Since that time it has become a classic and distinctive feature of the Ritual.

If the flags were escorted into the lodge room, they are escorted out before closing. The same detail which participated in the flag escort at the opening should be utilized. As before, the flag ceremony is conducted in accordance with the laws and customs of the country in which the lodge meets.

## *OF RULES OF ORDER*

A meeting composed of numerous individuals from a diversity of backgrounds and opinions needs a framework to oversee the process of discussion and debate. The solution for this dilemma is adopting rules of order that govern who may speak at what time and how **propositions** that come before the body are debated and ultimately disposed of.

While a lodge may indeed formulate their own rules of order, the standard set of parliamentary rules used in most bodies within Odd Fellowship is Robert's Rules of Order. It was first published by General Henry Martyn Robert in 1876.[17] As stated directly in the published text, the purpose of Robert's Rules of Order is "TO ENABLE ASSEMBLIES OF ANY SIZE, WITH DUE REGARD FOR EVERY MEMBER'S OPINION, TO ARRIVE AT THE GENERAL WILL ON THE MAXIMUM NUMBER OF QUESTIONS OF VARYING COMPLEXITY IN A MINIMUM AMOUNT OF TIME AND UNDER ALL

KINDS OF INTERNAL CLIMATE RANGING FROM TOTAL
HARMONY TO HARDENED OR IMPASSIONED DIVISION
OF OPINION."[18]

Robert's Rules of Order is centered around the notion of
a motion or formal proposal for the body to take a particular
action. In most cases, a motion may be made by any member of
the assembly through the verbal form "I move that . . ." which
further requires a "second" to indicate that at least one other
member of the body agrees with the proposal. Once a motion
has been made and seconded, it is restated by the chair and is
then on the floor, indicating that it is under active consideration
by the body and may be debated and ultimately voted on.

Per Robert's Rules, every member has the right to speak
on the merits of the motion at least once when called upon by
the parliamentary chair. Once every member who wishes to do
so has spoken once, the chair may call upon each member who
wishes to speak a second time. No one may speak a third time
on the matter unless given leave by the body. After all have
spoken their piece, the chair repeats the motion and calls for the
vote, after which the chair states the result to the assembly.

Beyond a simple motion to adopt a decision, referred
to as the "main motion," additional types of motions may be
made to alter the main motion or to dispose of it. "Subsidiary
Motions" allow for altering or addressing the motion on the
floor, as in the "Motion to Amend"; "Motion to Table"; "Motion
to Postpone Indefinitely," which kills the motion on the floor;
the "Previous Question," which calls to end debate and move
to voting; or the "Motion to Refer" to committee or otherwise.
There are also "Privileged Motions" which take precedence
over other business due to their urgency, including the "Motion
to Adjourn" or "Raising a Question of Privilege" such as to
make it easier to hear by turning up the speaker system or
make a determination as to the rights of a member. "Incidental
Motions" relate to procedural questions that arise in the course
of the business, such as the "Point of Information" to request

| Action | What to Say | Can interrupt speaker? | Need a Second? | Can be Debated? | Can be Amended? | Votes Needed |
|---|---|---|---|---|---|---|
| Introduce main motion | "I move to…" | No | Yes | Yes | Yes | Majority |
| Amend a motion | "I move to amend the motion by…." (add or strike words or both) | No | Yes | Yes | Yes | Majority |
| Move item to committee | "I move that we refer the matter to committee." | No | Yes | Yes | No | Majority |
| Postpone item | "I move to postpone the matter until…" | No | Yes | Yes | No | Majority |
| End debate | "I move the previous question." | No | Yes | Yes | No | Majority |
| Object to procedure | "Point of order." | Yes | No | No | No | Chair decision |
| Recess the meeting | "I move that we recess until…" | No | Yes | No | No | Majority |
| Adjourn the meeting | "I move to adjourn the meeting." | No | Yes | No | No | Majority |
| Request information | "Point of information." | Yes | No | No | No | No vote |
| Overrule the chair's ruling | "I move to overrule the chair's ruling." | Yes | Yes | Yes | No | Majority |
| Extend the allotted time | "I move to extend the time by ___ minutes." | No | Yes | No | Yes | 2/3 |
| Enforce the rules or point out incorrect procedure | "Point of order." | Yes | No | No | No | No vote |
| Table a Motion | "I move to table…" | No | Yes | No | No | Majority |

further factual information on the matter at hand; the "Point of Order" to challenge an error in the procedure followed or to "Appeal the Ruling of the Chair," which allows the majority of the assembly to overturn a parliamentary decision by the chairperson.

The final category of motions permitted are "Motions that bring a question again before the assembly," which allow for reconsideration of questions that had previously been disposed of, such as the "Motion to Take from the Table" and the "Motion to Reconsider," to bring back a question which had already been settled but may only be made by a member who had previously voted on the prevailing side.

Robert's Rules of Order Newly Revised[19] contains further explanations of the foregoing as well as numerous other types of motions which may be useful in the transaction of business for a lodge. It is intended to provide for any parliamentary question which may arise, ranging from methods of voting to nominations and elections to the formulation of agendas and reports of committees.

All officers who may be called upon to chair meetings and all members who wish to participate in the proceedings would do well to familiarize themselves with the contents of this work to participate fully and effectively. An investment of time is necessary to become fluent in the rules of order, but this is time well spent as it will ultimately lead to smoother and more participatory meetings where everyone's voice can be fully heard and considered.

## OF VISITING A LODGE

Visiting other lodges is a right possessed by all Odd Fellows in **good standing** and can be both pleasant and informative. Each lodge has a different style and may conduct its business differently. Seeing the myriad of forms that Odd Fellowship can take can only help expand a brother or sister's horizons. It can also be a great way to see some friendly faces while away from home if there is a local lodge available. All Odd Fellows would be well advised to familiarize themselves with procedures for visiting lodges so they can avail themselves of these opportunities.

If visiting a lodge within their own **jurisdiction**, a brother or sister must merely possess a **dues card** and know the term password and the password of the degree in which the lodge is open. When visiting another state, province, or country which has its own separate Grand Lodge, the term password is of no use, and the **Annual Traveling Password** must be consulted. The Annual Traveling Password is uniform for all lodges under the Sovereign Grand Lodge and may be requested from the Noble Grand of a member's lodge. Should the Noble Grand not possess the password, they may receive it from their District Deputy Grand Master.

When visiting, it is wise to arrive before the start of the meeting, and it may also prove useful to contact the lodge in advance so as to be expected. The lodge being visited must examine the potential visitor to ensure that they are qualified to enter the lodge in the degree it will be open in. In some cases, the Noble Grand may appoint an Examination Committee for this purpose. The **examination** consists of questions regarding the Secret Work. If the visitors' dues card appears valid and they can pass an examination on the work of Odd Fellowship, they will be admitted to the lodge and welcomed as a guest. Some lodges will have a **visitor's book** to sign.

Although visitors are welcome to attend any part of a lodge meeting, so long as they have attained the appropriate degree, it is essential to remember that they do not possess all the rights of a member of that lodge. They may be called upon to speak, but they do not possess the right to vote. It is considered bad form for a visitor to weigh in on lodge business unless asked directly to give input. When visiting, a brother or sister should remember that they represent their lodge and always act with courtesy and respect.

## OF VISITING AS A BODY

Visiting as a body was commonplace in times past, but more recently has mostly fallen into disuse. It occurs when a **quorum** of members from one **local lodge**, including either their Noble Grand or Vice Grand, decides to visit another local lodge all together. In this instance, the Noble Grand or Vice Grand of the visiting lodge may give all the signs and passwords of the degree for them. If an examination is necessary, then the Noble Grand or Vice Grand may be examined on behalf of the entire lodge as well.

It is the officer's responsibility to lead the visiting lodge delegation, ensuring that all members under their charge are in proper regalia and are qualified to sit in the degree the lodge is open in. Upon giving the alarm at the inner door, the officer will state their title and the name and number of their lodge, indicating their intention to visit as a body. The officer's statement will be repeated by the Inside Guardian to the Vice Grand of the lodge being visited and by the Vice Grand to the Noble Grand. The Noble Grand **calls up the lodge** and issues the command to admit them, which the Vice Grand conveys back to the Inside Guardian. The visiting lodge is then admitted and processes into the lodge room, utilizing whatever **floorwork** is customary in the **jurisdiction**.

The visiting lodge may line up in the center of the floor in whatever arrangement allows them to fit comfortably in

that space. It may be desirable to use a V formation with the
Noble Grand and Vice Grand at the point of the V and the rest
of the lodge fanning out towards the front of the lodge room.
The Noble Grand or Vice Grand of the visiting lodge gives the
appropriate sign of the degree and, after receiving the response
from the Noble Grand of the lodge being visited, presents the
officers and members of the visiting lodge. It is unnecessary
to introduce the visiting brothers and sisters individually, only
to name the body as a whole.

The Noble Grand of the lodge being visited should
welcome the visitors in their own words and invite them to be
seated. Once all the visitors are seated, the Noble Grand may
**seat the lodge.**

## OF DECORUM

While the lodge is open, all members must wear an Odd Fellows
**collar** or another badge of rank or office within the fraternity.
No one is permitted to speak or vote during a meeting without
wearing this regalia. It may include a collar, chain, or cord
indicating degree: white for Initiatory, pink for **First Degree,**
royal blue for **Second Degree,** or scarlet for Third Degree.
Badges of office may similarly take the form of collars, chains,
or cords and may be issued by a local lodge, Grand Lodge, or
by Sovereign Grand Lodge. Each will have a different emblem
indicating the symbol and nature of the office occupied. Collars
and other regalia also exist for past offices held, such as Past
Grand, Past District Deputy Grand Master, or Past Grand
Master. A member is always entitled to wear an item of regalia
from such a past office. In addition to those items of regalia
worn on the neck, **pocket jewels** are typically worn on less
formal occasions, including those for current or past Grand Lodge
or Sovereign Grand Lodge officers. In most lodge halls, there
is an anteroom that contains collars or other regalia for use by
members or visitors. When entering prior to opening or **working
one's way into a lodge** that is already open, one should don one
of these items unless one has already brought one's own regalia

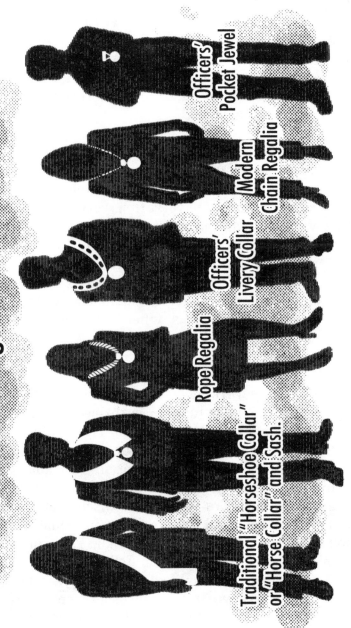

Odd Fellows Regalia in Current Use

Officers' Pocket Jewel

Modern Chain Regalia

Officers' Livery Collar

Rope Regalia

Traditional "Horseshoe Collar" or "Horse Collar" and Sash.

Aside from the collars and other regalia worn at regular meetings, most lodge officers also have designated robes and hats used for degree work. These vestments were historically also used in street parades and in formal group portraiture. Expected standards of secrecy in many quarters within the Order have changed over the last century, so a member should check with their own lodge or jurisdiction before taking photographs of officers wearing robes.

During a meeting, all members who wish to speak should direct their questions, comments, or motions to the Noble Grand. In fact, the entire meeting could be considered to be analogous to a conversation between the Noble Grand and the various lodge members. Cross-talk between members during a meeting is not officially permitted. However, many Noble Grands will allow it when a direct conversation between two members will facilitate the necessary information being shared with the lodge more expeditiously. Certainly, it should never be permitted in cases where the members are debating or tensions are elevated.

The prohibition on discussing matters that are political or sectarian in nature is a long-standing imperative within the lodge. This rule, which is enshrined in the Ritual of the Order, exists to maintain a spirit of fraternalism. All can then work together productively without engaging in those divisive topics that cause heart-burnings or ill will among people. The proscription is targeted solely at discussions within formal lodge meetings, with members welcome to discuss anything they wish with their brothers and sisters in an informal context, even if it should happen within the lodge hall. Even in cases where it is technically permitted, an Odd Fellow should think carefully before introducing such subjects and always strive to preserve peace and harmony with their brothers and sisters whenever possible. The precise nature of what constitutes "political" or "sectarian" within the eyes of the lodge is also highly subjective. Indeed, the discussion of specific political parties or political candidates clearly falls within this category. Still, for matters of human rights and social policy, the answer is far less clear, as Odd Fellows have historically been at the forefront of some of these issues in a nonpartisan and often united manner. As there are no clear written guidelines on this matter, a lodge would be well-advised to adopt its own suitable interpretation, respecting the feelings and sensibilities of their particular members, while not impairing the ability of lodge members to participate in the proud tradition of laboring for social improvements and the common welfare of all existing within Odd Fellowship.

There is also a general prohibition on engaging in **electioneering** inside or outside of the lodge room. This refers primarily to promoting a specific candidate standing for election at the local lodge, Grand Lodge, or Sovereign Grand Lodge level. The term is sometimes also applied to publicly supporting or opposing Grand Lodge or Sovereign Grand Lodge legislation outside of the official channels provided for debate and discussion within the context of a legislative session. This latter form is far more of a gray area, and standards regarding this may vary from one jurisdiction to another. In either case, there is no prohibition on speaking privately to one's friends or colleagues regarding personal opinions on candidates or legislation. What is generally considered problematic is to publish articles in newsletters, post on social media, or otherwise publicly campaign. Those holding high office or positions of great influence should be especially careful not to put their finger on the scale, as their words may have an outsized effect on how others will vote and could even be construed as applying pressure towards a specific outcome.

One of the many ways to show respect in the lodge is by standing up to speak, similarly to how one might stand in the presence of a king or queen. In this case, one is demonstrating respect for the lodge as a whole rather than for an individual, however. Obviously, it is not required in the case of a member who, for reasons of disability or infirmity, cannot stand comfortably for the time required, and they should be encouraged to remain seated as needed.

When speaking, Odd Fellows also use specific modes of address to indicate respect for the individual being addressed. When addressing the Noble Grand or Vice Grand of the lodge during a meeting while they are exercising their office, the convention is to address them by their title. Other officers are often referred to by their office as well while fulfilling their duties in a meeting, though this is not as consistently applied. The respect bestowed upon the Noble Grand of the lodge, in particular, is so profound that even a visiting Grand Master or Sovereign Grand Master will use the title when addressing them. If no other title is utilized, the proper form of address is Brother or Sister, adding the surname of the individual being addressed. In the present day, it is actually more common to see the given name of the individual appended rather than the surname, but this is not the traditional usage.

How a brother or sister should walk around the lodge room is also prescribed. While a meeting is open, only the Warden walks around the room unless the Ritual requires it or someone needs to leave or enter the lodge room. If, for example, a member has written materials they wish to have circulated to the others in attendance, the Noble Grand will generally call upon the Warden to collect the papers and distribute them. When the Warden or other members move around the room, they are not permitted to walk directly in front of the Noble Grand's station. Instead, if they wish to cross from one half of the lodge room to the other, they must progress as far as the Chaplain and Past Grand's stations, which in most lodge halls are halfway between the Noble Grand's and Vice Grand's stations, before crossing. There is no one consistent explanation given for why this tradition exists, but it is nearly universal. The major exception is when the Warden steps directly in front of the Noble Grand's station during the **Honors of the Order**.

Two officers occupy positions so significant to the working of the lodge that they may not leave their stations unoccupied, namely the Noble Grand and Vice Grand. The Vice

Grand has charge of the inner door and is thus responsible for determining who may properly be admitted. The Noble Grand is engaged in overseeing the lodge's entire operation, including the regulation of discussion and other business. In cases where these officers need to vacate their stations while a meeting is in progress, their respective Right Supporters have the privilege and responsibility to occupy their chairs. It is particularly important to remember that the Noble Grand may not engage in a debate from the **principal chair** and should voluntarily step aside if they wish to speak on the merits of a motion on the floor.

In the course of lodge meetings, it is often necessary for a member or visitor to be escorted around the room. This can occur in various situations, such as when a new member needs to proceed to the Secretary's desk to sign the **Members' Register**, when a member is to be presented with an award or **jewel**, or when a visiting dignitary is escorted to a seat. The escort procedure involves the escorting officer, who will often be equipped with a baton, advancing to the location of the officer being escorted and bowing. If a baton is used, it is held in the right hand and tucked in near the stomach during the bow. If the brother or sister bowing is not using a baton, the right arm is held across the stomach with the hand flat and the palm facing inwards while the bow is made. The individual being escorted bows simultaneously and in a like manner to the escorting officer. The individual being escorted follows behind the escorting officer until the desired location is reached, after which the escort concludes with another simultaneous bow.

In some instances, there will be more than one individual escorted at a time. Depending on the circumstances, this may be performed with one column of members or two, sometimes with two escorting officers, such as in the case of a **joint public installation**. When two columns are used, the brothers and sisters in the same row will often link arms. In all cases, only the front row will bow to the escorting officer or officers.

## OF OFFICIAL VISITS

An official visit or "visitation" occurs when an officer from the district, Grand Lodge, or Sovereign Grand Lodge level attends a local lodge on a formal basis. This occurs most frequently when the District Deputy Grand Master visits, which occurs bi-annually in most jurisdictions. They are accompanied by the District Deputy Grand Marshal if not the entire district officer suite. The Grand Master also makes similar visits accompanied by the Grand Marshal or other Grand Lodge officers on a schedule that tends to vary based on the jurisdiction's size. In some jurisdictions, the Deputy Grand Master and Grand Warden are also assigned official visits by the Grand Master or the Grand Lodge. Theoretically, the Sovereign Grand Master could make an official visit to a local lodge, but this happens far more frequently on the Grand Lodge level.

The specific ritual that accompanies the official visit varies by jurisdiction, but there are certain commonalities regardless of locale. A marshal should be designated in advance to perform the escort. This will usually be the District Deputy Grand Marshal or Grand Marshal if they are present but may be another district or Grand Lodge officer otherwise. If the visiting dignitary does not have their own marshal or another officer available, it is up to the lodge to provide one. If the visiting dignitary is the Grand Master or another Grand Lodge officer and the District Deputy Grand Master is present, that officer traditionally performs the escorting duties. Failing that, the Noble Grand generally appoints the Conductor to act as an escort. However, it may be desirable to appoint a different officer if they are more experienced in escorting.

The visiting dignitary may be in the lodge room at the opening, but if so, they will retire during Introduction of Visiting Members with the stated intention of returning for an official visit. At this time, it is traditional for the dignitary to request all elected and past elected officers of all grand bodies to retire for an escort at the same time. Optionally, fifty-year members may be invited to retire, and in some instances there is a more recent trend that new members of the Order who have been Odd Fellows for less than one year are also invited. It goes without saying that any elected or past elected officers from Sovereign Grand Lodge should be invited. All who retire must do so in form.

Before admission to the lodge room, the District Deputy Grand Marshal, Grand Marshal, or any other officer who has been selected to perform escort lines up those being escorted from lowest to highest rank. This facilitates introducing them in the correct order after admission. When the District Deputy Grand Master, Grand Master, or other dignitary is admitted for the official visit, they are announced at the door by the Inside Guardian to the Vice Grand. The announcement is repeated by the Vice Grand to the Noble Grand. It is customary for the Noble Grand to call up the lodge at this time out of deference to the honored guests. The dignitary and any others entitled to escort are admitted in a single group. After they enter in form and are recognized by the Noble Grand, the escorting officer announces the titles of all those being escorted in the order they have been arranged, saving the principal dignitary who is making the official visit for last.

Directly after introducing those being escorted, the **Honors of the Order** are given by the lodge. Only elected and past elected officers of Grand Lodge or Sovereign Grand Lodge are intrinsically entitled to the Honors. The one exception is that District Deputy Grand Masters who are representing the

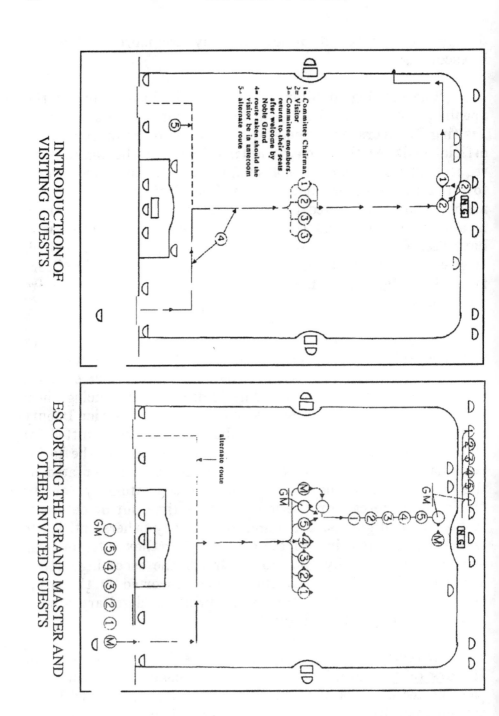

INTRODUCTION OF
VISITING GUESTS

1 = Committee Chairman
2 = Visitor
3 = Committee members,
returns to their seats
after welcome by
Noble Grand
4 = route taken should the
visitor be in anteroom
5 = alternate route

ESCORTING THE GRAND MASTER AND
OTHER INVITED GUESTS

alternate route

Grand Master on an official visit are also entitled to the Honors. Because the District Deputy Grand Master is only entitled to the Honors by virtue of representing the Grand Master, they should not receive the Honors during instances where the Grand Master is actually present. Thus, it is strongly recommended that the Grand Master not attend visitations made by their District Deputies. All those being escorted who are not entitled to the Honors, often including the marshal who introduces those being escorted, should take one step back directly prior to the Honors being given. After the Honors, it is considered polite for the principal dignitary being escorted to thank the body for the Honors, which in the case of a District Deputy Grand Master should be stated to be on behalf of the Grand Master.

The Noble Grand should welcome the principal dignitary and others receiving escort and instruct the escorting officer to escort the principal dignitary to a seat at the Noble Grand's right. At this time, the escorting officer leads the entire line to the Noble Grand's station. In turn, each officer shakes hands with the Noble Grand before finding a seat in the lodge, except for the principal dignitary who accepts the designated seat to the Noble Grand's right.

The meeting proceeds normally unless an installation is to occur, in which case the particular ceremony for installation selected by the Noble Grand-elect and **installing officer** is utilized. Also, during Good of the Order, it is customary that District Deputy Grand Master, Grand Master, or other principal dignitary be invited to speak last. All announcements or other matters to come before the lodge during Good of the Order should be disposed of before calling upon the principal

dignitary. The only business to occur afterward should be the actual closing of the lodge.

## OF SWITCHING BETWEEN DEGREES

Originally, lodges did most business in the Third Degree, though nowadays this has been changed to Initiatory Degree, so that all brothers and sisters have the opportunity to vote on most business of the lodge, even if they have not yet completed their degrees. From time to time, a lodge will need to switch to the other degrees to vote on the conferral of degrees or for the degree conferral itself. Normally a lodge will open initially on the Initiatory Degree and then switch to whichever degree is needed for the purpose at hand.

When switching degrees, the Noble Grand first calls up the lodge and requests the Warden declare the lodge closed in the current degree. If the lodge is moving up in degree, it is next necessary to ascertain that everyone present has already received that degree and is thus qualified to be in a lodge open in that degree. Therefore, the Warden is asked to determine that all present are qualified by requiring the degree password. The procedure for this is identical to taking up the password at the beginning of a meeting, except that only the password of the degree is given. As in opening a meeting, the Conductor may be asked to assist if there are a large number of members in the room. After it has been determined that all are qualified, the Noble Grand requests the members give the sign of the degree. The Noble Grand responds with the proper sign, after which the Noble Grand requests the Warden declare the lodge open in the new degree. Following this, the Noble Grand seats the lodge.

The process is simpler when moving down in degree because, in that case, it is already known that everyone present belongs to the lower degree, so it is not necessary to take up the password. It is also not necessary to give the sign of the new degree. As in moving up, however, the Warden is still required to declare the lodge closed in the higher degree and open in the lower degree.

## OF DEGREE WORK

Only a local lodge may initiate new members or confer degrees, making it the most crucial body in the Order. The degree work is a significant part of what separates an Odd Fellows lodge from many other types of non-profit organizations, laying the foundation for the lodge's fraternal nature. In past epochs, every lodge was responsible for conducting the degree work itself. It was performed frequently due to the multitude of new members coming in and the popularity of degree work among existing lodge members as a form of entertainment.

Nowadays, many lodges do not possess the resources to conduct their own degrees. Some are limited by the number of brothers and sisters capable of performing the various roles.

Others may lack the regalia and props necessary to adequately perform them or the training and experience to put on a credible degree ceremony. For lodges capable of bestowing the degree, it can serve as a major rallying point for the members and can deepen the understanding and connection they have to the principles and work of Odd Fellowship. Many a lodge which may not have performed the degree themselves in decades has been aided in their revitalization efforts by reinstating this salutary practice.

To gain the advantages of performing the degrees even in cases where some of the needful resources may be lacking, it is commonplace to see multiple lodges working together to perform degree work. This can be organized around district lines or any other convenient grouping of lodges to ensure there are sufficient officers to carry out the required roles. Even in this case, the lodge which is hosting the degree work in their hall is considered the lodge officially bestowing the degree and should call a **special meeting** for that purpose if it is not on a regular meeting night.

When one lodge performs the degree for a candidate belonging to another, it is necessary for the latter to deliver a letter certifying that the candidate or candidates in question have been duly elected to membership in the lodge or are eligible to receive the further degree requested. This letter should ideally be signed by the Noble Grand, attested by the Secretary, and **sealed** with the lodge's official seal. However, in cases where this is not possible, any letter from the lodge requesting the degree may be accepted at the discretion of the lodge conferring the degree. After reading all such letters, the lodge will take a vote on bestowing the degree on the candidates requested. No such vote is generally required for the candidates originating from the lodge conferring the degree. If, however, the candidate has not yet been duly elected to membership or to receive the degree at a previous meeting, then it is necessary to do this before proceeding on to the degree.

Even when the brothers and sisters from the lodge of the candidate receiving the degree are unable to confer the degree themselves or even to assist in performing it, it is highly desirable for as many of them as possible to be in attendance. Receiving the degrees of Odd Fellowship is a serious matter, an occasion which should ideally be of great importance in the candidate's life. It does not reflect well the members and on the Order if they neglect to attend and support their lodge's candidates as they undergo this significant rite of passage. By being present and among the first to congratulate our new candidates, one demonstrates the veneration one holds for the

Order, the inculcation of its lessons, and the esteem one has for the candidates as individuals. Quite simply, if the work is taken seriously by the members, the candidates being initiated will do so as well, so long as they have been selected with sufficient care.

In jurisdictions where many lodges have difficulty mustering the resources necessary for putting on a degree, a common practice is to engage in **Degree Rally** days or Three Degree Days on which multiple degrees are conferred on a large class of candidates. As with the recorded forms of the degrees, these are responses to the difficulties of this age and are not an ideal way to bestow the degrees in a manner that allows the candidates to fully absorb them. It may be the best solution for certain lodges and jurisdictions, and it is undeniably a superior experience for brothers and sisters to see a live degree in some manner, so long as it is performed with proper care and solemnity. These special days for the conferring of degrees will often be organized on a district, regional, or Grand Lodge level.

## OF DRAPING THE CHARTER

The lodge has a designated ceremony for honoring the memory of a departed brother or sister in the form of draping the charter. This ceremony may vary from one jurisdiction to the next. Still, certain key features are consistent in all locales. Most notably, the procedure involves the Warden utilizing a cloth drape to physically cover the charter, symbolizing that the lodge's vitality has been diminished by the loss of the individual. In some jurisdictions, the drape is moved into position by both the Warden and the Conductor, utilizing their staves rather than touching it directly. The charter customarily remains veiled for thirty days after first being covered. Other features of the procedure typically include announcing the departed member's Initiatory, degree, and key officer dates as well as their total length of service to the lodge. There is also often an opportunity for lodge members to speak about their memory of the fallen

comrade. The ceremony can and should be personalized to be meaningful to the departed and their surviving brethren.

## OF NOMINATIONS AND ELECTIONS

As a democratic body, the lodge selects its key officers by way of a vote as it does with most other business to come before the lodge. The length of a term of office is determined by the frequency with which a lodge meets. Most lodges currently meet twice a month and elect new officers once a year. In times past, it was more typical to meet once a week and to elect new officers once every six months. This second pattern is still used in a few lodges today. In all cases, though, the timing of nominations and elections must be in accordance with the **constitution** and by-laws of the lodge.

The process begins with First Nominations, which in a lodge meeting on a standard, bi-monthly schedule will usually be the first meeting in October. During nominations, the Noble Grand opens the floor to nominations for each of the elected offices in turn, beginning with Noble Grand and proceeding through Vice Grand, Secretary, Financial Secretary, and Treasurer. In most lodges, there will also be at least one Trustee position coming open, which will also be nominated at this time. Any member of the lodge in good standing may nominate any eligible member for an office. It does not require a second. However, no member can be made to stand for office against their will, so the Noble Grand should ascertain that all brothers and sisters nominated accept their nominations.

The basic requirement to be eligible for elected office is that the member must have served at least two terms as an appointed officer previously. For Noble Grand, however, the requirement is at least one term as Vice Grand. In cases where no brothers or sisters who are eligible for a given office are willing to serve in that office, one who does not possess the requirements may be nominated and elected, provided that they receive written dispensation to serve in that office before being installed. Said dispensation may be granted by the District Deputy Grand Master or directly from the Grand Master.

Following First Nominations is Second Nominations, which is usually held during the second meeting in October for a bi-monthly lodge. The reason for having two separate meetings to nominate is that it allows all those who were unable to make it to the first meeting a second chance to nominate an individual of their choosing, should they be dissatisfied with what transpired originally. This prevents any surprises from occurring which might otherwise deprive a member of the ability

to vote for a candidate of their choice. Second Nominations take the same form as First Nominations except that they come up during Unfinished Business and include the reading of previous nominees by the Secretary prior to nominations being opened. Lodges will sometimes hold Elections at the same meeting as Second Nominations, and this is entirely reasonable.

Elections often take place the first meeting in November for a bi-monthly lodge. Should any office have only a single nominee, the common practice is for a member to move that "where there be but one nominee for an office that the election be by acclamation collectively." Should this **motion** be seconded and passed, the lodge has opted to adopt a special procedure for quickly dispensing with unopposed candidates for office. A common misconception is that the passage of this motion constitutes the election of these officers, but it is actually only the first step. Instead, after the procedure is ratified, the Noble Grand reads off all those unopposed offices and candidates and then calls for a **voice vote** on whether they shall all collectively be elected. Should there be a single voice of dissent, the lodge must revert to the standard election procedure by secret ballot. If only a single office is unopposed, then the motion is to "elect by acclamation," omitting the word "collectively."

In cases with more than one candidate, the election is conducted by secret ballot, one office at a time. The Noble Grand requests the Warden to hand out paper ballots, which should have been prepared in advance by the Secretary, and asks each candidate for the office to appoint tellers to help tally the vote. As with voting on any other lodge business, only members in good standing should be permitted to vote. After the Noble Grand has ascertained that all entitled to ballot have done so, the Warden collects the completed ballots and proceeds to announce the name on each ballot one at a time while the tellers look on to ensure the names are correct. The Secretary repeats each name aloud, keeping track of the vote with tally marks and saying the word "tally" after completing a set of five tally marks. Once the result has been fully tallied, the Secretary announces the winner.

## OF INSTALLATION OF OFFICERS

Following elections, the new officers must undergo an installation ceremony before assuming their respective offices. The installation ceremony is generally performed as soon as is practicable once the new term has begun. For most lodges, this will mean installing the officer in January. The installation is most frequently performed by the District Deputy Grand Master. However, it may also be performed by a Grand Lodge officer or by any Past Grand. Ideally, all the installing officer parts should be filled, but it may also be performed solely with the District Deputy Grand Master and District Deputy Grand Marshal if those are the only officers available. The Junior Past Grand has the right and privilege to perform the Acting Past Grand duties for the installation unless they wish to waive that right, in which case any Past Grand may serve in that capacity.

When performed by the District Deputy Grand Master, the installation is declared to have been performed "in regular form," whereas if the Grand Master presides, the installation is "in ample form." When performed by any other Past Grand, the installation is simply "in form." If the officer parts are filled by Grand Lodge officers, they use their own titles instead of the standard district-level titles. If the Grand Master is presiding over the installation, any officers serving on the installation staff who are not actually the corresponding Grand Lodge officer are referred to in an acting capacity. For example, the Past Grand acting as Grand Marshal would be addressed as the "Acting Grand Marshal."

Although the Ritual only provides for a regular, **closed installation**, multiple other forms of the installation ceremony are used, depending on the jurisdiction. Only Odd Fellows may be present in a closed installation, and the gavel is utilized to call up or seat the lodge. Anyone may attend a **public installation**, but the audience is asked to stand or be seated verbally. A joint public installation occurs when more than one lodge is installed simultaneously, most frequently an Odd Fellows Lodge and a Rebekah Lodge. If both types of lodges participate, there are installing officer parts for both the District Deputy Grand Master from the Odd Fellows and the District Deputy President from the Rebekahs. There are also two corresponding Marshals. Some jurisdictions also have a **dinner installation** that takes place seated around a table without floorwork. In many lodges, after the installation is complete, it is customary for a Past Grand jewel to be awarded to the outgoing Noble Grand if they are a new Past Grand. This presentation is most often made by the outgoing Right Supporter of the Noble Grand or by a dignitary such as the District Deputy Grand Master or an officer of the Grand Lodge if one is present. Many lodges like to have a **collation** after their installation even if they don't have refreshments at most of their meetings.

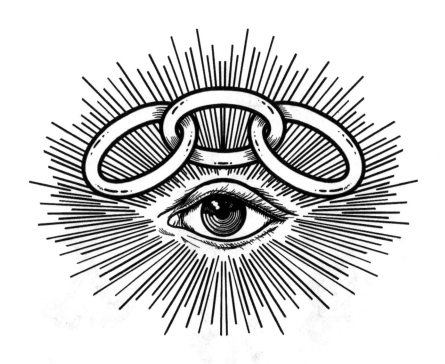

# CHAPTER VIII

## ON THE ELECTIVE OFFICES

### *OF THE NOBLE GRAND*

The Noble Grand is the highest officer in a <u>local lodge</u>. They are stationed in the central seat on a raised dais at the far end of the room from the <u>inner door</u>. Their emblem is crossed <u>gavels</u> signifying their authority over the lodge. For degree work, their robes are scarlet trimmed in gold. They wield a gavel, not only as a symbol of parliamentary authority but also for practical use while chairing the meetings.

SUBORDINATE-LODGE JEWELS.

Vice Grand.

Past Grand.

Noble Grand.

Guardian.

Conductor

Warden

Per. Secretary.

Treasurer.

Rec. Secretary.

The Noble Grand is responsible for appointing all appointed officers for the term, except for the Vice Grand's Supporters. They are also responsible for appointing all lodge committees unless otherwise noted in the lodge **by-laws** or other applicable Odd Fellows legal **codes**. Generally, before assuming office, the Noble Grand will put together a "program" for the term, which primarily consists of a calendar of events.

During meetings, the Noble Grand presides as the parliamentary **chair,** ensuring that the rules of debate are followed. While there is no rule precluding the Noble Grand from consulting with a **parliamentarian** or other authority on rules of order, this is generally not needed at the local lodge level where thorny parliamentary questions are somewhat less likely to occur. Learning how to wield the gavel effectively is a significant challenge that a new Noble Grand must face if they have not served in a similar position in a fraternal or other parliamentary-style organization. A careful balance must be struck between taking a firm hand to keep the meetings civil and on track and being permissive when needed to encourage participation and good feelings among the brothers and sisters. New Noble Grands inevitably take some time to develop this finely-tuned balance. The majority start out overly indulgent, and a minority begin overly draconian.

While presiding, it should be the goal of the Noble Grand to ensure that all voices are heard on any matter to come before the lodge and that a member or small group of members aren't able to dominate the discussion or hold the lodge hostage to their particular goals and opinions. The Noble Grand would be well-advised to be lenient with the rules, such as allowing discussion to occur without a **motion** on the **floor** while the meeting is proceeding harmoniously and expediently. When the tone becomes more acrimonious or the hour is late, the Noble Grand should enforce the rules of debate firmly and fairly to keep the meeting amicable and efficient. An effective Noble Grand should be able to dispense with business rapidly so that the attendees have ample time to socialize with their brothers and sisters after the formal meeting is concluded.

It is also worth noting that unlike the leaders of many other types of organizations, the Noble Grand does not possess much direct authority. Instead, the Noble Grand's role is to facilitate the lodge's decision-making process and other business. In some senses, the Noble Grand actually has less direct power than other lodge members because the Noble Grand customarily doesn't even vote on motions before the lodge except to make or break a tie. If there is one less vote against a motion than there is for it and the Noble Grand casts a vote against it, the result is the motion failing due to not having a majority. Thus, the Noble Grand may always cast the deciding vote when applicable. The reason behind this practice is to avoid depriving the Noble Grand of their intrinsic right to cast a vote as a member of the body when said vote would be determinative. In practice, this does not come up often, and the Noble Grand is further expected to refrain from even debating business while occupying their chair, to maintain impartiality. As a result, the Noble Grand mostly wields authority through influence with other members and would be well-advised to cultivate the social and collegial relationships necessary to exert leadership over the lodge. This is invaluable training for life, wherein one must often work with those over whom one has no formal authority. The Noble Grand is also permitted and expected to ballot on membership applications, advancing brothers and sisters to the next degree, and electing officers for the lodge.

## OF THE VICE GRAND

The Vice Grand is the second-highest officer in a local lodge. They are stationed in the central seat on a raised dais at the near end of the room to the inner door. Their emblem is an hourglass with double lines in the center, signifying that their time to become Noble Grand draws near. For degree work, their robes are blue trimmed in gold. Like the Noble Grand, they wield a gavel for practical use during the meetings. Though it doesn't often happen in practice in most lodges, the Vice Grand is fully empowered to use the gavel to maintain order in the lodge as a supplement to the Noble Grand.

As with many other second-in-command positions in other organizations, the office of Vice Grand primarily exists to have a substitute in the case of an absence by the Noble Grand and to help train new individuals to assume the mantle of Noble Grand the following year. As such, the Vice Grand is best advised to become familiar with the role and duties of the Noble Grand and to devote time to planning their expected term as Noble Grand for the following year. The Vice Grand also has particular charge over the inner door and is responsible for directing the Inside Guardian to discharge their duties regarding admission to the **lodge room**.

The Vice Grand is empowered to appoint the two Supporters of the Vice Grand and would be well served by appointing experienced individuals who can instruct them in their duties as Vice Grand when needed, both during and outside of meetings. In some lodges, there is an expectation that the Vice Grand's Supporters will move up to become Supporters of the Noble Grand when the Vice Grand is elevated to that office. The Vice Grand also has the privilege of appointing one member to all **Interviewing Committees**.

Additional duties may be assigned to the Vice Grand by the Noble Grand or based on the particular traditions of the lodge or **jurisdiction**. For example, it may be commonplace in one locale to have the Vice Grand chair the Finance Committee. In contrast, in another, it may be customary for the Vice Grand to superintend refreshments for the lodge's meetings. The lodge's by-laws may require the Vice Grand to serve on certain committees or in specific other roles. Still, as with many other enduring traditions, aspects of the role may not be written in any formal document whatsoever.

## *OF THE SECRETARY*

The Secretary, also often referred to as the "Recording Secretary," as distinguished from the Financial Secretary, is stationed at a desk to the Noble Grand's right. Their emblem is crossed quills and an open book, signifying their involvement with the written records of the lodge. The Secretary has official charge of the lodge's **seal**, which is used to indicate the lodge's approval of documents, such as the **annual term report** or a letter sent on behalf of a member. The Secretary also has custody of the lodge's **minute** book and **members' register**.

The Secretary is arguably even more critical than the Noble Grand to the effective functioning of the lodge. While the Noble Grand must ensure the harmony of the lodge, the Secretary is responsible mainly for its productivity through careful record-keeping and handling of incoming and outgoing correspondences. In olden times, there was often also a separate Corresponding Secretary responsible for correspondences in addition to the separate Financial Secretary which still exists today. In some lodges, correspondences are reviewed by the Secretary and the Noble Grand before the lodge opens so that only those which are required or are adjudged to be suitably of interest to the lodge are read.

The Secretary's minutes constitute the official record of what transpired at meetings, including all decisions of the lodge. It is of critical importance that they are accurate, complete, and written objectively. From reading the minutes, a member should be able to accurately reconstruct all motions made at the meeting, including the final outcome and any actions to be taken. However, it is not necessary to include the substance of the discussions themselves, and one should certainly not include anything resembling a full transcript. Best practice includes noting who made each motion, and many lodges also include the identity of the brother or sister who seconded a motion in the record. Generally, the exact vote total need not be recorded, except in special cases, such as a **roll call vote**, or if required in the by-laws or other code of Odd Fellows law.

The Secretary is also responsible for producing an annual term report for the lodge on the forms provided for that purpose by their Grand Lodge. This report, which may also be referred to as an "annual **per capita** report," typically includes lodge financials and a roster of current officers and members, noting any additions or subtractions. This report must be submitted promptly each year, as Grand Lodge must have an accurate picture of membership in the jurisdiction and the health of each lodge. Submission of the term report is also necessary as a prerequisite for the annual installation of officers to be held and, if not filed on a timely basis, may ultimately result in the **arresting of the lodge's charter**. While this report is the Secretary's particular responsibility, the other officers and members should also take an interest in ensuring this crucial report is submitted.

The Secretary or other **desk officers** are further responsible for ensuring any necessary annual non-profit organization reporting requirements handed down by the country, state, or province in which the lodge is located are complied with. In the United States, this may include the **990, 990-EZ, 990-N**, or e-Postcard form, depending on the gross receipts or total assets of the lodge, and the **990-T** if the lodge has a substantial amount of income unrelated to the lodge's core mission as a non-profit. The officers should consult with an accountant or other suitable professional regarding state filings if in doubt as to how to prepare these reports. Failure to comply may result in a loss of tax-exempt status or other penalties.

## OF THE FINANCIAL SECRETARY

The Financial Secretary is stationed at a desk to the Noble Grand's left, alongside the Treasurer. Their emblem is similar

 to that of the Secretary, but omitting the open book. In this case, the quills signify the Financial Secretary's responsibility for maintaining payment and membership records. They keep track of payment of dues and any other assessments or fees from the membership and issue **dues cards** to those members in **good standing**. All incoming money should pass through the hands of the Financial Secretary before being provided to the Treasurer for deposit. Some lodges, particularly smaller ones, opt not to have a separate Financial Secretary and instead combine the office's duties into those of the Secretary.

The records kept by the Financial Secretary allow the lodge to know which members are paid up in their dues and other fees, the primary requisite for being in good standing. Only members in good standing are permitted to vote or otherwise transact the business of the lodge. A member who is not in good standing cannot attend any lodge except for their own. The Financial Secretary should strive to ensure all members who are in **arrears** on dues, assessments, or any other indebtedness to the lodge are reminded to pay. It should be noted that members are most frequently behind on their financial obligations to the lodge due to simple inattention and not due to a desire to withdraw from participation. The Financial Secretary should send out a **notice of arrears**, sealed with the lodge's seal, once the brother or sister is behind on their debts. This is generally done after eleven months of nonpayment. Once the member owes the sum of at least one year of dues and has been duly notified, they may be **suspended** for nonpayment. In the course of their duties, the Financial Secretary may also become aware of financial hardships suffered by individual members; for this reason, discretion should be regarded as an imperative virtue of the office. In most lodges, the Financial Secretary is also responsible for generating annual or other periodic financial reports for the Grand Lodge or civil authorities.

## *OF THE TREASURER*

The Treasurer is stationed at a desk to the Noble Grand's left, together with the Financial Secretary, if there be one. Their emblem is crossed keys, signifying their function of protecting the money and assets of the lodge. The Treasurer keeps a ledger and is the principal financial officer of the lodge. Generally, the Treasurer is also the  primary officer to possess and make use of signing authority on the lodge's operational accounts. They are to pay all bills which have been properly voted on by the lodge.

It is especially imperative that the individual serving as Treasurer is above reproach in all of their business dealings with the lodge. If the lodge's policies only require a single signature for drafting checks and one is due the Treasurer, the Treasurer should seek out another member with signing authority to avoid any possible accusation of foul play. The Treasurer should also studiously avoid any possible conflict of interest arising from their position in the lodge, as is wise for any lodge officer.

## *OF THE TRUSTEES*

Trustees are elected by a lodge if their by-laws or the laws of their jurisdiction mandate it. They may vary in number depending on the lodge's by-laws, with the most frequent numbers being three or five. In most cases, they serve a multi-year term, with their election staggered to result in one new trustee taking office each year. In cases where a trustee leaves office before the end of their term, the lodge may opt to elect multiple trustees simultaneously with one open office for a longer time period than the other.

The expected duties of trustees may vary considerably between lodges or jurisdictions because they are generally not spelled out in great detail in the codes of law. Different lodges may own different types of property. Fundamentally, a trustee's responsibility is to manage capital assets for the lodge. Lodges may possess substantial investments in stocks, bonds, or other liquid assets. In this case, the trustees must make decisions regarding the purchase, disposition, or management of these investments. The trustees should strive to be prudent with the lodge's invested funds, ensuring that the principle is preserved if not enhanced and that the lodge only withdraws a sustainable income from these accounts. If they are not well-versed in investment strategy, they would be well-advised to consult with a competent investment advisor or another professional in this area. A lodge may exist for hundreds of years. Still, for it to remain prosperous, every generation of officers must heed well their fiduciary responsibility to the lodge and its members.

Lodges may also possess real estate in the form of lodge halls, cemeteries, rental properties, parcels of land, or others. The trustees are also responsible for managing and protecting these highly valuable assets. The key role of the trustees here involves making investment decisions regarding these assets. However, in many lodges, the trustees might also have a role in arranging for repairs or other necessities for a building's upkeep. Other lodges may have a Building Committee which handles the more mundane aspects of caring for the building or even be part of a **hall association** in which one or more lodge forms a separate legal entity to handle ownership of and matters relating to the lodge hall.

The trustees' role is entirely focused on assets and property and not on taking leadership or ritualistic role within the lodge. Therefore, they have no designated station in the lodge room or **regalia** denoting their office. Trustees may serve concurrently in most other lodge offices, though it is not usually considered proper to be Noble Grand, Secretary, Financial Secretary, or Treasurer at the same time.

# CHAPTER IX

## ON THE APPOINTIVE OFFICES

### *OF THE WARDEN*

The Warden is stationed at the chair in front and to the right of the Noble Grand. Their emblem is crossed axes, which hearkens back to former times when the Warden would carry an axe which he would use the flat side of for collecting charitable donations for the benefit of needy members. The axe is also a symbol for progress, representing humanity's ability to conquer the natural world. For degree work, their robes are most often black, though other colors are used in some lodges. The Warden is the highest-ranked appointed officer in the <u>line</u> and carries out a variety of ceremonial functions within the lodge.

The Warden is officially responsible for preparing the **lodge room** before meetings, including initiations. When setting up for a regular meeting, it is standard to place the **regalia** for each officer at their station, set out the **gavels** for the Noble Grand and Vice Grand, and also deposit the Bible and any other holy books on the Chaplain's station. Serving as Warden thus provides an opportunity to learn the emblems and stations of all the offices of the lodge for those who may not yet have committed them to memory.

During meetings, the Warden is responsible for taking up the passwords during the opening. The Warden is the only officer expected to walk around the lodge room during meetings and may be directed by the Noble Grand to **escort** another member or visiting dignitary or to carry papers or other items between stations or to the brothers and sisters on the sidelines. The Warden also plays a major role in balloting on new members, draping the **charter**, and other lodge ceremonies. They are further tasked with making the members comfortable while in the lodge and should strive to ensure that all have what they need.

## OF THE CONDUCTOR

The Conductor is stationed at the chair in front and to the left of the Noble Grand. Their emblem is crossed rods or staves, signifying the role of the Conductor in escorting the candidates around the lodge room during degree work. For degree work, their robes are black. During a regular lodge meeting, substantially fewer duties devolve on the Conductor than the Warden, but the Conductor is charged to assist the Warden as needed and will often be the one tapped to fill in when the Warden is absent. Indeed, the Conductor may be thought of as both the assistant and trainee of the Warden in preparation for advancing to that position the following year in lodges which utilize the **progressive line**.

## *OF THE SCENE SUPPORTERS*

The Scene Supporters are stationed in the two chairs in front of the Vice Grand's station. Their emblem is a torch, symbolizing the knowledge they help bestow upon the candidates in the **Initiatory Degree**. For degree work, their robes are white. Their duties are focused entirely on degree work, and they have no special function during any other lodge meeting. In a lodge with a progressive line in operation, they are only a way station between the more operative roles of Inside Guardian and Conductor unless the lodge follows the venerable practice of having each officer perform the part into which they have been installed for degree work.

## *OF THE INSIDE GUARDIAN*

The Inside Guardian is stationed at the chair nearest to the **inner door** of the lodge room. Their emblem is crossed swords, signifying their role in protecting the lodge from any intruders. Instead of a robe, the Inside Guardian wears a coat of armor which may be of any color. In olden times, lodges were often guarded with real weapons, indicating the importance members attributed to the lodge and its private business. The primary responsibility of the Inside Guardian is to guard the inner door of the lodge room.

Whenever an **alarm** is given at the door, the Inside Guardian should respond, whether or not the alarm was given correctly. The Inside Guardian opens the **wicket** and inquires "Who comes there?" They are to relate whatever information they receive about the individual seeking admittance to the Vice Grand, who has official charge of the door. In regular circumstances, the Vice Grand will respond "Admit them if correct," and the Inside Guardian is then tasked with verifying that the arrival is in possession of the correct password. If the password is given correctly, then the Inside Guardian opens the door to allow the member to enter. Alternatively, where there is a visiting dignitary or group of dignitaries seeking admission, the Inside Guardian will be ordered to simply admit them. During degree work, the Inside Guardian should consult the **Ritual** to determine the proper response to candidates seeking admission. The Inside Guardian should also be sure that everyone given permission to enter is in the proper regalia.

In the prescribed format wherein there is also an Outside Guardian, the Inside Guardian only asks for the password of the degree that the lodge is open in. The prevailing custom among lodges today, however, is not to have an Outside Guardian stationed in the **anteroom** and in this case, the Inside Guardian should be certain to require both the **term password** and the password of the degree in which the lodge is open. When there is an Outside Guardian stationed in the anteroom, the Inside Guardian must inform the Outside Guardian whenever the lodge is closed in one degree and opened in another so that the Outside Guardian may properly fulfill their own duties.

## OF THE OUTSIDE GUARDIAN

The Outside Guardian is the only officer stationed outside of the lodge room during a meeting, officially occupying a position in the anteroom. Their emblem is identical to that of the Inside Guardian, consisting of crossed swords with the same symbolism of protecting the lodge. Although they occupy a role in the ritual apparatus of the lodge, they nevertheless do not have an assigned costume for degree work.

While in past epochs, it was a strict requirement and expectation that the Outside Guardian would remain in the anteroom guarding for the duration of the meeting, this is seldom practiced today. Often, the easiest way to find a brother or sister willing to serve as a traditional Outside Guardian is to encourage someone from another nearby lodge to **associate** with the lodge and even potentially arrange a swap of associate members willing to serve in this capacity. Two lodges may thereby procure the services of an Outside Guardian without requiring an existing member to miss out on the business meetings.

The Outside Guardian ensures that no one approaches the inner door without being in possession of the term password and wearing the proper regalia. They are to ascertain the opinion of the Noble Grand in any case of doubt as to the right of an individual to enter the lodge room. This may be done by communicating through the Inside Guardian and Vice Grand. The Outside Guardian must also bar everyone from entering during the opening and closing of the lodge as well as degree work, **closed installations**, or any other ritualistic work not open to the public.

Having an Outside Guardian stationed in the anteroom is important not only for the measure of security it provides, but also because the Outside Guardian acts as a host or greeter for all members arriving after the lodge is opened. The Outside Guardian is always kept informed by the Inside Guardian as to what degree the lodge is open in and can inform any tardy brother or sister, enabling them to give the correct password and **sign**. The Outside Guardian may also assist arrivals with locating the proper **collar regalia** to wear into the lodge room. If a visitor is not a member of the Order but nevertheless requires admission to the lodge room, the Outside Guardian may convey the message to the Noble Grand via the Inside Guardian and Vice Grand, allowing for a **recess** to be called or other provisions made to accommodate the new arrival.

## OF THE CHAPLAIN

The Chaplain is stationed at the podium along the wall to the left of the Noble Grand. Their emblem is the Holy Bible, signifying their role in leading the spiritual or devotional

exercises of the lodge. For degree work, their robes are reminiscent of ecclesiastical dress, often similar to a surplice or similar vestment. The Chaplain is a relatively recent addition to the Ritual, only having been in existence since the early 20th century. Prior to that, the Noble Grand was the primary priestly figure in the lodge menagerie, delivering many of the lines during degree work that are now recited by the Chaplain

The Chaplain recites the **opening and closing prayers** recorded in the Ritual as well as any other such recitations as are necessary or desirable in the course of the work of the lodge. They also play a key role in funeral services and attending to the sick or infirm members of the lodge via the Visiting Committee. The Chaplain may also serve as a spiritual advisor to the members of the lodge, assisting in matters of ethics or morals. It is important for the Chaplain to be sensitive to the needs of members hailing from all different faiths even if those faiths may differ substantially from their own. Odd Fellowship is non-sectarian in nature and the Chaplain should therefore strive to refrain from using any liturgical materials or concepts which are particular to one religion unless everyone in the lodge agrees. The intention is not to prevent a lodge from reflecting the religious predilections of its members, but rather to ensure that the rights and sensibilities of all are respected, including guests to the lodge.

## OF THE JUNIOR PAST GRAND

The Junior Past Grand, also known as the "Acting Past Grand" or simply the "Past Grand," is stationed at the podium along the wall to the right of the Noble Grand. Their emblem is the Heart in Hand, superimposed on a pentagram, signifying that Past Grands

should exemplify the precept that an Odd Fellow should always receive another whole-heartedly. The pentagram further alludes to the five degrees of Odd Fellowship which existed throughout much of the 19th century prior to the adoption of the four-degree system in use today, indicating that the Past Grand has mastered all of them. For degree work, the Past Grand's robes are scarlet trimmed in white. The Past Grand delivers **charges** during degree work, but aside from that has no particular responsibilities in the lodge. Their station has been referred to as the "most comfortable seat in the lodge" because they have completed their term as Noble Grand, one of the most difficult and demanding positions in the lodge, and are now entitled to repose. It may also be thought of as a place for the outgoing Noble Grand to cool off from their multifarious involvements with the lodge before diving into any other lodge responsibilities.

## OF THE SUPPORTERS
## OF THE NOBLE GRAND

The Supporters of the Noble Grand are stationed flanking the Noble Grand. Their emblem is a single gavel, signifying their attachment to the Noble Grand, whose symbol is the gavel. For degree work, their robes are scarlet trimmed in gold, but less ornate than the robe of the Noble Grand. They have ritual functions during the meeting, but also serve in an important advisory capacity for the Noble Grand. The Right Supporter should definitely be a Past Grand, and ideally the Left Supporter should also have served in the office

During meetings, the Right Supporter assists the Noble Grand in declaring the lodge open and closed. They are also responsible for assuming the station of the Noble Grand when the Noble Grand needs to vacate it temporarily in the course of a meeting. This can happen because the Noble Grand needs to exit the lodge room to attend to personal business, or it can also occur when the Noble Grand wishes to debate a **motion** on the

<u>floor</u>. A scrupulous Noble Grand will also surrender the chair when a matter comes before the lodge which might constitute a conflict of interest for the Noble Grand. The Right Supporter should be sure to advise the Noble Grand when a situation arises that necessitates the Right Supporter assuming the gavel. The Left Supporter of the Noble Grand officiates in the position of Right Supporter when the Right Supporter is absent. Both officers are responsible for observing that the members give the signs correctly, but would be well-advised not to call them out publicly during the meeting. As with any ritual or procedural mistakes that do not actually impede the flow of the meeting, it is always best to inform the brother or sister privately after the fact. The Left Supporter is further charged to verify that members who enter the room are clothed in the proper regalia, though this should not be necessary if the Outside Guardian or Inside Guardian notify members who have forgotten to don their regalia while the mistake requires less effort to correct.

## OF THE SUPPORTERS OF THE VICE GRAND

The Supporters of the Vice Grand are stationed flanking the Vice Grand. Their emblem is a simple hourglass, signifying their attachment to the Vice Grand, whose symbol is the hourglass. For degree work, their robes are blue trimmed in gold, but less ornate than the robe of the Vice Grand. Like the Supporters of the Noble Grand, they have ritual functions during the meeting, but also serve to advise the Vice Grand on the administration of the duties of the office. As in the case of the Noble Grand Supporters, the Right Supporter should definitely be a Past Vice Grand and ideally the Left Supporter should also have served in the office.

## OF THE MUSICIAN

The Musician is officially stationed to the left of the Conductor, but in practice is likely to sit at the piano or other instrument they play. Their emblem is a lyre, signifying the music they produce. They add musical accompaniment not only to the odes and the national anthem, but also to the process of escorting members around the room when necessary. A good lodge musician will always have a march available to perform when time needs to be filled while escort is occurring and can adjust the pace or  start and stop whenever needed. In the Initiatory Degree there are several places indicated for musical accompaniment, including the **Initiatory Ode,** as well as portions of the degree where solemn music may be played.

Arranging the music adeptly is also possible when operating recorded music, but is far less flexible than what a skilled performer can achieve. There is also the possibility of using non-traditional instruments. The key is to use whatever instrument the Musician is comfortable with and to keep it enjoyable for all. There are recommended melodies listed for the odes in the **charge book** which may be utilized, but there is also nothing to stop an enterprising Musician from choosing their own to suit their own distinctive taste. This position is considered optional and is one of the chairs least frequently filled, but lodges would do well to consider finding one for their officer staff if at all possible.

## *OF THE COLOR BEARER*

The Color Bearer is stationed to the right of the Warden. Their emblem is a flag, signifying that they carry the flag during the ceremonies of the lodge. This too is a position that lodges rarely fill even if they do possess sufficient members to do so. Most lodges refrain from escorting the flag, preferring to have the Warden post it prior to the start of the meeting. 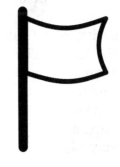 The Color Bearer would be well-advised to study the laws and customs of their country surrounding the presentation, retiring, and caring for the flag.

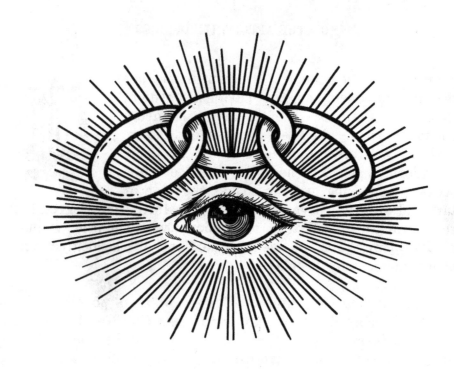

# CHAPTER X

## ON COMMITTEES AND THEIR WORK

### *THEIR PURPOSE, COMPOSITION, AND FUNCTIONING*

Well-regulated committees are a significant factor in the operation of a successful lodge. Committees have the opportunity to discuss complex issues at length without monopolizing the time and attention of the entire lodge. They can also be used to research a topic when further information is needed before acting or to take any action that has already been decided on by the lodge. The other big advantage of committees is that having a smaller group to consider a decision can produce a better result than a larger one. When a discussion involves more than a handful of participants, the conversation's overall unity can degrade, and the discourse can suffer from shallowness. There may also be members who can make invaluable contributions but

might otherwise be silenced by more dominant personalities when in a larger setting. Committees can thus provide an excellent forum for less outgoing members to shine.

The two basic types of committees are standing or regular committees and special or ad hoc committees. Standing committees are appointed, usually at the first meeting after installation, for the term. Special committees may be appointed at any time and only exist until the purpose for which they were created has been accomplished.

Standing committees should be appointed by the Noble Grand unless otherwise specified in the lodge's **by-laws**. In some cases, the by-laws may mandate that particular officers, such as the Noble Grand, Vice Grand, or Chaplain, be appointed to serve on or chair specific committees. In most lodges, the Noble Grand is considered an **ex-officio** member of all committees, which means they are on the committee by virtue of their office of Noble Grand. When composing a committee

for purposes of deliberation on a question, the best practice is
to select individuals whose viewpoints span the full spectrum
of lodge opinion. If the committee only embodies a narrow point
of view, it is far more likely that the committee's work will
spill over onto the **floor** of the lodge. Brothers and sisters
may feel that their perspectives have not yet been expressed
and may strive to ensure their voices are heard. This can
unnecessarily prolong discussion on the topic at a lodge meeting.
If neither explicitly stated nor otherwise predetermined, the
first brother or sister named when the committee is appointed
is the **chairperson** of said committee.

The chairperson of a committee is the primary individual
responsible for convening the committee and facilitating the flow
of discussion and decision making on the committee, similarly
to the presiding officer of a lodge. However, there is rarely
an expectation that a committee's chairperson will refrain from
making, debating, or voting on **motions**. This is a departure
from common practice on the floor of lodges or other larger
bodies. In smaller committees, the chair will often also be the
one taking **minutes**. However, a larger committee may wish
to elect a secretary to do so. There is also sometimes a vice-
chair appointed or elected to serve as a backup when the chair
is not available. If the chair fails to convene the committee
as necessary, a meeting may also be called by two or more
members. Committees are generally also empowered to elect a
new chair or other officer should they wish to do so.

The manner in which committees conduct their business is
frequently more informal and with less protocol and procedure
than a lodge. Ex-officio members may attend and vote at
any committee meeting when they choose to do, but they
need not be counted when **quorum** for the committee is being
determined unless they have also been appointed to the committee
independently of their office. Nevertheless, any committee
charged with making a recommendation or any other decision
should use voting or **unanimous consent** to fulfill their duties.

When the Noble Grand calls for reports of committees during a lodge meeting, it is customary for the committee's **chair** to be the one giving the report. However, any committee member may be permitted to give the report, particularly in the chair's absence. While a standing committee may be expected to report at every lodge meeting, a special committee typically reports less frequently. Generally, the special committee only reports when it has completed its purpose or when necessary to update the lodge on its progress. Accordingly, two types of reports may be delivered by a special committee, a partial report or a final report. After a final report, the special committee is dissolved. Traditionally, standing committees are also expected to deliver final reports, but generally not until the end of the term for which they were constituted.

In the course of their deliberations, committees do not always achieve unanimity. The majority view of the committee is accepted as the primary report returned to the lodge. Should there exist a minority faction within the committee who agree on a result at variance to that of the majority, they too are permitted to give a report to the lodge, though this is not required. If desired, it should be done directly after the report of the majority, but before voting on any directive put forward by the majority of the committee. Any lodge member may offer an objection to hearing the report of the minority, and if a single member objects, the lodge votes by a simple majority on whether to hear the minority report. Should the committee members in the minority not have one consistent position on the matter, individual committee members may be permitted to give their own reports at the discretion of the lodge. Once all committee reports have been received, if an action is recommended, the motion made will typically be to "accept" or "adopt" the majority recommendation of the committee. If this motion passes, the recommendation is enacted by the lodge, with no further motion necessary. In some lodges, however, to avoid possible confusion about what is being voted on, a separate motion is required to commit the lodge to a course of action.

## OF FINANCE COMMITTEES

A finance committee reviews and approves the bills to be paid at each meeting of the lodge, as has already been discussed. If no separate budget committee or similar exists, the finance committee is also responsible for putting together an annual budget. At the end of the year, the finance committee audits the Financial Secretary, Treasurer, and Trustees' books. Therefore, the finance committee should not include any of these individuals so that it can act as a disinterested party in the accomplishment of said audit. As this committee is expected to participate in every meeting of the lodge, the members appointed should have a good attendance record in addition to being scrupulous in matters of business.

## OF VISITING COMMITTEES

Visiting committees played a far more prominent role historically than they do in most lodges today. They usually included the Noble Grand, Vice Grand, and the Chaplain once that officer was added to the traditional set of appointed officers in the early 20th century. They also included other lodge members specifically selected to assist in the work of the committee. The committee would visit and comfort sick members, but it had an additional major purpose, which may be surprising to some brothers and sisters today. That purpose was to verify that the member truly was sick and that their illness was not the result of their own negligence or poor decisions. The pecuniary benefits which lodges provided to sick members were often quite generous and were therefore subject to fraudulent claims. Furthermore, a member was not entitled to receive said benefits if the illness resulted from irresponsible behavior, such as excess consumption of alcohol or other intoxicants. Medical doctors were sometimes consulted to ensure the claim against the lodge was valid and should indeed be paid. This original function is essentially non-existent today. Now that benefits are seldom paid, most lodges do not even bother appointing this committee unless required to do so by their by-laws.

Today, this committee can still play a valuable role. Visiting the sick is far less common than it used to be, but can still be a source of solace and comfort for the infirm. It may be desirable for the committee to make arrangements to visit brothers or sisters in the hospital or their homes. It may be sufficient simply to organize sending cards, flowers, or baskets of fruit on behalf of the lodge. Small gestures can go a long way to remind ailing members that the lodge is thinking about them and cares about their well-being. People do not usually forget those who supported them in their hour of need.

## *OF MEMBERSHIP COMMITTEES*

A membership committee can be invaluable in assisting a lodge in the attracting of new members as well as the retention of existing ones. The committee may bring in new members in various ways, including, but not limited to, holding lodge open houses or other events to which prospective members are invited to meet some of the brothers and sisters and see the lodge hall. Most passersby have no inkling of what takes place in the lodge hall in many cities or towns. They may be interested in attending merely to satisfy their curiosity. The committee may develop a program to focus on recruiting a particular set of demographics or shared interests, which may bolster or complement the current set of members.

The retention of existing members is even more important than the recruiting of new members to the success of a lodge. Far too often, lodges experience a revolving door phenomenon wherein they rapidly bring in new members and lose members in sufficient numbers to offset any gains. If a member joins but finds nothing for them in the lodge, they are more than likely to depart posthaste. An effective membership committee can prevent this unfortunate turn of events by seeking to understand the needs of the various constituents of the lodge community.

"Committees Illuminate the Whole Lodge

## *OF BUILDING COMMITTEES*

Many lodges that own halls find it practical to assign a
committee specifically to look after the lodge's repair and
upkeep and restocking supplies, and managing the rentals if
applicable. While the lodge's trustees are responsible for the
building in a legal and financial sense, a Building Committee
can handle the multiplicity of minute tasks associated with
operating a communal property. Without a committee serving
this purpose, a lodge may find itself without certain necessities
unexpectedly. Worse, it may also fall into disrepair if it lacks a
designated set of individuals to monitor the physical structure,
infrastructure, and furnishings.

At least some of the individuals assigned to a Building Committee should ideally have a background in building repairs and maintenance. It would be ideal to find a lodge member who is a construction professional to chair or serve on this committee, but this will not be possible for every lodge. If there is interest in decorating the lodge, it may also be helpful to appoint a member with a design background or a strong interest in design. Having the hall be comfortable, attractive, and safe is required for the lodge to be successful because few people enjoy spending time in a shabby, dilapidated structure that is crumbling around them.

Some lodges will hire a lodge member or outsider as a hall manager to oversee the facility, including hiring service providers and administrating rentals. Conflicts of interest may arise any time a lodge hires a member. In these cases, it is best to clearly define designated tasks and accompanying compensation. Earnings should be reasonably consistent with the industry's norms and standards. Similar conflicts of interest may also occur in the fairly common situation where a renter of the hall becomes a member, often at the urging of the lodge members themselves. In these cases, the renter should ask to recuse themselves from voting on any decisions that impact their hall rental.

Another practice utilized in many lodges in the **hall association.** This is a separate legal entity, usually a corporation which holds title to the lodge hall instead of the lodge itself. There can be a variety of reasons for a lodge to establish a hall association. In some cases, a hall association may solely be composed of the members of a single lodge. In many of these cases, the basic intent is to circumvent the reversionary interest the Grand Lodge holds on the lodge's assets. These types of single-lodge hall associations are therefore often prohibited by a prudent parent body. On the other hand, a multi-lodge hall association can bring harmony to the governance of a shared facility through the establishment of clear rules and regulations.

## *OF SOCIAL COMMITTEES*

A Social Committee is responsible for the planning and execution of social events for the lodge. In many lodges, particularly smaller ones, this committee does not exist. Instead, event planning is handled on an ad hoc basis with a special committee for each event. It may also be combined with the responsibilities of a Service Committee and others to form a broader Events Committee, which is responsible for all events hosted by the lodge. The chair and other members should be capable event planners, skilled at navigating the manifold moving parts necessary to organize a successful social event. It may be particularly desirable to ensure that at least one committee member is well-acquainted with how to prepare or secure refreshments as these are integral to success for many classes of social events.

In larger, successful lodges, there typically exists a wide variety of interests on the members' part. The committee should be careful to ensure that the variety of events held by the lodge is representative of all the members' interests, not merely a vocal minority. For event types that do not fall within the committee members' interests or expertise, the committee should be sure to consult with the members who do possess those interests to achieve success. Particularly large

or complex events often should be assigned their own special committee rather than being handled by a more generalized social committee.

## OF SERVICE COMMITTEES

The lodge's calendar should not only include events designed for the entertainment and enjoyment of the lodge but also for the good of the community and society at large. A designated Service Committee can be an effective way to maintain a full complement of these events. A similar skill set is required as in the planning of social events. Still, there should also be an emphasis on building partnerships with other organizations. It may be beneficial to have at least one committee member who is well familiar with the non-profit sector or with the administration of social services, as knowledge of these may make it easier to find appropriate opportunities for the lodge to make a positive impact.

Many lodges have become complacent in the forms which their service to the community takes. It is far less effort to merely write a check to a charity than to deploy the lodge members out in the world to lend a hand more literally. To remain shut within the four walls of the <u>lodge room</u> would be a mistake, however. Not only is working directly with those in need often more efficient or effective, but it's also more rewarding for the volunteers and reminds all of the responsibility Odd Fellows have to those less fortunate than themselves. All lodges should seriously ponder how they can become more involved in service.

An effective way to motivate the committee members and the lodge to participate fully and wholeheartedly is to select causes that are of particular interest or arouse the members' sympathies. This may depend on what type of community the lodge exists in and what needs are most pressing. Some perennial issues such as homelessness and food insecurity will be applicable in any location.

## OF BY-LAWS COMMITTEES

The By-Laws Committee is not necessarily a standing committee. In some lodges or <u>jurisdictions</u>, it may be appointed every year as per by-laws or other <u>codes</u> of law, while in others, it may only be appointed when deemed necessary. If the jurisdiction requires that the by-laws be amended on a set schedule, such as every fifth year, then the By-Laws Committee is responsible for reviewing the existing by-laws and recommending suitable improvements. In instances where the By-Laws Committee has been appointed specifically because the lodge has determined a particular amendment is required, the committee is merely tasked with devising how to best achieve the lodge's goal, including drafting specific language for the amendment.

All lodges may wish to consider appointing this committee every year, however, because there is always a need for the

lodge to monitor changes in Odd Fellows legal codes emanating from their Grand Lodge or Sovereign Grand Lodge. When those bodies alter the law, it already overrides any contradiction in the lodge **constitution** or by-laws, but this can confuse the members who may not always remember to look in all the different law sources. Thus, it is best to update lodge by-laws any time they come into conflict with another source of law having greater precedence.

## OF EXECUTIVE COMMITTEES

It is not always practical to have the full lodge vote on business, particularly if an urgent need to pay a bill or make a decision comes in between the regularly scheduled meetings. While the lodge could call a **special meeting** to address these, a more agreeable solution may be to permanently establish an Executive Committee to handle such matters as they arise. In order to be able to act with the full authority of the lodge, the details of the committee and its operation must be spelled out in the lodge's by-laws. The most common approach is to define the Executive Committee as being composed of the elective officers of the lodge, though sometimes the Acting Past Grand may be included. Other individuals may be part of the committee as well, if desired. The exact powers granted should be detailed to avoid any possibility of controversy arising from its operation.

An Executive Committee may meet in person, over the phone or videoconferencing, or may even potentially vote on business over email if permitted. Careful records should be maintained of all Executive Committee decisions. They should be reviewed at the first available meeting of the lodge following the determination. By requiring all decisions to be ratified by the entire lodge, the committee's power is checked, and the ultimate power to decide remains with the whole body where it ought to reside. By enabling immediate action while preserving democratic principles, the Executive Committee provides a useful tool for the lodge to function while not able to meet. It is heartily recommended for all lodges to consider utilizing.

## OF SPECIAL COMMITTEES

Special committees may be appointed to handle many different types of functions ranging from the ordinary to the sublime. Their purpose could be as simple as arranging the chairs in the lodge room or as lofty as drafting a new mission statement to guide the lodge for years to come. They are often created spontaneously during meetings, arising from the judgment of the Noble Grand or the collective deliberations of the members. The only immutable rule is that the committee must have a single, clearly defined purpose. Once this purpose has been completed, the committee dissolves back into the nothingness from which it sprang.

Perhaps the most frequent use of special committees is to plan a one-time event, especially in lodges that do not possess any standing committees for event planning. In this case, the chair and members simply make whatever arrangements are necessary for the event, make interim reports on their progress as desired, and then make a final report once the event has been successfully held. In addition to the result achieved, including the number of attendees and any financial results, their final report could also include anything they learned in planning and executing the event, which may be of general interest to the lodge. The committee may be assigned a budget by the lodge upfront or may periodically request funds as needed while the event arrangements progress.

Another exceedingly common use of special committees is to gather further information and make a recommendation on an issue that has come before the lodge. The whole lodge need not entertain a prolonged discourse on the relative merits of different models of an item of equipment to be purchased. Instead, the matter is often disposed of through the means of a special committee. This sort of committee may only need to meet a single time to review whatever relevant materials are available and formulate a recommendation to deliver at the subsequent meeting. It is generally better to use a committee rather than a single individual to engage in information gathering. This ensures a higher level of objectivity due to the members' respective biases, ideally counterchecking one another.

The lodge may find that the same brothers and sisters may repeatedly volunteer for special committees and the minor tasks that they preside over. It is best, however, to work towards involving a wider variety of members whenever possible. Not only should one seek to avoid exhausting the generous souls who always want to help, but engaging a larger portion of the lodge provides the members with a stronger connection to the lodge and its work. It is especially beneficial to draw upon the newer members of the lodge who may not yet feel fully attached and who also may proceed with the task at hand with a higher level of enthusiasm than the grizzled veteran.

# CHAPTER XI

## ON LODGE FINANCES

### OF FINANCIAL PRACTICES

Income to the lodge should be first delivered to the Secretary so it can be noted in the **minutes.** In the case of dues or other payments from members, it must also go to the Financial Secretary if there is a separate officer, so that the brother or sister's account with the lodge may be kept current. Finally, income should be placed in charge of the Treasurer, who is responsible for depositing it into the lodge's bank account. It is to be entered in the ledger or other financial records maintained by the Treasurer and Financial Secretary.

Expenditures are also first delivered to the Secretary, who enters them into the minutes and fills out a **warrant** to be signed by the Noble Grand and the Finance Committee. No

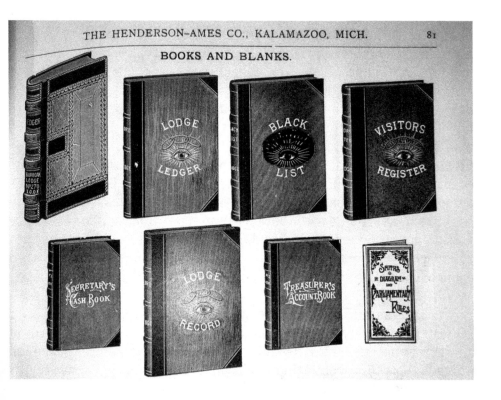

bill may be paid without the vote of the lodge unless the lodge has made provisions to allow for this in the **by-laws** between meetings in the form of an Executive Committee or another similar method. Lodges often have bills to pay, which may have deadlines before the next stated meeting, so making provisions to legally pay bills in between meetings is wholeheartedly recommended. In cases where they have been approved between meetings, they must still be documented in the usual manner, and the approval granted between meetings must be reported to and ratified by the lodge.

Even in this era of electronic payments, nearly all lodges pay bills almost entirely through the use of checks. A very common requirement is that the check must be signed by two individuals with signing authority for the lodge, ideally including the Treasurer. Common sense should be used when determining who may sign a check on behalf of the lodge. For example, it might raise questions if reimbursement was paid to a member after having been signed only by the individual and their spouse. However, checks may not be practical for items such as utilities, which may be best handled by automatic debit to ensure they are paid on time. The lodge may vote to authorize automatic billing, but this too must be reported to and ratified by the lodge as well as properly accounted for in the records. Lodges are also permitted to use debit cards, credit cards, or digital payment services, subject to all the same restrictions as other forms of payment unless specifically forbidden in the laws operative on that lodge. To properly utilize newer payment methods, a lodge would be well-advised to specify the procedures for their usage in the by-laws to ensure that proper procedures and accountability are in place.

Lodges using older record-keeping systems may keep records primarily in written form within a book. There is an increasing trend to switch to modern approaches based on spreadsheets or accounting software. In all cases, however, a record needs to be made available to the lodge officers or any other member on demand. Financial records are also checked by the District Deputy Grand Master or by Grand Lodge officers or other agents on a regular schedule and when there is cause to investigate or audit the lodge's financial practices. The required records should be delivered forthwith in response to any legitimate demand from these individuals. It is also a laudable practice to maintain paper copies of financial records in the lodge hall so that they may be inspected at will. The general standard for length of document retention is seven years, after which they may be safely discarded.

## OF DUES

Originally, dues collected from the members were the primary means a lodge used to sustain itself financially. This remains true in lodges that are not blessed with large endowments or investments and do not have an income-producing property. These lodges do not have the luxury of keeping dues low

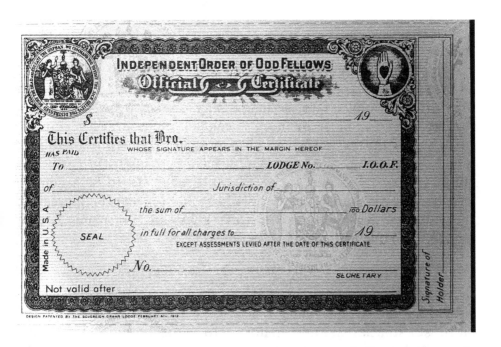

and must charge enough to fund the lodge's operation. Many contemporary lodges do possess substantial financial resources, however, due to the prudent financial stewardship of previous generations, or in some cases, one or more mergers resulting in the sale of a superfluous lodge hall. Even in these more prosperous lodges, dues serve a valuable purpose: keeping the membership rolls limited to those who place at least some nominal value on their affiliation with the Order. For a well-heeled lodge, the dues may be quite low indeed. Still, even the mere effort of arranging to make payment betokens a basic level of commitment. There is also something to be said for the proven wisdom that a person will often assign more worth to that in which they invested than that in which they have not.

The price of dues is conventionally set within the lodge's by-laws, along with the schedule by which they become due. The price will often include multiple tiers, generally one price for full members and another, usually lower, for **associate members**. The reason for this price discrepancy is that a lodge only pays a **per capita** tax to the Grand Lodge based on full members, and this cost is not insubstantial. There is no requirement that the lodge charge less for associate membership, and instances have occurred where lodges charge more to disincentivize associate membership. In addition to these two prevailing pricing tiers, a lodge may devise others, such as pricing tiers for older or more financially constrained members. In some instances, there may be **non-contributing members** who do not pay at all. Lodges may have provisions in their by-laws, setting their dues price for full members to be a certain amount above the per capita. When the per capita increases, these lodges need not hastily draft a by-law amendment with a corresponding increase in the dues price.

The dues schedule is subject to considerable variation as well. In most cases, nowadays, dues are collected annually. However, in earlier times when dues would constitute a far more substantial amount relative to household incomes than today and meetings were more frequent, they would even be paid weekly. A lodge may opt for allowing dues to be paid more often, such as bi-annually or quarterly. Still, even when this is an option, most members will pay in advance for a full year to avoid the inconvenience of more frequent payments. The date that dues are payable can vary based on the lodge's fiscal calendar or other considerations. The two most common arrangements are for dues to be payable as of the first day of the calendar year or the first day of the term, should it differ from the calendar year.

A member must be paid up on their dues as well as any other outstanding debts to the lodge to be considered in **good standing**. Dues must be paid on or before the date they are due, a practice often referred to as "dues paid in advance." Even if dues are a single day late, the member is no longer in good standing, meaning that they are deprived of most of the rights they would otherwise possess as an Odd Fellow, including the right to receive the **term password**, visit other lodges, vote in lodge, stand for election, or be installed into an office. If the member's lodge has pecuniary benefits, such as a **sick benefit** or a **death benefit**, the member is generally not eligible for these either until they return to good standing. The member's **home lodge** must also be in good standing by having filed any necessary term reports and paid per capita or any other indebtedness to the Grand Lodge. Otherwise, none of the members of that lodge can be in good standing, regardless of having actually paid their portion of the per capita as part of their dues. It is also possible for an entire Grand Lodge to lose their standing should they not meet their reporting or financial obligations to Sovereign Grand Lodge, though this is less common. A member who is currently under **suspension** is not in good standing, regardless of their payment status with the lodge.

## OF ASSESSMENTS

When a lodge is unable to raise sufficient funds to pay its expenses, it may levy an assessment upon its membership to procure additional income. The standard form of an assessment is a flat fee, which is required of all lodge members, though it may be stipulated in the lodge's by-laws that assessments are only obligatory to certain classes of members. For example, in a lodge with a non-contributing member, they may also be exempt from paying assessments. As with dues, if a member neglects to pay the amount required, they are no longer in good standing.

Assessments are rarely used in most lodges, though at one time, they were quite routine. In particular, they were brought to bear to support needy members during the epoch before formal sick benefits, and other benefits were devised. The member's circumstances would be brought up in open lodge, and those assembled were asked to open their hearts and purse strings. Odd Fellows lore tells that the practice originally included the Warden of the lodge traversing the **lodge room** with axe extended, collecting donations from the brethren on the blade. This was a voluntary assessment, but assessments took on the involuntary character they possess today in later

times. They were the prevailing method of providing for death benefits, in particular. Death benefits, which remain in force for numerous lodges even if they remain untouched in recent times, were intended to assist the member's surviving spouse or family members in affording the cost of a decent burial.

Another type of assessment, which is exacted only against a single member, is a fine. However, this is also seldom used in practice nowadays. An attentive brother or sister may recall that fines are alluded to in the **charge** delivered by the Noble Grand during the opening of the lodge. In olden times, a list of fineable offenses and their attendant quantities would likely have been put in writing, perhaps even in the lodge's **standing rules.** Conduct resulting in a fine would have included items such as cursing during a meeting or engaging in other forms of unruly behavior. Today, a lodge would be far more likely to use the other major remedy at the Noble Grand's disposal: instructing the Warden to **escort** the offender out of the lodge room. It was also once common for fines to be issued for failing to attend meetings, failing to attend to the responsibilities of offices held or committees assigned, or the more general category of "conduct unbecoming an Odd Fellow." These types of issues are far more frequently addressed through the process of removal from office or committee.

## OF OTHER FORMS OF INCOME

Beyond the standard methods of collecting dues and assessments, there are numerous other ways that a lodge can bring in income. Events, particularly those open to the public, often have admission fees. These are usually priced just to cover the cost of putting on the event in most cases, though, and sometimes not even that. Beyond the admission fees, events can also generate income through sales of food and drink, raffles, or auctions. Often for raffles or auctions, the prizes are donated by lodge members. This can be an excellent way for participants to get superfluous items out of their homes and generate some income for the lodge in the process. One Odd Fellow's trash is another Odd Fellow's treasure. Another widespread practice is the 50–50 Raffle in which the prize awarded is 50% of the revenue from raffle ticket sales, with the lodge keeping the remaining amount. Most frequently, raffle and auction income are used to generate funds to be used for charitable donations.

Lodges that have been in existence for longer periods of time are able to fund themselves comfortably through a combination of investment income and property rentals in many cases. Property rentals take two principal forms, rental of designated commercial spaces within the lodge hall and rental of the lodge room or banquet space. Designated rental spaces are more desirable because they generate more consistent and predictable income. They also involve less inconvenience caused by having to move around furniture or otherwise alter the space to account for different types of usage. For lodges which do not have separate rental spaces, considerable income may be derived from renting out parts of the hall at a daily or hourly rate. Popular renters for hall facilities include other

clubs or hobbyist groups and individual life cycle events such
as birthday parties, wedding receptions, or memorial services.
In all cases of lodge rentals, it is extremely important that the
lodge ensure it is protected through proper lease agreements,
suitable insurance policies, and adequate security personnel or
monitoring of the site when needed.

## OF EXPENDITURES

Lodges are permitted to expend money for any purpose in
accordance with the aims of Odd Fellowship, including items
such as lodge hall maintenance and upkeep, office supplies and
equipment, events and refreshments, publicity or promotional
materials, member relief, charitable donations, member travel
reimbursements, and Odd Fellows <u>regalia</u> or other ritual items.
However, one should always ensure that the expenditure is
permissible with respect to the lodge's by-laws as well as other
applicable Odd Fellows laws and that proper procedures are
followed in the approval and disbursement of allocated funds.
Often, the form this approval will take is a vote of the lodge
before a member makes the purchase with their own funds.
In these cases, the item's precise cost may not be known, and
the remedy is for the lodge to set a maximum pre-approval
amount for the member to keep the cost below. Alternatively,
an event may be allocated an overall budget with the particular
purchases left to the committee's discretion for planning the
event.

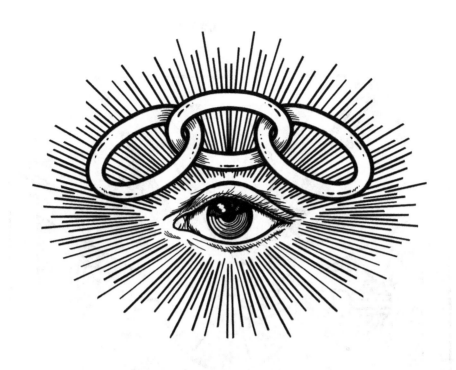

# CHAPTER XII

## ON THE LAWS OF THE ORDER

### *OF PRECEDENCE OF LEGAL AUTHORITY*

Odd Fellowship is an organization governed by its own laws at all levels, and as such, it provides guidance on how to resolve contradictions between the various sources of Odd Fellows law. The highest authority is the **Ritual**, which includes the contents of the **charge book** and any other publications from Sovereign Grand Lodge containing the ceremonies of the Order. Second in precedence comes the Constitution and Code of General Laws issued by the Sovereign Grand Lodge. Third is the **constitution**, **by-laws**, and **standing rules** of the Grand Lodge, whose **jurisdiction** the legal question falls under. Fourth is the constitution, by-laws, and standing rules of the lodge. Fifth is Robert's Rules of Order Newly Revised, which may be relied upon for all matters not covered in the previous documents.

At every level of governance there is also an internal
order of precedence. A constitution supersedes by-laws. By-
Laws, in turn, prevail over standing rules. The lowest form of
precedence is tradition or custom, which may be overturned by
any written laws or with a simple vote of the body.

## OF THE POWER OF INTERPRETATION

Any brother or sister is qualified to formulate their own
opinions on interpreting the laws as written. Still, only certain
officers have the formal power to issue interpretations which

are binding upon Odd Fellows bodies and individuals. A Noble Grand is the legal decisor for their lodge, so long as no ruling on the matter has already been issued by a higher authority. The lodge may vote to overturn the Noble Grand's ruling. It may also be appealed to the District Deputy Grand Master for the district that the lodge belongs to. All legal decisions solicited from the District Deputy Grand Master must be requested in writing. That officer should render their ruling in writing, including citations of all relevant <u>code</u> passages and providing a copy to the Grand Master in addition to the petitioners.

The Grand Master of the Grand Lodge having jurisdiction should review all decisions made by the District Deputy Grand Masters. They have the option to overturn those rulings by issuing a formal ruling in writing, citing all relevant code passages, and indicating the new interpretation to be observed by all Odd Fellows and lodges in the jurisdiction. An individual or a lodge may also directly appeal the ruling of a District Deputy Grand Master to the Grand Master by petitioning in writing. The rulings of the Grand Master are binding until the Grand Lodge meets. At this point, they are all subject to review by the Judiciary Committee of the Grand Lodge. The Judiciary Committee presents their findings regarding the decisions of law the Grand Master has made during the term to the Grand Lodge, who will then vote to adopt or reject the committee's recommendations. Rulings that are not reversed by the Judiciary Committee or the Grand Lodge become precedents, binding on the Grand Lodge until the Grand Lodge adopts further legislation on the matter through the normal legislative process. In some jurisdictions, it may also be customary for the Grand Lodge to pass legislation affirming the Grand Master and Judiciary Committee's ruling by committing it to the corpus of law in <u>bill</u> form.

The Sovereign Grand Master and Sovereign Grand Lodge have the authority to overturn decisions by Grand Lodges through a similar process to that effectuated by the Grand Master and Grand Lodge. A decision from the Sovereign Grand

Master may be requested only by a grand body, a Grand Representative, or the official head of any unit of the Order under Sovereign Grand Lodge's direct supervision, such as a lodge which does not fall within the jurisdiction of any Grand Lodge. This decision must be requested in writing, and the resulting ruling must also be rendered in writing to take effect. The ruling is to be considered binding until Sovereign Grand Lodge meets. At this point, all official rulings are reviewed by the Committee on Judiciary and then acted on by the assembled Grand Representatives in a like manner to a Grand Lodge acting on rulings from the Grand Master.

The Committee on Legislation has official responsibility for preparing legislation to enact the Grand Representatives' rulings if necessary. In a case where the Sovereign Grand Master's home jurisdiction is involved, the power of interpretation may be delegated from the Sovereign Grand Master to the Deputy Sovereign Grand Master or Sovereign Grand Warden to avoid any semblance of conflict of interest. Sovereign Grand Lodge also retains a Committee on Appeals and Petitions to consider appeals filed with the Sovereign Grand Secretary after the Sovereign Grand Lodge's ruling has been reviewed by the Committee on Judiciary.

One of the most commonly quoted passages in all the legal codices of Odd Fellowship is the "Laws to be Liberally Construed" passage. This passage reads as follows, though slight variations may be found in different jurisdictions: "THE RULES AND REGULATIONS SET FORTH IN THE CONSTITUTION AND CODE OF GENERAL LAWS SHALL BE LIBERALLY CONSTRUED. THE CHIEF CONCERN SHALL BE FOLLOWING THE SPIRIT OF THE LAW AND THE GOOD OF ODD FELLOWSHIP RATHER THAN HARSHLY ENFORCING RULES TO THE LETTER OF THE LAW."[20]

On the surface of it, this passage may seem to engender a willful disregard for the literal meaning of the laws, should they contradict a notion of the Good of the Order as formulated in the mind of the interpreter. The concept of liberal construction in legal interpretation is not specific to Odd Fellowship. Instead, it is part of the general judicial tradition prevailing amongst many polities and organizations. It is intended to be utilized in cases where the written text leads to ambiguity, fails to address the question at hand, or results in an outcome that is not the statute's intent. In these limited situations, it permits the decisor to use their own judgment of the particulars of the situation in addition to the literal meaning of the language set down so as to avoid a miscarriage of justice. Thus, it should be invoked sparingly, and certainly not in cases where it would do violence to the terms of the provision by separating words from their natural meanings.

An interpreter of Odd Fellows law would do well to remain well within the possible literal meaning of the applicable provisions while also striving to ensure that their ruling is just, fair, and following the precepts and principles of Order. If it has been determined that the laws themselves do evil rather than good, the proper remedy is not to interpret them out of existence but rather to change the laws through the legislative process provided for that purpose. When formulating an interpretation, a simple strategy may be employed to ease the undertaking. One should begin with the principal source, the Ritual, and work one's way down the order of precedence, noting any potentially relevant passages along the way. When reviewing them, it is entirely possible that some will be in direct conflict with each other. In those cases, it is important to be mindful of the precedence of authority and to disregard the lesser of the sources. In some rare instances, one may even discover contradictory passages within the same document. In these cases, judgment might provide for either one being given priority, depending on the peculiarities of their contents and placement. It could also be beneficial to consult a dictionary if the meaning of any of the terms in a provision is not clear.

In cases when the law is silent on a matter, there are multiple strategies to employ. One might draw a logical analogy

with a similar situation for which the law is provided and reason from this how the authors of the operative laws may have decided. In a case where no such analogy may be drawn, or intent gauged, an interpreter of Odd Fellows law would always do well to look to the Good of the Order and meditate carefully on what outcome would result in the greatest good for the institution. The power of interpretation is mighty, a potent tool of benevolence in the hands of the just and the pure of heart.

## OF CHARGES AND TRIALS

Although Odd Fellowship inculcates its participants with respect for established laws that protect all individuals' rights and preserve the common good, these high standards may not be upheld by all members at all times. When an offense against the Order's laws is committed, regulations exist to determine appropriate consequences for such violation that the lodge may be restored to peace and harmony.[21] The term used for such action is to bring **charges** against the errant member. The laws governing this process are perhaps the most complex and intricate in all of Odd Fellowship. The following is an attempt to explain them as simply as possible.

In cases where a member has been convicted of a crime, the matter should be brought to the Secretary of the member's lodge, the Grand Secretary, or Sovereign Grand Secretary. If verified, the member is to be expelled from the Order without requiring the trial procedure. Generally, a brother or sister may not be subject to charges or **expulsion** for actions committed before becoming a member. However, if membership was obtained under false pretenses, it may be revoked. In cases where a civil judgment has already been obtained against the member regarding personal business dealings, it is not subject to charges within Odd Fellowship unless there was a finding of fraud on the part of the member.

Charges may be brought against any member of the Order by any other member using the Trial Code forms found in the Sovereign Grand Lodge Code of General Laws.[22] The completed "Charges and Specifications" form is filed with the lodge Secretary of the accused. It should be recorded in the **minutes** of the lodge. Charges must be filed within the statute of limitations of ninety days of the alleged offense. Notice of the charges having been filed is delivered to the accused using the form prescribed for that purpose. The notice form should also be presented to the Noble Grand of the lodge.

The charge for an offense against the Order is stated as "conduct unbecoming an Odd Fellow" but further specification should be given in one of the following categories: acquiring membership by misrepresentation; printing or distributing Odd Fellows materials such as forms or rituals without authorization;

illegal use of the lodge seal; exposing books or records of the lodge; identifying a member who opposes admission of a candidate; attempting to fraudulently obtain pecuniary or other benefits; attempting to misappropriate or embezzle lodge funds or property; acquiring passwords by false representation; organizing, participating in, or affiliating with an organization composed of Odd Fellows whose objects or purpose is in conflict with the Order; engaging in **electioneering** or political methods for selecting officers; using abusive or profane language in the lodge, on lodge property, or in a public space when members or the general public are present; issuing communications to the jurisdiction without permission of the Grand Master or other principal officer, aside from newsletters or magazines; gambling in the **lodge room** during a meeting; failure to report fraudulent claims for benefits or assistance; spreading false or malicious allegations against another member; promulgation of spurious written or unwritten information; conviction in a court of law for an offense evincing a serious lack of character; exclusion from membership or other discrimination based on race, ethnicity, sex, gender, sexual orientation, religion or other social identity, or age, aside from the minimum age required to join the unit; misfeasance, malfeasance, or nonfeasance while in office; or any other offense deemed to be conduct unbecoming an Odd Fellow. The charges stated should specify the time, place, and circumstances of each offense by the accused.

Upon receipt of the charges, the Noble Grand is required to appoint a **Special Deputy** who is initially responsible for meeting with both the accuser and the accused to determine if the matter may be resolved without having to go to trial. Both parties are to be apprised of what would be involved in a trial so that they can determine their preferred course of action. Whenever possible, it is best to address the issue which led to the charges without putting the lodge through the controversy and unpleasantness of a trial. If both parties agree to drop the charges, the matter is concluded, but if either party seeks a trial, they have a right to proceed with one. The Special Deputy reports the outcome of this initial meeting to Noble Grand.

Should the charges go to trial, the Noble Grand appoints a Trial Committee, which consists of five lodge members. The first member so named contacts the other members to convene an organizational meeting within thirty days. At this initial meeting, the committee elects a **chairperson** and a secretary. The accused, the accuser, and the Special Deputy are to be notified in writing of the composition of the committee and given the opportunity to challenge for cause up to three members of said committee. The reason for such an objection must be returned in writing within ten days of receipt. The challenge is adjudicated by the Noble Grand, who is empowered to select suitable replacements. Further challenges may be issued to the replacement committee members in a like manner.

The accused, accuser, and Special Deputy are also to be notified of the trial's date and time, which is selected by the Noble Grand. A trial date may not be on a Sunday, as this is the sabbath for many members of the Order. Should the accused observe a different day as their sabbath, they may object to the trial being held on that day in writing to the Trial Committee at least one week before the scheduled date. This objection must be honored. The trial's venue is to be determined by the Noble Grand and must be within the jurisdiction of the accused. The trial must be held within ninety days of the charges being filed, or the charges are to be dismissed without prejudice, meaning that the accuser may file similar charges for the same infraction at a later date. Notification for the parameters of the trial is provided on the form provided for that purpose by Sovereign Grand Lodge. It is to be considered properly delivered if left at the residence or delivered by registered mail.

While awaiting trial, the accused member retains all rights of membership in the lodge except for **transferring** to another lodge or obtaining a **withdrawal card**. However, the accused should be temporarily removed from holding office in the lodge pending the completion of the trial. Should the trial result in an acquittal, the member must be restored to their former office. The accused may not be punished in any other manner until the trial has been completed. If the accused does not appear at the time and place specified for the trial, the trial may proceed in their absence. Alternatively, the Trial Committee may issue a **resolution** that the accused who fails to appear is in contempt of the lodge and is to be expelled.

Those bringing the charges are responsible for selecting the prosecutor for the trial. The prosecutor may call witnesses and present evidence but may not themselves serve as a witness. The accused may choose to represent themselves or may alternatively be represented by another Odd Fellow who has received the same degrees as the accused who will speak, call witnesses, present evidence, and render arguments in their place. **Quorum** requirements for the Trial Committee to operate are that all five members must be present, with a simple majority determining all questions to come before the committee except for procedural matters. No one is permitted to attend the trial other than the accused, their representative, the accuser, the prosecutor, the witnesses, the Trial Committee, and the Special Deputy. The Trial Committee members may not serve as witnesses, and the spouse of the accused may not be called as a witness unless the offense was against the spouse.

The trial begins with a reading of the charges against the accused. Should any of the charges not include sufficient specificity for the accused to understand them and provide for their own defense, the accused may object to the charge, and the accuser is given leave to immediately amend the charge. If the accuser cannot provide a specific charge, the accused may move to have the charge dismissed. For each charge, the accused must enter a plea of "guilty" or "not guilty," or alternatively admit to the facts and justify their actions. They may also contend that the matter is outside of the lodge's jurisdiction or that the complaints contained in the specifications are frivolous.

All witnesses are to be sworn in with the oath or affirmation, "Do you swear, or affirm, to tell the truth, the whole truth, and nothing but the truth?" The witness is to respond, "I do," "I so swear," or "I so affirm." No charges referred to the Trial Committee may be dismissed except by unanimous vote or by the accuser withdrawing them. The Trial Committee must hear all witnesses called by both parties and must deliver a ruling on each charge after hearing and considering the evidence presented. The opposing party may cross-examine the witnesses after the direct examination from the party who called them. The Trial Committee may also question the accused, accuser, and witnesses directly during their testimony. The Trial Committee has the authority to determine the admissibility of any testimony or evidence presented.

Should any designated witness be absent from the proceedings, testimony by that individual is permitted in the form of a written deposition. The party requesting the deposition lists the questions to be answered and submits them to the lodge Secretary, who then relays them to the opposing party. The opposing party has one week in which to submit their counter questions if desired. The questions are compiled by the Secretary and transmitted to the Noble Grand or other presiding officer nearest to the witness request that the local lodge or unit take a statement from the witness accordingly. The presiding officer or their designee then has thirty days to secure the deposition, propounding every question from the list. The witness is then required to subscribe to the truthfulness of the answers provided by attesting with their signature. The member taking the deposition also signs and affixes the seal of the lodge. The materials are returned to the Secretary and furnished for the trial.

Immediately following the trial, the Trial Committee deliberates privately to render a decision of "guilty" or "not guilty" on each charge specified and to determine punishment if the accused is found guilty of one or more charges. When determining the penalty, the committee begins by considering the highest penalty of expulsion and, if that fails, proceeds through **suspension** and reprimand. If suspension is selected, the length of suspension is to be set by **motion**, not to exceed one year. The outcome of the trial must be determined within one week of the trial. The result is to be reported in writing within fifteen days by the Trial Committee Secretary to the accuser, accused, Noble Grand, Special Deputy, and accuser's lodge. The minutes and all evidence of the trial are also delivered to the lodge's Secretary as a permanent record. These minutes should include: the date and place of each meeting and the parties present; the charges and specifications and the pleas or answers returned by the accused; all points raised and the decisions made thereon by the Trial Committee; any exception taken by the accused or accuser; oral evidence provided by the witnesses; any documentary evidence submitted; and the final decisions of the Trial Committee on the charges. All members of the Trial Committee must sign the report.

In the case of expulsion or suspension, the Secretary of the Trial Committee must notify the lodge Secretary, the Grand Secretary or Sovereign Grand Secretary, and all other Odd Fellows units to which the member belongs, including the reason for the suspension or expulsion.

If the verdict is that of expulsion, the individual's membership is terminated in the lodge and all other units of the Order. However, they may apply for readmission after three years from the imposition of punishment unless there was also a conviction in a civil or criminal court, or the individual had agreed in writing not to reapply for membership. Any such readmission must follow the normal course of an application for membership, including interview and balloting. Application must be made to the lodge from which the individual was expelled.

If the verdict is suspension, membership is not terminated, and the member is required to continue paying dues and any other fines or assessments that may arise but is not entitled to any of the rights or privileges of membership. At the end of the suspension period, the member is restored to regular status unless they have been suspended for nonpayment or expelled for cause during the intervening period.

If the verdict is reprimand, then the custom is for the Noble Grand or a Past Grand to call the member onto the <u>floor</u> and deliver the reprimand in open lodge before the members present. This should also be recorded in the meeting minutes.

The accused has the right to appeal the Trial Committee's decision to the Grand Lodge by using the designated form provided for that purpose by Sovereign Grand Lodge. The appeal is to be examined by the Grand Lodge Appeals and Petitions Committee or the equivalent thereof, along with all the materials from the original trial. The appellant must be present at the Grand Lodge session in which the appeal is to be heard. The findings of the Appeals and Petitions Committee are reported to the Grand Lodge, which proceeds to either adopt or not adopt the committee's recommendations on the disposition of the appeal. If the Trial Committee has cleared the accused on the charges specified, no appeal is permitted by the accuser.

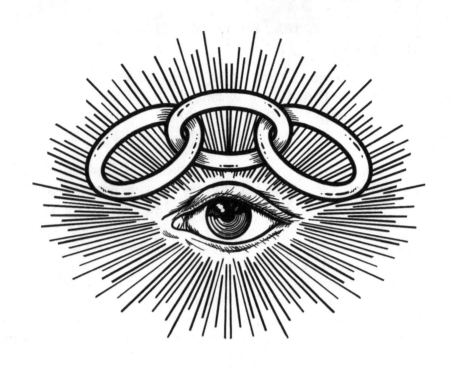

# CHAPTER XIII

## ON EVENTS AND THEIR PLANNING

### OF GENERAL CONCERNS

As has been discussed, a variety of different committees or individuals may be responsible for event planning, but regardless of who does the organizational work, the principles remain the same. The first thing to bear in mind is that an event should be planned sufficiently far in advance to allow for all necessary arrangements to be made without an unpleasant and ineffective rush. Naturally, the duration of time constituting this will vary considerably with the event's size and complexity. One should always leave a little bit more time than one expects to need due to the possibility of unforeseen circumstances arising. When first getting into event planning as an individual or a lodge, it is best to begin small with a simpler and easier to operate event, one without a lot of moving parts. One will potentially be bringing together new volunteers, many of whom may not have a lot of skills and experience relevant to the task at hand. By having success in a simpler or smaller event, the team can gain valuable experience and greater confidence to move into more ambitious events later on.

As with any other collaborative work, each participant will bring unique skills and experiences to the table. When assembling an event-planning team, one should be sure to include all the expertise and abilities necessary to carry out the desired event. There may be volunteers who are interested in helping but may not lend themselves to any of the roles

envisioned by the lead planner. In these cases, it is often worth devising a custom role well suited to each individual, even if those tasks may not have been considered essential to the event's original vision. Finding ways to involve as many members as possible will bear fruit through a more engaged and active lodge.

Events that are open to friends and family of existing members or the general public can be an effective means of broadening the lodge's social base and making further connections in the community. At any event where non-members are present, it is especially important that the program be engaging and enjoyable so that the visitors come away with a positive impression of the lodge and of Odd Fellowship. It is also imperative to ensure that the brothers and sisters make an extra effort to be friendly to the new arrivals, including them in conversations and seating them at tables with existing members, where applicable. Making a good impression on visitors is the best way to maximize the chances of transforming them into prospective members.

## OF ROLL CALL DINNERS

Roll Call Dinners are a traditional event in many lodges, often taking place on the anniversary of the lodge's institution. They include a meal that may be catered or provided by the members, either as a potluck or using a pre-planned menu. During an appropriate interval in the dinner, the Secretary is called upon to "read the roll." The ideal time to do this may be between dinner and dessert. The Secretary reads the names of each lodge member aloud, beginning with the one who joined the lodge earliest and proceeding in order through the latest initiates. In each case, the date of joining or the number of total years as an Odd Fellow is read. Those assembled cheer or applaud each member in turn. The member being honored by having their name and seniority announced rises to acknowledge the recognition. This event is useful for bringing the lodge together to indicate the value accorded to every member.

## OF GUEST SPEAKERS

Hosting a guest speaker can be a simple event to plan since the speakers themselves plan the materials they present. The lodge needs to provide adequate facilities such as a podium and microphone or a television or projection screen for a slide presentation. To ensure the event runs smoothly, cooperation with the speaker is required in advance so that any possible technical issues can be resolved and everyone is on the same page regarding the facilities available for the lecture. Beyond that, comfortable seating for the audience with an unobstructed view of the speaker and light refreshments are usually all that is needed.

Topics for guest speakers may vary substantially based on the interests of the members and what speakers are available. It is unlikely that one topic will be found which everyone in the lodge shares an interest in, so rotating speakers and topics from one event to the next is highly recommended.

Topics could be historical, literary, artistic, scientific, technological, or charitable, to name a few basic categories. It may even be desirable to invite a speaker from the lodge or a different lodge to speak on an Odd Fellows topic. One popular example is to have a representative visit from one or more Odd Fellows appendant bodies to inform the members assembled as to the fraternal opportunities awaiting them should they join that body. These groups exist for Odd Fellows who wish to participate in additional degrees and get to know members from a wider geographical area.

## OF CONCERTS

Another event which has a long history in the Order is having live musical performances. When most lodges were larger during earlier epochs, a lodge might even have its own house orchestra or band. While having a sufficient number of musicians in the lodge is less common today, any lodge can bring in outside entertainment of this sort so long as they possess adequate facilities. The first and most important choice to make when planning such a performance is to determine whether the lodge wants to handle running the event or whether to hire one or more musicians and allow them to handle the promotions, setup, and production. The latter method may be especially desirable when the lodge does not yet have much experience running this type of event.

A concert should ideally take place in a room with good acoustics. In most lodges, the **lodge room** itself is likely to have the best acoustics, as they are designed to enable members at a meeting to hear each other speak. If any of the musicians will be using amplifiers or other electric apparatus, the planners should ensure that there are sufficient electrical outlets in the space for the performance. Different room arrangements are possible depending on the atmosphere desired, such as tables, rows of chairs, standing room, or a designated dance floor.

The easiest way to locate suitable performers is through personal connections. This is not always possible. One possible avenue is to contact a local music school and find out whether they have any students or alumni they can recommend. Social media or other online listings are also effective means for locating available talent.

It may also be sensible to partner with an external arts organization to form an ongoing relationship for the purpose of holding a recurring concert series. These may be located by contacting a local arts council or similar association and can result in a mutually beneficial ongoing relationship.

## OF GAME NIGHTS

Game nights are another event that can be held with very little planning or overhead. It could be as simple for a smaller lodge as acquiring a couple of decks of cards and a set of poker chips to allow for friendly games of cards with nominal betting. Remember that if any form of gambling is included, it

must be arranged in conformance with all applicable local laws and the lodge's own **constitution** and by-laws.

In addition to games of chance, there are numerous pre-packaged board, card, or role-playing games that members can bring to game nights. The lodge may also provide the games, depending on the members' preferences.

For a larger event, a good strategy is to have many different games available to choose from as the participants arrive. As with most other types of events, providing gracious, if modest, refreshments can make the difference between a good event and a great event.

## OF CRAFT FAIRS

Craft fairs provide an opportunity to show off the handiwork of the brothers and sisters of the Order and any other community members invited to participate. Many members possess expert skills in sewing, knitting, crocheting, drawing, painting, ceramics, woodworking, or metalworking, and these events can bring those talents to the fore.

Crafters often continuously produce new items from hobbies and may even have an excess of completed projects looking for good homes. There is often an element of fundraising in craft fair events, with proceeds potentially being designated to be donated to a particular charitable cause. Craft fairs are especially popular during the winter holiday season. They can provide a good source of hand-made items to be given as gifts.

## *OF CARNIVALS*

Carnival-style events can be very popular with families and children in particular. They can range in scale from making a few simple homemade carnival games all the way up to renting elaborate equipment such as a bouncy house.

At the more basic end, there are a variety of carnival games such as bean-bag tosses, can knock-downs, or a fishing game, which an enterprising lodge member may construct from readily available plans.

Purchasing rolls of tickets and carnival-style prizes may also enhance the carnival event, as can decorations and music to add to the atmosphere. Suitable sources of refreshments may include a hot dog roller, a theater-style popcorn machine, cotton candy, or snow-cones. As with other events held by lodges, this can be an appropriate event to label with a decidedly "odd" theme.

## OF HOLIDAY PARTIES

Holiday parties are a standard event for many lodges, some of which have a bustling schedule of seasonally appropriate celebrations year-round. Numerous occasions are satisfactory for lodge festivities, with a few perennial favorites. Christmas and other winter holidays are most common for lodge parties. For these, it is important to bear in mind that brothers and sisters may observe a variety of religious or cultural practices during this time of year, and that ideally at least some element of each should be incorporated to make sure all members feel included. It is best to avoid any overt display of religious

trappings unless everyone in the lodge subscribes to a similar religious tradition and is comfortable with the lodge doing so. Gift giving, raffle prizes, or auctions of seasonally appropriate items or gifts are always options. Lodge members may also enjoy participating in relevant songs or games. Some lodges use their annual winter holiday party as an opportunity to give out lodge awards, such as veteran pins, the Merit Award, or even an "Odd Fellow of the Year" award.

Another typical holiday for lodges to celebrate in the United States is Halloween, providing lodges with an opportunity to host a costume party or even a masquerade. Costume contests are one possibility, allowing creative lodge members to compete for prizes. Other appropriate festivities for this include perennial Halloween practices such as distributing candy or bobbing for apples. For a masquerade approach, Venetian-style masks may be obtained at a minimal cost from various vendors. Haunted houses are another option for larger lodges who might be able to muster a larger number of volunteers.

Thanksgiving provides an opportunity for lodges in the United States to reach out to those members of the community who may not have family or friends nearby with whom to share a Holiday meal. Even if most lodge members prefer to celebrate Thanksgiving privately, just a few volunteers willing to put on a communal meal will allow those who would otherwise not have a place to go to share one with their brothers and sisters from the lodge. This can be done with catering or through the culinary expertise of the members themselves. Do not underestimate how sharing in important cultural events can further the fraternal bond within the lodge. Depending on the country the lodge is situated in, there may be similar festivals where this approach would work.

What other holidays are popular for lodge celebrations is very much dependent on the local community. An Independence

Day or comparable observance could include a barbecue and even a small fireworks show. However, the latter should only be used if it can be done safely in conformity with local ordinances and regulations. Lodge members may also belong to a particular cultural or ethnic group with its own holidays that the lodge may choose to honor, such as St. Patrick's Day, Mardis Gras, Cinco de Mayo, or the Lunar New Year. Any time a holiday stemming from one particular group of people, particularly a group constituting a minority within the larger community, is being celebrated, it is vital to ensure that the proceedings are conducted in a way that is respectful to that group. It is usually best to have such an event spearheaded by a member of the relevant group to properly conform with their cultural norms so that it does not provoke offense.

## OF BARBECUES

Barbecues can provide a social event that is painless to organize and is also a crowd-pleaser. Ideally, the lodge owns a grill for use in these events. Even if one must be borrowed from a member, this may be easily accomplished. The trickiest part may be timing when the food is ready, though this is eminently feasible for a skilled grillmaster or chef. Menu selection can range from the classic hot dogs and hamburgers to more involved delicacies such as shish-kebab, steaks, chicken, or fish. Often barbecue cuisine is heavy on meat. So if anyone in the lodge maintains a vegetarian diet or has other applicable dietary restrictions, suitable alternatives should be available so far as is practicable. As with any other event involving food, securing an expected attendance list in advance can guarantee that everyone has enough to eat and a minimum amount of food goes to waste.

## OF PARADES

In the 19th century, marching in parades was standard for fraternal organizations and many other types of societies. It

"First Odd Fellows Rebekahs Rose Float, 1908"

allowed lodge members to demonstrate their pride in belonging
to the Odd Fellows and their status or rank within the Order.
These were grand undertakings with considerable formality and
ostentation. The members would often wear matched outfits
along with lodge **regalia** demonstrating their current position
or previous attainments. The marchers' arrangements were
determined by their role in the lodge or the highest degree
they had received. Due to the number of participants available,
lodges or Grand Lodges were able to hold their own distinct
parades in addition to participating in larger civic assemblies.

In the present day, most lodge organizations do not
possess sufficient numbers of brothers and sisters to have
a fully independent parade, but this doesn't mean that they
cannot engage in this age‑old practice of Odd Fellowship.
Local municipalities or other bodies may have parades on
holidays or other occasions where the lodge can register a

unit to participate, often at a minimal cost. For decades, Odd Fellows have participated in the Tournament of Roses parade held in Pasadena, California, on New Year's Day, including the production of elaborately themed floats bearing Odd Fellows and other honored guests. This event brings Odd Fellows from all over the world to participate in both the construction of the float and the parade itself. Even for a more modest parade, the lodge members may find it desirable to wear **collars,** fezzes, Patriarchs Militant uniforms, or other regalia showing off their affiliation. Marching in parades helps build awareness among the general public regarding Odd Fellowship and the **local lodge** or other body.

## *OF SERVICE EVENTS*

Serving the community is an essential role for an Odd Fellows lodge. While not every lodge has the resources to put on an elaborate service event, there are options available for participation at every scale. When first beginning, it may be desirable to engage as part of a larger event organized by another non-profit with compatible goals. Undoubtedly, there are many different worthy causes in each lodge's local community that could benefit substantially from additional volunteers. Food banks almost always need volunteers to help, for example. Even if they do not need more staff to work on-site, there are other possible ways to contribute, such as organizing food drives or linen drives consisting of blankets, towels, socks, or undergarments. Voter registration drives or volunteering to staff polling locations can also provide a way to contribute to civil society's functioning while avoiding anything inherently partisan or political in nature.

When choosing to organize a volunteer event internally, a lodge has a myriad of possible goals to select from, depending on the lodge members' interests and abilities. The best ways to help out in the local community may vary considerably, so it is well worth it to invest time upfront in determining how to be impactful with labor contributions. It is important to choose a cause that is well within the members' consensus, to maximize lodge participation while minimizing controversy. At least one member should be tasked with organizing the volunteer pool to ensure that all participants know what to work on and to attend to any concerns or questions which may arise. The selection of a time and location for the event should be informed by the availability of volunteer staff in addition to the cause being advanced. Rather than merely limiting participation to the lodge members and their immediate friends and family, advertising the event in suitable venues allows a lodge to cast a wider net for recruiting volunteers. This approach can lead to the lodge making contact with new individuals who have similar values and interests to the lodge. Over time, it can provide an excellent source for identifying suitable prospects for lodge membership. In all cases, it is paramount to provide volunteers with a positive experience and ample opportunities to feel appreciated and valued for their labor contributions. One option is to provide volunteer staff with customized t-shirts to wear during the event, a practice that can further improve the visibility of the lodge's own branding as well. Another possible idea is to hold a dinner or luncheon to honor internal and external volunteers for their contributions from time to time. Regardless of how the lodge chooses to do it, recognizing volunteers for their service is one of the best ways to ensure volunteers are available for future events.

## OF FUNDRAISING EVENTS

Not all lodges are blessed with having full coffers to draw upon for all of their expenses. For those who find they need to raise additional funds, there are numerous options for accomplishing this. Even if the lodge is already flush with cash, fundraising events to support a particular charity may be a desirable way to engage the community and may be more meaningful and satisfying to the lodge than simply writing a check out of existing funds. One tried and true approach is to hold a gala dinner and to charge for reserving a seat or table, with the difference between the price and the lodge's cost constituting the funds raised. This may be further supplemented with additional revenue from auctions, raffles, or the sale of premium refreshments such as alcoholic beverages if permitted by the lodge's by-laws. When holding such a gala, the fare served should be gracious enough that everyone who attends feels satisfied with what they were served but economical enough to raise a decent amount of money.

Another major category of fundraising events are those where the lodge members donate items they no longer need or services they can personally provide. This could take the form of a communal yard sale but could also be more specialized depending on the interests and abilities of the participants. Individual members may possess unique professional skills or talents that the lodge may not even be aware of until such a fundraiser is planned. The items or services can be offered for a fixed price or dispensed through a raffle or an auction. This approach is beneficial to those donating and allows them to clear additional space in their homes or receive greater recognition or publicity for the professional services they offer.

As an alternative approach, there are many opportunities available to partner with companies that specialize in assisting with fundraising through the sale of goods. Depending on the program, the lodge may be permitted to purchase some of the company's products at a special, discounted charity rate and then resell them at a profit to raise funds. In other cases, the lodge is responsible for taking orders in advance. Then the company delivers the items, with the lodge receiving a portion of the proceeds. Restaurants may also offer fundraising opportunities wherein meals are sold at a discounted price. The lodge is responsible for providing staff to serve the meals and bus dishes. Even if a business does not have a designated fundraising program, it may be possible to work out an arrangement to have items or services donated for the lodge to sell. This is particularly relevant for smaller, local businesses that do not have a formal program but may still be interested in giving back to the community.

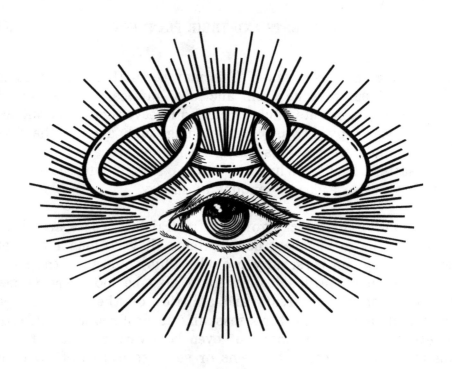

# CHAPTER XIV

## ON MARKETING AND PUBLICITY

### *OF NEWSLETTERS*

Lodges commonly use newsletters as a major method for dispensing information to their membership. These may be organized on a <u>local lodge</u> level, but also by district or other regional groupings if a single lodge does not possess sufficient writers or newsworthy topics to regularly fill an entire newsletter. Banding together between lodges also serves to keep each lodge informed of the activities members are engaged in beyond the lodge's four walls. Historically, newsletters have been printed and mailed or otherwise distributed in hard copy. More recently, electronic distribution methods have made it far easier to reach a larger audience faster and at a negligible cost in most cases.

One member is often designated as the editor and takes on the primary responsibility for soliciting articles from the wider lodge community. In a smaller operation, the editor may also be responsible for doing the page layout and distribution. However, these tasks may be delegated to other team members for a more ambitious newsletter project.

Topics to cover include upcoming events and reports on past events, giving absentee members or the general public a view into the lodge's accomplishments. Articles about the ideas, principles, and viewpoints of Odd Fellowship are also quite popular and help the members engage more fully with the Order's traditions. A "Noble Grand's Message," or similar communication from the District Deputy Grand Master or another officer, also serves to inform the lodge about the leaders who are presently serving them. It may also be desirable to highlight individual members' personal achievements and life experiences through reporting on topics like a new birth in the family, a course of educational study completed, or even an exotic vacation taken by a member of the lodge.

Whenever possible, articles should include pictures to break up the text and provide additional color to the dispatch. One noteworthy practice is highlighting the names of lodge members in the article by setting them in bold type to add to the satisfaction members receive from seeing their names and their friends' and colleagues' names in print. A representative newsletter requires contributions from many different members, so cultivating these authorial relationships is paramount to a successful newsletter.

## OF WEB SITES

In this age of electronic communication, having a strong web presence is critically important for a lodge that seeks to be relevant to younger people in particular. At the bare minimum, a lodge should possess a basic website. It should include the lodge's meeting times and location, mailing address, and a method of contacting the lodge. Ideally the means of contact should be a lodge email address or another electronic method.

In this busy and fast-moving era, a lodge that cannot be easily reached by the general public, and prospective members in particular, cannot realistically expect to thrive. Once the basics are in place, a lodge would also be well-advised to work towards including a full calendar of events, a summary of the purpose and nature of Odd Fellowship, and an online membership application. This allows candidates for membership to submit their information with a minimum of friction. It ought to be self-evident that the easier it is to apply for membership in the Order, the more people will do so.

A web site may also be superbly enhanced by the inclusion of graphics including Odd Fellows emblems and symbols as well as photographs of the brothers and sisters engaged in the work of Odd Fellowship in the lodge and out in the community. Photographs can provide an unmatched tool to demonstrate the membership's diversity, which should ideally span all ages, cultures, and walks of life from the surrounding environs. Some lodge web sites also incorporate more advanced features such as members-only sections that provide internal documents and coordination between committees and individuals in the discharge of their duties. A truly ambitious web strategy might also include the ability for members to make and track their dues payments or other indebtedness to the lodge.

The practical labor involved in establishing a web presence need not present an overwhelming burden for the lodge. If none of the members possess the requisite technical skills to do the implementation, numerous companies or individual web designers are potentially available, though this can be costly. Before embarking on such an endeavor, the committee or other individuals responsible should gather together all the materials expected to comprise the site so that no further delay is necessary after a web designer has been engaged. Ideally, rather

than being entirely custom-built, an effective web site should use a content management system. This allows non-technical members of the lodge's website team or, indeed, any authorized lodge member, to edit the content of the site without needing to go back to the designer to make a small change. When items like the lodge officers, events, or especially contact information are not kept current, the lodge's public image will suffer. No matter what strategy is used to build and maintain the site, the lodge should plan for updates to occur frequently and seamlessly.

## OF BLOGS

Blogs can also be a valuable way for a lodge to engage with its members and the general public. The word blog is a truncation of weblog. It refers to a website composed of a series of timestamped posts, most commonly displayed in reverse chronological order, with the most recent post appearing on top.

Unlike other media, blogs are often written in a very personal or informal style. In the context of Odd Fellowship, this medium is ideal for posting articles about Odd Fellowship or more journal-style posts about what is going on at the lodge. For example, a lodge may wish to use one to provide accounts of events held at the lodge, including photographs. Many blogs allow comments to be posted by readers and provide an opportunity for lodge members or visitors to give feedback or new ideas and connect with the bloggers. A blog may represent a single lodge, a district, **jurisdiction**, or even a group of scattered Odd Fellows who are united by an interest in a particular aspect of Odd Fellowship.

To set one up, it is necessary to first procure blogging software and a place to host the blog. There are numerous blogging platforms available for this purpose, which can be found with a simple online search, along with instructions for their use. Once the blog is ready to be launched, it should be borne in mind that regular posts are crucial to success. There is no precise interval of posting recommended, but weekly is a good cadence to start with. A simple trick for maintaining the regularity of posting is to write several posts in advance and then schedule them to be published with the desired frequency. The blog also need not be written entirely by one lodge member. It may be desirable to spread the work out and get a wider variety of viewpoints expressed.

## OF SOCIAL MEDIA

Social media has also increasingly become a crucial part of a lodge public relations strategy. Nowadays, the general population gets much of their news from various social networking applications, particularly amongst the younger set. Beyond news, it has also become the primary platform for disseminating event information and even receiving commitments to attend events.

Be warned, however, that attendees who respond that they will attend an event via social networking often have a lower likelihood of actually attending than those responding through traditional channels. Part of the reason for this is that it is so easy to find and respond to events in this manner that it doesn't indicate the same level of commitment that mailing back a card, making a telephone call, or even sending an email does. Even with this drawback, social media is now the premier way to get the word out about events and secure participation.

A comprehensive social media strategy should include postings to multiple platforms. The number of major platforms has increased steadily over time and will likely continue to evolve. Different platforms may reach different populations, so to get good coverage, it is beneficial to span several larger ones. It is often possible to have postings automatically cross-posted to multiple social media platforms. This should be considered a cornerstone of lodge social media best practices. Tools are also available to allow for scheduling posting in advance, allowing for the method of setting a series of posts up in advance to be delivered in sequence.

Topics for social media posts can span a variety of subjects. A good starting point is events the lodge would like to invite the public to. It can also be desirable to post retrospectives on events or lodge projects as they occur, including photos. In the latter case, one should always get permission before posting an image with an individual, particularly if they are not a lodge member. Other suitable topics for posts include information about Odd Fellowship in general, including articles written by members about Odd Fellows history, philosophy, and symbolism. The key is to keep posting regularly to show that the lodge is active and to engage with the audience.

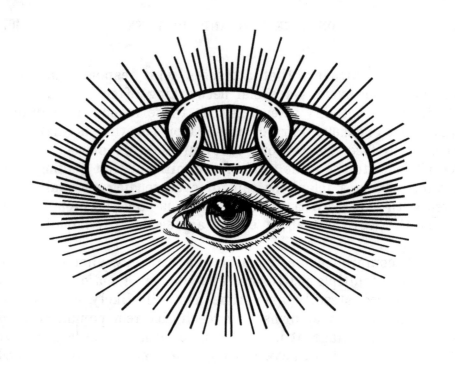

# CHAPTER XV

## ON RECRUITMENT AND TRAINING

### *OF SEARCHING OUT NEW MEMBERS*

No organization can survive without bringing in new members, and Odd Fellowship is no exception. Many lodges have asked themselves how they can do this, and various strategies have been tried. The truth of the matter is that no one approach will work everywhere. Every lodge has its unique strengths and abilities. Every lodge is situated within its local community, which may differ considerably, even from other lodges within the same district. While each lodge needs to find the answer for itself, certain commonalities in the types of strategies tend to be effective. The first principle most lodges internalize almost immediately is that a powerful way to get new members is simply to ask. They approach a fitting friend or acquaintance and propound the question.

Often it's not quite that simple, because one needs to know how to explain the Order to them. In the modern day, people don't usually have anything in their personal experience to prepare them for understanding precisely what Odd Fellowship is or what it does behind closed and mysterious doors. One approach is to work from analogy and describe what Odd Fellows are in terms of something they already know about in their own life. If a connection can be drawn between the teller and the told, then a bit of the subtle spark that powers Odd Fellowship can be channeled into the conversation. No two candidates have exactly the same reasons for joining the Order. Some are drawn to the **regalia** and formality, others to the venerable Ritual steeped in history, and others to the symbolism and philosophy that draws the new member to probe their innermost depths. One candidate may be motivated by Odd Fellowship's devotion to the principles of mutual aid

"Famous Odd Fellows of the Past"

and service to the greater cause of humanity, while another may merely be looking for a group of men and women to hail as brethren. Finding partners for shared interests and hobbies can also induce a prospective member to unite with the Order.

The initial catalyst to affiliate matters little because once the relationship is initiated, it will grow and evolve to encompass further facets of Odd Fellowship. Even should a candidate join for the wrong reasons, chances are that they will only linger for the right ones.

While the acquisition of new members is imperative to grow, the retention of those members is paramount in many ways. Having traversed the portal, should a fledgling brother or sister find nothing to hold their interest, it will surely wane. The meetings they attend must be collegial and gratifying. Should they instead be confronted with anger or monotony, they will not return once their initial fervor has subsided. The actions taken by the lodge and the environment it formulates will seal the fate of the initiate. The degree work bestowed upon them will also solidify their impression for good or for ill. The degrees must be conveyed lovingly and with care for the foundational messages of Odd Fellowship. Should the lodge not demonstrate through its deportment a dedication to the Order's principles and practices, there is no reason to expect the initiate to hold them sacrosanct either.

It is often said that a new member should be put to work immediately to engage them fully and give them a reason to remain. They must indeed be given a role and a voice, but this must be done mindfully. If the brother or sister is assigned only the basest or most menial of labor, the effort to involve them will surely prove fruitless. Instead, the lodge must carefully consider each initiate's nature and only attach them to a meaningful role. A suitable committee may be found to appoint them to, or an upcoming event may be found which would benefit from their talents and interest. The lodge should also listen carefully and attentively to the new ideas the member brings and give them due consideration. Often the very best ideas come from more recent members who are unfettered by constraints of conventional thinking. New members should be given the space and support to pursue these proposals for the betterment of all. If a brother or sister finds a fertile bed to plant their seeds in, they will soon send forth deep roots to anchor them to the bedrock of the Order. Even if a proposition is flawed or impractical, it should still be received with the utmost care. The lodge cannot expect the new member's concept of Odd Fellowship's possibilities to be fully formed. Any feedback must be handled with kindness and sympathy so that the brother or sister comes to understand they are valued and appreciated within the lodge.

## OF MENTORSHIP

The availability and commitment of a suitable mentor for a new member can also be a significant factor in how well they are integrated into the fabric of lodge life. Should one of the elder brethren form a solid bond with the newer, that relationship will bolster their involvement. This role includes reminding them of meeting times, helping them to learn and remember the **signs** and passwords, encouraging them to advance through the degrees, and introducing them to other brothers and sisters. One often overlooked but important function is to acculturate the mentee into the numberless and sometimes subtle norms of the lodge, including how to walk around the **lodge room**, conduct oneself during the meeting, engage in parliamentary debate, and address officers and members. Having a guiding hand to help make sense of the potentially overwhelming expanse of customs and usages ensures far greater comfort to the new participant.

In some lodges, it is customary for the brother or sister who proposed the candidate to membership to take primary responsibility for mentoring them beyond their initiation, but this is not a requirement and may not be ideal if the **sponsor** is still fairly new. Above all, the mentor should be a person of sensitivity. They must discern the needs of the mentee and work to meet them at their current level in a supportive manner. The lodge might select a mentor who has common interests or a common background with the new member, to provide an immediate affinity. So long as their concerns are being addressed, the new member is sure to have an improved induction into the lodge than if left to their own devices.

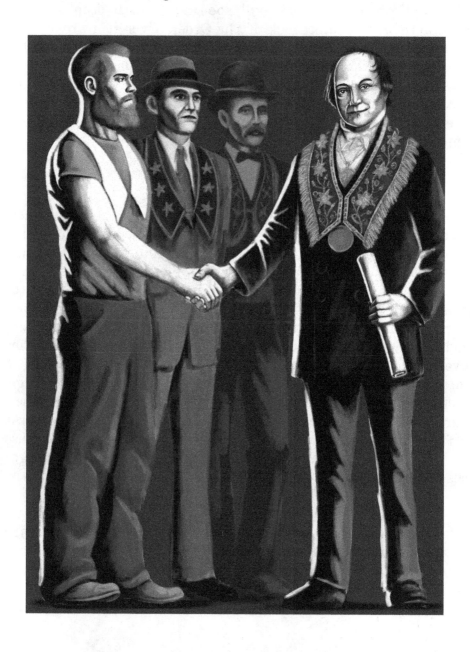

# CHAPTER XVI
## ON DISTRICTS

### THEIR NATURE

The lodges within a geographical vicinity are combined to form a district, which can vary in geographic size and number of lodges. The district exists to foster cooperation and fraternal relations between Odd Fellows in different lodges. It also provides a convenient way to disseminate information and guidance from Grand Lodge and the Grand Master to the <u>local lodges</u>.

While it is possible to have a district composed of a single lodge in the case of an isolated lodge with no natural neighbors, this obviates most of the advantages of having a district. Notably, a district serves to allow for coordination between lodges to collaborate on larger projects or events. It also further provides a wider possible audience for any programs put on by a constituent lodge. In some cases, the district lodges are in frequent contact with each other and share in Odd Fellowship's work, but in others, the lodges stand alone to varying degrees. While it is undoubtedly the choice of the lodge and its members whom they wish to associate with, if a lodge is not participating actively in the district, it is not reaping the ample rewards to be found there.

In some districts, in addition to their role in performing installations and other ritual functions, the district officers have further responsibilities. Some districts have district funds collected from the individual lodges and managed by the District Deputy Grand Secretary and District Deputy Grand Treasurer that may be disbursed for the needs of the district. Some **jurisdictions** may also have district-level committees to further the work of the Order on a district level. In such cases, the district committee appointments are most often made by the District Deputy Grand Master.

## *THEIR OFFICERS*

A district is led by a District Deputy Grand Master appointed by the Grand Master upon the recommendation of one or more lodges in the district. To be eligible for such an appointment or any other district-level office, an Odd Fellow must be a Past Grand in **good standing** within a lodge in the district. Many districts have an arrangement wherein each lodge gets to take a turn in selecting the candidate to be recommended to the Grand Master for the following year. Customarily, the lodge making the initial recommendation contacts the other district lodges to inform them. The other lodges may send the Grand Master their own letters of support for the candidate.

The District Deputy Grand Master is responsible for appointing the other district officers, including a District Deputy Grand Marshal, District Deputy Grand Warden, District Deputy Grand Secretary, District Deputy Grand Treasurer, District Deputy Grand Chaplain, and District Deputy Grand Guardian.

"DDGM Emblem"

These officers are largely parallel to the corresponding offices of a local lodge, except for the District Deputy Grand Warden, who fills the position of the Vice Grand. Some may choose to appoint district officers primarily from their own lodge, where they know the members best. Selecting from among as many of the different lodges in the district as possible, however, can serve to bring greater unity and participation to the district. It is also an excellent opportunity to involve newer Past Grands so they can begin to get more involved in Odd Fellowship beyond their local lodges. The most critical officer to select is the District Deputy Grand Marshal, who will ideally accompany the District Deputy Grand Master on all official visits. This can also be a good training position for one who aspires to become District Deputy Grand Master in the future. The other officers must be willing to attend and participate in installations at the district lodges, which will be their most important duty.

Having a full slate of officers helps in putting on a credible installation ceremony, though, in a pinch, this may be done with only the District Deputy Grand Master and District Deputy Grand Marshal by having the District Deputy Grand Master perform all the other officer **charges**. When appointing district officer positions, one should be mindful of the offices that individuals might hold in their local lodges. For example, it is best to avoid appointing someone who is Secretary of their local lodge to be District Deputy Grand Secretary. This avoids the awkward situation of a person having to install themselves or shuffle the staff at the last minute.

The District Deputy Grand Master's responsibilities always include making some number of official visits to each lodge in the district, though that number may vary by jurisdiction. Often, the first visit will be made as soon as possible after the District Deputy has been installed and includes the District Deputy presenting the **commission** they received from the Grand Master and informing the lodge of the Grand Master's programs for the year. When a second official visit is made, that one is usually after the new officers of the local lodges have been installed and may include instruction and training for the new officers. On all official visits, the District Deputy is expected to address the lodge. Besides covering the required information about the Grand Master's programs and other jurisdictional or district activities, it may also be valuable to cover topics related to Odd Fellowship's meaning and practices or its symbols and traditions. The District Deputy is charged with guiding lodges and members. Still, any corrections that need to be made in the lodge's practices are better delivered to the Noble Grand or other officers privately rather than in front of the entire lodge. The District Deputy should also spend time getting acquainted with the lodge members to help build the spirit of fraternity within the lodges.

The annual installation of officers constitutes another major purview of the District Deputy Grand Master and staff. It may not be undertaken until the District Deputy has verified that the lodge's **annual term report** has been completed and deposited with Grand Lodge or placed in the hands of the District Deputy, accompanied by all **per capita** funds due. The form of installation performed is at the discretion of the incoming Noble Grand. It may include a **closed, open, joint public,** or **dinner installation**, depending on what is permitted in the jurisdiction. When a joint public installation is employed in cooperation with the Rebekahs, it must be coordinated with the District Deputy President, who then officiates over the installation on an equal basis. Rehearsing with the officer team beforehand inevitably produces a superior result.

While a Noble Grand is the highest authority on the interpretation of the laws of the Order within the lodge, the District Deputy Grand Master may be called on to rule upon a novel question of law encountered by the lodge in the course of its work. This may be the result of an appeal of the Noble Grand's decision or a separate petition for clarification. Such a request must be made in writing, and the District Deputy must respond in writing for it to be considered a valid ruling. When making a ruling, the District Deputy should always rely on the Order's written laws, being mindful of the principles of precedence. Such rulings must ultimately be reported to the Grand Master for confirmation. No one needs to know all the laws by memory, but the District Deputy should know where to find the materials necessary to render a legal and just ruling. The law may not be clear, and the District Deputy needs to be prepared to exercise personal judgment based on their understanding of the law's letter and spirit. If the Grand Master has already ruled on a particular topic, the District Deputy's ruling must conform to this higher ruling.

The authority to issue select **dispensations** is delegated to the District Deputy Grand Master, but these may only include those particular dispensations recognized in the jurisdiction and enshrined in the Grand Lodge's **constitution** and by-laws. The most commonly requested dispensations in most localities are to hold **public installations** or to install lodge officers who have not met the stated requirements of previous offices held for their new offices.

On a fundamental level, the District Deputy Grand Master is the direct representative of the Grand Master in the district. This is the reason why the District Deputy receives the **Honors of the Order** on official visits, a privilege otherwise reserved for the Grand Master and other elected or

past elected officers of a Grand Lodge. As the Honors are only received by the authority stemming from the Grand Master, when the District Deputy receives them, they should thank the lodge for the Honors on behalf of the Grand Master. As the Grand Master's representative, the manner in which the District Deputy conducts themselves is a direct reflection on the Grand Master. Therefore, it is incumbent upon the District Deputy to make the best possible impression by dressing sharply, practicing their ceremonial role in advance, and, above all, always treating others with kindness and respect. Not every Odd Fellow has the opportunity to see and interact with the Grand Master directly, so the District Deputy will often be the main point of contact with the Grand Lodge and the Grand Master.

Additional responsibilities for the District Deputy Grand Master include attending official visits of the Grand Master within the district. The District Deputy must support the Grand Master and serve as marshal for them if none of their officers are present to perform in that capacity. This is true for any official visits conducted by the Deputy Grand Master or Grand Warden as well. The District Deputy is charged to ensure that the district's ritual work is performed in a proficient and dignified manner. Although not everyone can learn a part from memory, all can improve their role with practice even if they need to read from the book. While it is unrealistic for the District Deputy to expect perfection in ritual work, the key is to foster a culture wherein the ritual work of Odd Fellowship is taken seriously and performed with effort and care.

Should any lodge in the district violate the laws, rules, and regulations of the Order, it is incumbent upon the District Deputy Grand Master to serve as the eyes and ears of the Grand Master and alert them of any infractions. This includes the violation of any lawful commands that the District Deputy issues as part of their duties of the office. All Odd Fellows are

bound to obey the Order's laws so long as they do not conflict
with civil or criminal law or the member's moral duty.

Finally, the District Deputy Grand Master must render
a final written report to the Grand Master. In this report
is included a summary of activities, including official visits
made, installations performed, decisions rendered, dispensations
granted, and any other activities performed for the benefit of
their district. A statement of the condition of each lodge in
the District Deputy's charge should be included, as well as any
recommendations the District Deputy may have for the well-
being of the Order in their district, jurisdiction, and beyond.
Some jurisdictions require additional reports during the course
of the year, such as monthly or quarterly reports.

## THEIR MEETINGS

One of the most significant advantages of belonging to a lodge
organization is the opportunity to interact with high-quality
persons beyond one's own <u>home lodge</u>. In many districts,
district-wide meetings are held at least once a year to coordinate
between the district's lodges and facilitate cooperation and
participation in each other's events. The Noble Grands and Vice
Grands of the local lodges are invited and potentially other
officers as well. In some cases, a district meeting is open to
any member in good standing of a lodge in the district. Even if
there are presently no district meetings in the District Deputy
Grand Master's district, they may wish to consider starting one
to gain these important benefits for the lodges and members.

Typically, a district meeting will be scheduled and led by
the District Deputy Grand Master, with the District Deputy
Grand Secretary responsible for taking <u>minutes</u>. Some use
district meetings to harmonize the calendar for the coming year
so that all the lodges can attend each other's respective events.
There may also be other matters to discuss, such as working
together on initiations, service events, or social events. Having
a close-knit district can be a huge boon to lodges, especially

the smaller ones that might not be able to hold elaborate events without the cooperation of other lodges.

## OF LODGES OF INSTRUCTION

Holding a lodge of instruction for the district is a superb way to help educate the members of the district lodges about Odd Fellowship. The tradition is very deep, so there is always something new for any brother or sister to learn. The subject matter should be tailored to the interests of the members of the district. Some may be interested in understanding the meaning of our rituals, symbols, and philosophy. Others may want to know more about what charitable causes and what service opportunities the Order offers. Still others may want to learn more about what types of events they can hold to attract new members. It is also vital to make sure the teaching is at a level appropriate for the audience. One may be dealing with new members, fifty-year members, or a combination of everything in between.

While the District Deputy Grand Master should take the lead in planning a lodge of instruction in their district, they need not do all the teaching themselves. They may invite any knowledgeable member to assist with the teaching and can also contact the Grand Instructor to invite them to assist in locating an appropriate speaker or speakers for the event.

# CHAPTER XVII

## ON GRAND LODGES

### *THEIR COMPOSITION AND PURPOSE*

Grand Lodges are composed of all Past Grands in **good standing** of the lodges in the **jurisdiction**, who have received the Grand Lodge Degree. Each lodge elects representatives to their Grand Lodge from amongst its Past Grands. These representatives are empowered to cast votes on matters that come before the Grand Lodge in accordance with the will of their lodge. The number of allocated representatives is dependent on the size of the **local lodge**. In some jurisdictions, the **constitution** may also provide for additional voting members of Grand Lodge, such as current elected officers, Past Grand Masters, and District Deputy Grand Masters.

Grand lodges exist to promote the aims of Odd Fellowship throughout their jurisdiction and have a supervisory role over the local lodges. Promoting the aims of Odd Fellowship takes many forms. It encompasses both promoting Odd Fellowship to the general public and promoting the principles and traditions of Odd Fellowship within the Order.

Grand lodges meet once a year in regular session to vote on bills and resolutions that come before them, to amend the laws of the Grand Lodge or decide upon what course of action to take on issues. Grand lodges also elect and install their officers at the annual session. Additionally, special sessions may be called during the year if there is business that requires immediate action, though this is relatively rare.

Many Grand Lodges have also constructed Odd Fellows homes or camps to provide facilities for the use of Odd Fellows and their families jurisdiction-wide. Odd Fellows homes were particularly popular in the 19th century. They provided a way of taking care of elderly members who were not able to provide for their own needs or who preferred to live in a shared environment, together with their brothers and sisters. Initially, these homes were operated entirely by the Order. They featured communal-style living, but over time many of these closed or transitioned to being staffed and administered by commercial retirement home or assisted living management companies in a more contemporary style. At one time, the promise of having an Odd Fellows home available upon retirement as a perk of membership was very compelling to prospective and existing members, but as society has evolved, it has become less of a priority for most new members. Odd Fellows camps have been created for various purposes, including the establishment of summer camps for children of Order members or others and providing recreational facilities for members and their families, such as cabins, tent sites, and RV sites. These too have waned in popularity as the average age of members has increased, but are still very popular in some locales.

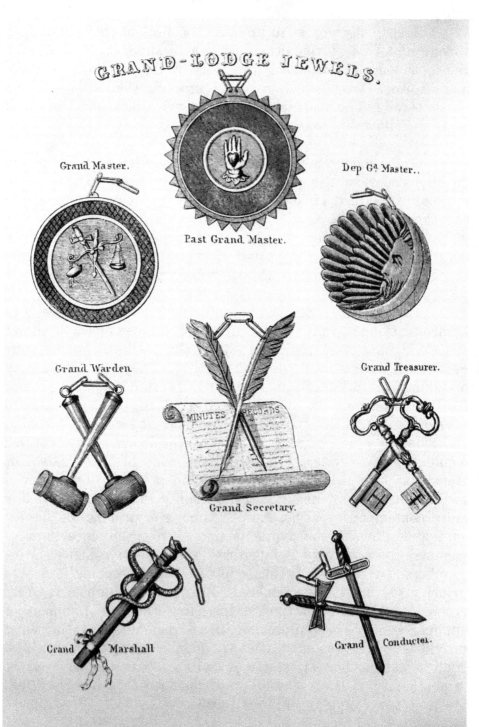

GRAND-LODGE JEWELS.

Grand Master.

Past Grand Master.

Dep G<sup>d</sup> Master.

Grand Warden.

Grand Secretary.

Grand Treasurer.

Grand Marshall

Grand Conductor.

## *THEIR ELECTED OFFICERS*

The elected officers of a Grand Lodge include the Grand Master, Deputy Grand Master, Grand Warden, Grand Secretary, Grand Treasurer, and Grand Representatives. The principal officer is the Grand Master, who has charge of all ritualistic functions within the jurisdiction, appoints officers and committees, and presents a program for the benefit of Odd Fellowship in the jurisdiction during their term.

The Grand Master is assisted by the Deputy Grand Master and Grand Warden. They are elected in a **progressive line** similar to the one used in a local lodge. While there is no guarantee that the Grand Lodge **line officers** will move up to the next office, and they must stand for election like any other elected officer, it is quite unusual to see a line officer fail to move up unless for reason of health or serious wrongdoing. This weighty custom of officers moving up is to allow the line officer to have two full years to prepare for the intense role of Grand Master and all the intricate logistics required. The duties for the three line offices have many commonalities across jurisdictions but tend to vary from one jurisdiction to another more than the equivalent roles at the lodge and district level. During sessions, the Deputy Grand Master sits to the right of the Grand Master and assists in keeping order, while the Grand Warden sits in the analogous location to the Vice Grand and correspondingly has charge of the **inner door**. The Grand Warden has the additional duty to confer the Past Grand Degree on new Past Grands who are joining Grand Lodge.

Other elected officers include the Grand Secretary and Grand Treasurer. They fulfill record keeping and financial functions similar to those of officers in a local lodge. Additionally, Grand Lodges elect one or two Grand Representatives, depending on the Grand Lodge's size. They represent the Grand Lodge in sessions of the Sovereign Grand Lodge in a like manner to lodge Representatives, acting on behalf of their lodges at the Grand Lodge. Grand Lodges are given the option to have an Executive

Committee composed of the Grand Lodge line and **desk officers** to make decisions and administer the programs and policies of the Grand Lodge while that body is not in session. Alternatively, the Executive Committee may be replaced by a Board of Directors, which is composed of additional elected Term Directors beyond the mandated line and desk officers. If Term Directors are utilized, they are not considered elected officers of the Grand Lodge and do not receive **regalia** or the **Honors of the Order** unless otherwise entitled to them. Term Directors may not serve more than three consecutive terms, though the length of the term may be determined by the Grand Lodge, up to three years. Grand Lodges are also permitted to establish additional elected offices if defined in their constitution.

## THEIR APPOINTED OFFICERS

Appointed officers for a Grand Lodge are selected by the Grand Master. The required appointed officers include the Grand

Marshal, Grand Conductor, Grand Chaplain, Grand Guardian, and Grand Herald. These officers correspond to the Warden, Conductor, Chaplain, Inside Guardian, and Outside Guardian of a local lodge. They fulfill primarily ceremonial functions during sessions, parallel to the equivalent officers of a local lodge. The Grand Marshal occupies the position of the Warden in a local lodge and has the responsibility of **escorting** the Grand Master and introducing all officers and dignitaries when appropriate. The Grand Guardian and Grand Herald correspond to the Inside Guardian and Outside Guardian, respectively. The Grand Master may also appoint a Grand Musician to perform on the piano or other suitable instrument so that Grand Lodge sessions will have musical accompaniment. As with elected officers, Grand Lodges may establish additional appointed positions, with the most common being a Grand Color Bearer to carry the flag of the country in which the Grand Lodge resides and a Grand Instructor who is responsible for training incoming District Deputy Grand Masters. The role of a Grand Instructor is unconventional because the majority of the work of the job is typically done before taking office, in the form of preparing educational materials and training the District Deputies during the session of the previous term's slate of officers.

In some jurisdictions, the custom exists for the Deputy Grand Master to visit the home lodges of each of the Past Grands selected to be the appointed officers for the following term. When this occurs, during Good of the Order, the Deputy Grand Master requests the **floor** and announces that the lodge member is to serve in the particular Grand Lodge appointed office and asks for the lodge's support of the member. The reasoning behind this custom is that, while being an honor for the lodge and the individual serving, the appointment is a minor imposition on the lodge because they will inevitably surrender some of that individual's time, which might otherwise be spent working for the lodge. The lodge may also be on the hook to plan a reception for the officer. To show their support for their member, the lodge may pass a **motion** indicating their support for the prospective officer. It bears mentioning that the lodge members should keep this information private within the lodge until the new officer is formally announced at the Grand Lodge sessions, so as not to detract in any way from the attention due the current officers.

The Grand Master also appoints the District Deputy Grand Masters for the term after receiving the recommendations from lodges of each district. The Grand Master is under no obligation to appoint the members so proposed and should choose an individual who will best represent the Grand Master within that district. As the District Deputy Grand Masters often must serve as the eyes and ears of a Grand Master, this is not a decision to be made lightly. Similarly, the Grand Master has the power to appoint **Special Deputy** Grand Masters to aid in the fulfillment of official duties such as performing an institution, observing or guiding lodges experiencing difficulties, or **arresting a charter**.

## *THEIR PROGRAMS*

Traditionally, the Grand Master composes a set of programs to set the term's theme. This may include selecting one or more emblems, a motto, watchwords, colors, flowers, songs, and projects, though other components of the program are possible as well. The emblems are frequently used on much of the paraphernalia produced for the term, including itinerary books, banners, and merchandise.

A banner is commissioned to commemorate the term, usually incorporating the Grand Master's name, the jurisdiction, the years, and the Grand Master's emblems. During earlier epochs, the banner may have been carried in parades. However, this usage is far less common today, when it is primarily displayed during sessions. Oftentimes, the **home lodge** of the Grand Master will also exhibit the banner in the lodge hall during and after the year.

Grand Masters also customarily produce merchandise with their emblems or alternative designs, to raise money for their charitable projects. The most common item to sell is a lapel pin, though many other items are possible, such as challenge coins, belt buckles, or t-shirts. This provides an enjoyable way to celebrate the term and the Grand Master while directing the proceeds to a worthy cause.

Grand Masters have the opportunity to accomplish much for the advancement of Odd Fellowship and those in need. Most choose one or two specific charitable causes to raise money for during their term. These can be a mix of both Order-specific and independent charities. It is undoubtedly worth considering choosing at least one external to the Order, to expand the reach of Odd Fellowship's good works and to help get the Order's name out in the public sphere. Order charities should not be neglected, however, because they are dependent upon the support of lodges and members for their continued existence and success.

The Grand Master often also puts together one or more projects for the Order's benefit directly. These projects could encompass almost anything related to Odd Fellowship in the jurisdiction and thus will differ from one locality to the next. If the jurisdiction is privileged to have its own Odd Fellows home or Odd Fellows camp, the project may serve to benefit those. Grand Masters have chosen to focus on bolstering specific aspects of the Order, such as public relations, Odd Fellows youth groups, lodge hall upgrades and improvements, or degree teams to serve the jurisdiction. Each Grand Master has their distinct interests within the Order. This allows the opportunity to focus on building the organization through various means.

The term's programs are often summarized within the itinerary book that each Grand Master publishes at the start of the term, typically in cooperation with the President of the Rebekah Assembly, who also puts forward their own programs within the same booklet. The itinerary book usually includes a photograph of the Grand Master and President, a listing of the Grand Master and President's programs, and a roster of Grand Lodge and Rebekah Assembly elected and appointed officers for the year, including contact information and each one's home lodge. The bulk of the materials consist of the itinerary itself, with a page for each month, detailing what official visits and other events the Grand Master and President will be attending each day. The itinerary provides an invaluable resource for officers and members to be informed about important occasions they wish to attend.

The new **term password** for local lodges, which in most jurisdictions runs parallel with the calendar year, is selected by the Grand Master midway through their term. The password selected is often related to the Grand Master's programs or desire to set the year's theme. It is communicated to the Grand Secretary, who distributes it to the District Deputy Grand Masters for communication to the local lodges at installation.

## THEIR OFFICIAL VISITS

A universal requirement for the Grand Master is to visit lodges around the jurisdiction during the term. The number of official visits made will vary depending on the size of the jurisdiction in question.

For smaller jurisdictions, it is expected that the Grand Master will visit every lodge during the term. For a larger jurisdiction where this is less practical, a rotating schedule may be in effect, requiring the Grand Master to visit a certain fraction of lodges so that all lodges receive a visit at least every few years. Some jurisdictions also allow or require the Grand Master to delegate a few of the visits to the Deputy Grand Master and Grand Warden, giving these officers an opportunity to learn and practice how to perform this vital function. It should be ensured that if a lodge receives one of these substitute visits from another line officer during a given year, the next visitation cycle will include the Grand Master directly. This guarantees that each lodge has the opportunity to regale the Grand Master at least once every few years.

Official visits from the Grand Master or other Grand Lodge officers take the same basic form as those of District Deputy Grand Masters.

## THEIR RECEPTIONS

Grand Lodges show their appreciation for their officers' diligent efforts through the practice of receptions. These are celebrations to honor and celebrate those who tirelessly contribute their time and energy to the Grand Lodge as an officer. In most cases, only the Grand Master and the appointed officers receive receptions. The Deputy Grand Master and Grand Warden do not have receptions because they will almost certainly receive one as Grand Master. The Rebekah Assembly also holds receptions for its own officers.

The form which receptions take varies according to jurisdiction, but there are two main variants. In some jurisdictions, the visitation is held when the Grand Master and staff visit the officer's home lodge. In others, the reception is an independent event, often held on a weekend or other time conducive to availability and travel. Receptions inevitably include a festive meal served to all attendees. During this banquet, the honoree is treated as an honored guest and often invited to receive their meal first.

In some jurisdictions, additional rules of protocol are observed at these and other formal Grand Lodge banquets, such as disallowing anyone to sit down until the Grand Master is seated or to arise from the table until the Grand Master has arisen. Obviously, in such cases, exceptions are made for any emergency needs of those attending.

Following or before the meal, the reception's formal program occurs, which also can be very different depending on the jurisdiction. In more austere versions, the assembled Grand Lodge officers and other guests who wish to speak take turns regaling the honoree with speeches demonstrating their appreciation, but far more involved variants also exist, with a formalized program. In these variants, the principal officer of each local body of the Order that the honoree belongs to may express a welcome on behalf of that body, such as their Odd Fellows lodge, Rebekah lodge, encampment, or Patriarchs Militant canton. A welcome is often also extended by the District Deputy Grand Master of the district.

Another standard component is greetings brought from the heads of the different branches of the Order for that jurisdiction, including the Grand Master, Rebekah Assembly President, Grand Patriarch of the Grand Encampment, and Department Commander of the Patriarchs Militant Department Council.

In the case where the Grand Master is being honored, Grand Lodge's greetings are instead offered by the Deputy Grand Master. A friend or relative of the honoree may be called upon to speak about the honoree's life history and any other relevant details they may wish to share during a more elaborate reception.

Giving gifts to a reception honoree is also a common practice. These may come from individuals or lodges or groups of officers. At receptions, it is often also customary for each guest to bring a card for the honoree with a modest sum of cash included, which helps the honoree offset the extensive travel cost that is often required of officers and not necessarily reimbursed from Grand Lodge funds.

If a more elaborate reception is held for an individual officer, the responsibility of planning it usually devolves upon their home lodge. A more recent trend is sometimes to combine multiple officers into a single reception to avoid holding as many such events each year jurisdiction-wide. The advantage of this, beyond merely saving on costs and effort, is that it can often lead to better attendance, since different guests come to support different officers. The downside is that it can detract from the individual officer receiving attention and recognition. One middle ground that combines the advantages of both approaches is to pair Grand Lodge honorees with Rebekah Assembly honorees of the equivalent office or from the same region.

## THEIR SESSIONS AND CONVENTION

Unlike a local lodge, which generally meets once or twice a month, a Grand Lodge conducts most of its business within a single annual session, also referred to as a convention, when the business session is combined with various banquets or other ancillary functions. This event, which typically spans several days and may occur in a hotel or other large venue, far exceeds a local lodge in formality and ceremony. It also provides an opportunity to reconnect with old friends and meet other Odd Fellows from all over the jurisdiction. In most cases, one must register in advance before attending. If serving as a representative, the lodge must also have submitted its list of elected representatives to be permitted to vote. Usually, a convention credential will be issued at the registration table, to be worn as the session's official regalia. This will distinguish between an officer, representative, or non-voting guest. Initially, only Past Grands were permitted to attend Grand Lodge sessions as guests, and the Grand Lodge operated entirely in the Grand Lodge Degree. Today, however, Grand Lodges are permitted to admit all **Third-Degree** members to sessions. To accommodate this, Grand Lodges may now open in the Grand Lodge Degree, confer the Grand Lodge Degree on new Past Grands, and then move down to the Third Degree for the remainder of sessions so that the Third-Degree members may be admitted. The Grand Lodge then returns to the Grand Lodge Degree shortly before closing, after asking all who have not received that degree to retire.

**Quorum** for a Grand Lodge session requires the attendance of a minimum of seven Past Grands in good standing from the jurisdiction, representing at least three lodges, per Sovereign Grand Lodge's requirements. If there are fewer than five lodges in good standing within the jurisdiction, then a majority of lodges are required to be present for business to be transacted. While these are the minimum requirements, each Grand Lodge is empowered to set higher minimums for a quorum in their constitution and by-laws.

The schedule of a Grand Lodge convention depends considerably on the convention's overall elaborateness and duration. Certain common elements will almost always be present regardless. A convention often has an opening ceremony or welcome. It must also include the requisite time allocated to the sessions themselves. The sessions most often begin in the morning each day with a break for lunch, potentially followed by an afternoon session if needed. Afternoon periods may also be used for committee meetings or special events. Banquets or lunches are scheduled for the entire assembly or select groups of participants. A memorial service is often scheduled to remember Odd Fellows and Rebekahs who have died during the previous year. If there is a Grand Instructor in the jurisdiction, that individual may lead a training course for the incoming District Deputy Grand Masters during the sessions, potentially the day before the formal start of the sessions. In some jurisdictions, the nomination and election of officers for the following term happen on separate days of the sessions, but in others the nominations are held immediately prior to elections. There may be an opportunity for the Grand Master-elect to formally introduce their programs, newly appointed officer teams, and committee appointments and to seek approval from the body. This may happen while the current Grand Master is visiting the Rebekah Assembly with their team of officers. The installation of new officers elected and appointed at sessions is permitted to occur in open sessions before closing or after sessions have been closed on the final evening, as determined in the constitution and by-laws of the jurisdiction. The officers of the Grand Lodge and Rebekah Assembly are generally installed together in a **joint public installation**. It is most common for Grand

Lodge and Rebekah Assembly sessions to run in parallel with each other in the same venue and share in the meals and social or ceremonial events. As membership in the two organizations increasingly overlaps, it may be desirable to schedule them consecutively or in alternation, to allow those voting members of both bodies to participate fully.

At the start of sessions for each day, or at a minimum on the first day, there may be a flag ceremony presided over by a Grand Color Bearer, which will typically also include a non-denominational prayer delivered by the Grand Chaplain. The Grand Marshal may escort in all the other Grand Lodge officers each day, and on the first day of sessions the Grand Marshal may also introduce each officer in turn. If there is a Grand Musician, that officer performs musical accompaniment throughout the various ceremonies. The entire assembled body often joins in song for the National Anthem and the **Opening Ode**.

It may be necessary to admit dignitaries from other branches of the Order or others who may not possess the requisite degrees to be present at the session. This should be done in a **recess** of the Grand Lodge. An officer of Sovereign Grand Lodge is provided as a visiting dignitary to observe the sessions and address the body on behalf of Sovereign Grand Lodge. This dignitary is to be provided with an escort and a seat of honor during the proceedings.

During sessions, specific protocols are observed to enable all present to understand what transpires. Any reports, legislation, or resolutions submitted before the jurisdictional deadline are printed in the Advance Proceedings and distributed to all participants. After each day of sessions, **minutes** are compiled and printed for distribution to the participants the following day, along with any other reports that have been submitted. When addressing the Grand Lodge, each member must state their name and their lodge number after receiving the floor from the presiding officer. Voting occurs through a **voice vote** or any other voting mechanism recognized by

Robert's Rules of Order. For voting on elections, a paper ballot was historically used, which can be quite time-consuming. More recently, grand bodies have begun adopting electronic voting systems to eliminate the tedious counting previously required. Any method may be used, so long as it is reliable, secure, and, in the case of elections, preserves the ballot's anonymity.

Seating is assigned for Grand Lodge officers, who hold stations in the **Grand Lodge room** in accordance with the Ritual, as well as other key officials, who sit on a raised dais with the Grand Master, Deputy Grand Master, Grand Secretary, Grand Treasurer, and other dignitaries, such as the **Parliamentarian** and the **chairperson** of the Assignments Committee. Other committees or groups of members, such as Past Grand Masters, are provided with tables for their use. If there is one, the Parliamentarian sits adjacent to the Grand Master to make parliamentary determinations as requested.

Though the Grand Lodge convention contains highly scripted and scheduled programming, some of the most valuable opportunities for networking and deepening one's knowledge about Odd Fellowship occur outside of a formal setting. Casual conversations held during meals or even in the hallways of the venue may expand horizons and nurture the fraternal bond between brothers and sisters from all across the jurisdiction. After the event, one may return home with a new perspective and new ideas to bring back to one's local lodge. The opportunities available for advancing the Order's aims merely by conversing in an informal setting should not be underestimated.

At the end of annual sessions, Grand Lodges traditionally end through a declaration of adjournment "Sine Die." This is a legal term originating from Latin, literally meaning "without day" and indicating that the body is adjourning without setting a specific time to meet next. The reason for this particular language is to allow the Grand Lodge to adjourn the meeting without dissolving the body, permitting the body to meet again later in the year should a special session be necessary. The alternative would be to require the election of new representatives to form a new Grand Lodge voting body, so this technique is highly valuable for the flexibility and convenience it offers a Grand Lodge.

After the annual session has been completed, the Grand Secretary works with others to produce a Grand Lodge Journal of Proceedings, which memorializes the session's business for posterity. At a bare minimum, it includes the complete advance proceedings, all reports and legislation presented to the body, any matters held over to the following year, and the minutes from each day of sessions. Bills, resolutions, recommendations, and reports should be numbered to facilitate easy indexing and readability of the material. The journal can also contain supplementary information such as photographs of officers and their contact information. It is often also desirable to include lists of District Deputy Grand Masters, past presiding or elected officers, and statistics on Odd Fellowship's condition in the jurisdiction and the various lodges' health.

## THEIR SPECIAL SESSIONS

Should urgent business need to come before a Grand Lodge during the year, a special session may be called to address it. The Grand Master has the power to call a special session, giving a minimum of 30 days' notice to the lodges of the jurisdiction. The notice must include the time and place of the meeting as well as the purpose. No business may come before a special session which is not included in the purpose for which it was originally called. A special session may also be called by a minimum of seven Past Grands in good standing from the jurisdiction, hailing from at least three different lodges or the majority of lodges in good standing. In emergency cases where it is not possible or practical to have the usual in-person meeting, Sovereign Grand Lodge allows for voting to be conducted by mail so long as no more than two **propositions** are presented, and the pros and cons for each proposal are fully disclosed.

## THEIR COMMITTEES

As in a local lodge, Grand Lodges do much of their work through committees. The size and scope of Grand Lodge is far beyond that of a local lodge, so a larger number of committees are needed than most lodges have. As in local lodges, there are multiple classes of committees with standing or "sessional" committees typically fulfilling the majority of their duties during the annual sessions and most other regular committees having responsibilities over the entire year. The Grand Master also has the right and privilege to appoint special committees as desired. Usually, the first member named to a committee is the chairperson, and the second member named is the vice-chair, who presides in the absence of the chair. Most committees are appointed entirely by the Grand Master. However, the constitution and by-laws may mandate that officers be appointed to certain committees by virtue of their office. Regulations generally prohibit a member of Grand Lodge from being appointed to more than one standing committee. As standing committees often have their own tables during sessions and are expected to fulfill crucial functions in the course of Grand Lodge business, this is an eminently sensible requirement.

The particular standing committees appointed in each Grand Lodge are enshrined in the constitution and by-laws, along with any specific requirements for who must or may be appointed. There are common standing committees that are utilized in most jurisdictions for the smooth handling of Grand Lodge business.[23] However, the names and precise roles may differ between jurisdictions. Additionally, precisely which committees are defined as standing also varies from one jurisdiction to the next.

Committees are closely involved in the legislative process at sessions of a Grand Lodge, beginning with the Assignments Committee. This committee rules on what other standing committees should be assigned each piece of legislation, resolution, or officer recommendation to render an opinion before reporting back to the Grand Lodge. In most cases, only two members are needed for this committee, with one fulfilling the role and the other acting as a backup or alternate. The committee members should have a good understanding of the legislative process and which committees are relevant for each item to be considered.

The Legislation Committee reviews legislation submitted to the Grand Lodge to verify it is in the proper form and not in conflict with the laws of Sovereign Grand Lodge or the Grand Lodge itself. The committee may also assist Grand Lodge members with drafting or revising their legislation in advance to ensure compliance. Working on this committee can be quite involved. The volume of submitted legislation is often substantial, but reviewing and responding to incoming legislation before the start of sessions makes the workload significantly more manageable.

The State of the Order Committee opines on pending legislation concerning the general welfare and activities of Odd

Fellowship. Their mission is to assess which legislation is ultimately for the Good of the Order and recommend accordingly. Like the Legislation Committee, it often has to review large quantities of legislation, and its recommendations carry significant weight. The committee's annual report should also render a statement on the current condition of the Order in the jurisdiction, which may include one or more recommendations for the betterment of Odd Fellowship in the jurisdiction. Similar to officer recommendations, any such recommendations are referred to the Assignment Committee for referral to such standing committees as are relevant to the subject matter at hand.

The Rebekah Matters Committee serves as a liaison between the Grand Lodge and the Rebekah Assembly for matters related to Rebekah legislation. It is similar to the Legislation Committee but only addresses legislation within the purview of the Grand Lodge's legislative authority pertaining to the Rebekah Assembly or Rebekah lodges. The members serving on this committee should have received the **Rebekah Degree** and be knowledgeable about the needs and concerns of the Rebekah branch of Odd Fellowship.

Other standing committees serve a primarily legalistic or judicial function. The Judiciary Committee is responsible for reviewing all interpretations of Odd Fellows law formulated by the Grand Master during the term. It presents recommendations to the Grand Lodge on whether the interpretations are to be upheld or overturned, subject to the approval of the Grand Lodge itself. When interpretations are upheld, the Judiciary Committee should submit legislation to commit the interpretation to law for posterity. In this manner, the Judiciary Committee ensures that the laws are interpreted consistently from one term to the next. The Judiciary Committee may also be called upon by the Grand Master during the year to render advisory opinions on the proper interpretation of the laws. The committee may also be responsible for approving the content of instructional materials published by the Grand Lodge for use within the jurisdiction.

The Appeals and Petitions Committee receives any appeal from the decisions of the Grand Master during the term and renders an opinion for the consideration of the Grand Lodge. All appeals or petitions must be provided to the Grand Secretary in a designated written form to be considered valid and taken up for a determination. As with any other committee, a recommendation is issued, and the final decision rests in the hands of the fully assembled Grand Lodge voting members. If there is no separate appeals committee, these responsibilities may rest with the Judiciary Committee.

The Finance Committee is responsible for reviewing any Grand Lodge expenses before payments are issued. This includes reviewing any reimbursement requests made by Grand Lodge officers or other authorized individuals for official travel or official expenses. It is also often responsible for drafting the Grand Lodge budget to be presented at the regular session should there be no separate Budget Committee.

There are also several committees whose responsibilities specifically relate to the annual sessions themselves. The Credentials Committee performs the critical function of determining who is eligible to vote at Grand Lodge sessions through careful checking of **dues cards**, credential forms, and records of elected representatives. The committee issues all attendees an appropriate badge indicating their rank and voting status. They usually staff a registration table where attendees check in upon arrival. Each day of sessions, the committee reports the total number in attendance and number eligible to vote. While this may not seem like exciting work, it is required for the fair and legal conducting of the business of the Grand Lodge and should be entrusted to experienced members who will safeguard the integrity of the process.

The Courtesies Committee participates in the welcoming and escort of visiting dignitaries, including officers from Sovereign Grand Lodge or the heads of other branches of Odd Fellowship. They may also have a role in supporting distinguished visitors to the jurisdiction during their visits, such as assisting with transportation and serving as a tour guide for the vicinity. The Courtesies Committee should strive to ensure that the dignitaries in their charge have an enjoyable visit and are accorded personal introductions to officers and members from the jurisdiction.

Finally, there are a few commonly used Grand Lodge committees whose roles are primarily during the part of the year when Grand Lodge is not in session. The By-Laws Committee reviews the by-laws or by-law amendments submitted by local lodges for approval by the Grand Lodge before taking effect. The by-laws must be in proper form and in compliance with all applicable requirements in the Ritual, Sovereign Grand Lodge's Code of General Laws, and the constitution and by-laws of the jurisdiction. They should not be internally contradictory or to the detriment of the good of the order.

The Convention Committee is responsible for the planning and execution of the Grand Lodge convention. This includes addressing such topics as securing a location and producing a daily schedule. During the convention, one or more committee members serve as liaisons with the venue and any other vendors assisting with the convention arrangements. They may also field questions from convention participants who have any concerns about the accommodations or amenities.

The Communications Committee assists in jurisdiction-wide communications. This can include jurisdictional newsletters, magazines, websites, blogs, or social media efforts. Ideally, this committee should include members familiar with modern electronic communications or who are at least prepared to educate themselves in current trends for disseminating publicity materials or other pertinent information.

The Relief Committee addresses any issues related to relief projects to benefit Odd Fellows in the jurisdiction. Depending on the jurisdiction, there may be funds designated

for the relief of members. Those jurisdictions who do not have such programs may wish to consider adding them. Mutual relief is one of the primary purposes of our Order which is no longer addressed by the local lodges in most cases. The committee may be able to assist members who have been impacted by fire or natural disaster. This should be handled as objectively as possible, with designated financial or other assistance provided when well-defined conditions have been met.

## THEIR REPORTS

All committees and elected officers are required to produce an annual report which is submitted to the Grand Lodge for consideration at its regular session. Reports should include a

summary of the officer or committee's activities during the
year, any pertinent findings, and optional recommendations for
a course of action to be taken by the Grand Lodge. Depending
on the laws of the jurisdiction, a committee may be responsible
for an initial report and interim reports in addition to the final
report delivered prior to the annual sessions. During the annual
session, committees are responsible for drafting and submitting
reports on any matter referred to that committee. Joint reports
are to be signed by members of the various committees to
whom the matter was referred.

## THEIR LEGISLATIVE PROCESS

A Grand Lodge will often receive a large volume of legislation
from among the lodges, representatives, and officers of Grand
Lodge, so having a well-defined process for addressing it allows
Grand Lodge sessions to proceed efficiently and effectively.
There are three primary tracks for legislation: bills, resolutions,
and recommendations. A bill is required to make a permanent
change in the constitution or by-laws of the Grand Lodge and
must clearly state the textual revisions desired. A resolution
provides for an immediate course of action to be taken by the
Grand Lodge and is only in force until the following year's
sessions. Recommendations are extracted from the reports of
the Grand Lodge officers and certain committees and follow
a similar course of action to resolutions. If an officer or
committee desires to make a recommendation that requires a
change in the laws, a bill should be submitted in addition to
the recommendation provided in the report.

Any voting member of the Grand Lodge, including officers
and representatives, is empowered to submit legislation. A
local lodge may also submit legislation if the legislation has
been presented at a lodge meeting and ratified by a majority
of the members present. Legislation may also originate with a
committee or Board of Directors if that entity has approved
the legislation during one of its meetings.

When preparing legislation, it is recommended to first review all applicable existing laws, wherever they may be in the Ritual or legal <u>codes</u> of Sovereign Grand Lodge or the Grand Lodge. This serves not only to ensure that there are no conflicting laws that would take precedence over the new legislation but also that any bill is placed in the most appropriate location within the Grand Lodge's own codes of law. When in doubt about the proper format in which to submit a bill or resolution, a member is advised to consult with past Grand Lodge journals to see examples and to work directly with the Legislation Committee as far in advance of sessions as possible. By submitting well in advance, it is possible to resolve any potential issues with the legislation more easily before they are brought to the floor. Depending on the laws and practices of the jurisdiction, bills may need to either be submitted by a stated deadline in advance of sessions or alternatively have an emergency clause attached indicating why the particular matter needs to be addressed immediately. Any bill considered under emergency provisions must receive a two-thirds majority vote to be brought to the floor for consideration and then pass with a three-quarters majority of voting reps present, rather than the standard two-thirds majority, before becoming law. In some jurisdictions, bills must generally lay over for a year before being acted on.

A bill to permanently amend the legal codes of a Grand Lodge requires submission in the proper form, which contains the phrase "be it enacted by the Grand Lodge" and only addresses a single subject. The bill should reference the specific chapters, sections, subsections, paragraphs, and page numbers of the laws to be enacted, amended, or repealed. It should also indicate the changes with strikethrough for deletions and underlining for additions. The Assignment Committee dispatches the bill to one or more Grand Lodge standing committees that evaluate its merits according to that committee's role. For example, the Legislation Committee evaluates whether the bill is in proper form and is free of any conflicting laws which would render it invalid. In contrast, the State of the Order Committee evaluates whether the new law proposed is ultimately to the benefit of Odd Fellowship in the jurisdiction, and the Finance Committee renders judgment on the financial feasibility of any alterations to the Grand Lodge's income or appropriation of funds proposed. All bills should be referred to the Legislation Committee at a minimum.

Following committee review, one of the committees to which the bill has been referred delivers a report to the floor of the Grand Lodge, citing the bill and indicating whether the committee recommends the bill or whether it should "stand on its own merits," which means that the committee cannot give it a positive recommendation. In the case of a positive recommendation, the Grand Lodge then takes up the question of whether to accept the committee report. If the positive report is accepted, then the underlying legislation is also enacted. If the bill stands on its own merit, then the proponent or another voting member is permitted to move the bill directly from the floor of the Grand Lodge to attempt to secure its passage.

Debate on bills follows the standard approach of Robert's Rules of Order or any alternative rules of order adopted by the Grand Lodge. In all cases, the bill's proponent should be given time to speak on behalf of the bill initially and also before the final vote. Amendments may be considered from the floor, but no amendment offered may be considered if it alters the bill's original purpose.

Under normal circumstances, a bill requires a two-thirds majority to pass, though this may instead be a three-quarters majority if submitted using an emergency clause. Grand Lodges may also mandate higher majorities as necessary to pass bills under other circumstances. Even after being passed by the Grand Lodge, bills do not take effect until they have been submitted to Sovereign Grand Lodge. The Grand Secretary sends the legislation to the Sovereign Grand Secretary, who, in turn, passes it to the Sovereign Grand Warden. The Sovereign Grand

Warden makes the initial assessment, which is then approved or rejected by Sovereign Grand Lodge.

A bill takes effect the first of January following passage, so long as it has received ratification from Sovereign Grand Lodge. The main exception to this is a bill with an emergency clause that immediately goes into effect after being ratified by Sovereign Grand Lodge. If a Grand Lodge does not take up an adequately prepared and duly submitted bill during the session, it is held over until the following year, at which point it should be placed on the agenda before the new bills submitted that year.

Resolutions, which exist to mandate a particular course of action, follow a similar trajectory to bills. with a few notable exceptions. They are submitted similarly but should instead contain the phrase "Be it resolved by the Grand Lodge." As with a bill, a resolution may only pertain to a single matter. If it is to appropriate funds, it must layover for at least two days before being voted on unless passed by general consent unanimously. In most cases, they need not be referred to the Legislation Committee, as they do not produce any changes to the codes of law. If appropriating funds, they should go to the Finance Committee. In most cases, resolutions only require a simple majority. After being passed, resolutions take effect immediately and only have force and effect until their purpose has been accomplished or until the end of the term. Annual budgets are generally passed by resolution.

Recommendations are comparable to resolutions in effect and course of action but instead originate from an officer or committee's report. In most cases, the reports of officers and committees are accepted separately from the recommendations contained therein. The recommendations are referred by the Assignments Committee to whichever committee or committees are best equipped to evaluate their merits. Recommendations may be made by a minority of a committee in addition to those made by the majority. In this case, both are addressed separately by the committees and the body.

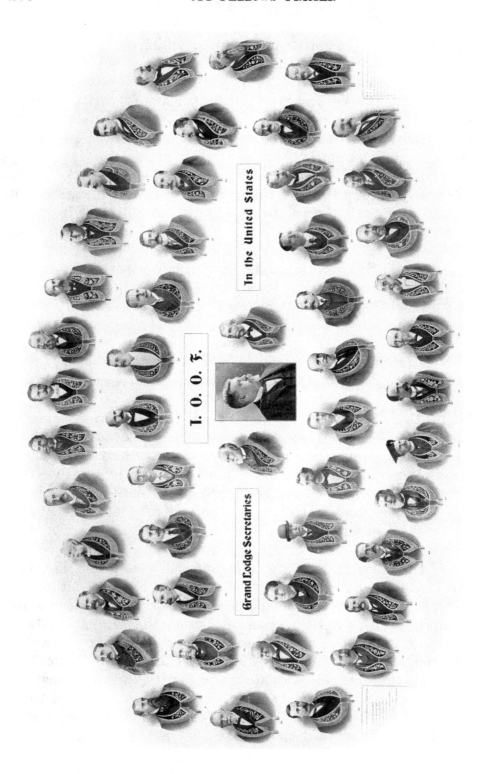

## THEIR ELECTIONS

For many attendees, the election of new officers is one of the highlights of the annual sessions, when the Grand Lodge selects who will lead it for the coming term. The process of standing for election varies from one jurisdiction to another, but certain features are standard. In many jurisdictions, the candidates must submit a statement of qualifications giving their biographical background, history with the Order, and any relevant views they would like to share about the future direction which the Grand Lodge should take. They may also be responsible for securing an endorsement from their home lodge, indicating that the lodge supports them in seeking office. To be eligible for elective office, the candidate must be a Grand Lodge member in good standing. Nominations are held, during which any member of the Grand Lodge or a friend or family member of the candidate who may not necessarily be a Grand Lodge member is permitted to nominate the candidate. In most cases, during the nomination, the nominator is only permitted to state the nominee's name, lodge, and the position they are nominated for.

The election follows nominations, usually on a separate day of sessions. Candidates standing for office may be allowed to speak briefly on their qualifications and their plans and ideas for the Order before voting occurs. This is most common with candidates for Grand Warden, who are likely to advance to the post of Grand Master and thus play a significant role in Odd Fellowship's future within the jurisdiction. In some jurisdictions, however, nominees do not speak on their own behalf, and instead the individual nominating them speaks briefly about the nominee. The Credentials Committee may also be called upon to ensure that the candidates meet the candidates for office following nomination.

Once the election begins in earnest, doors are sealed to prevent anyone from entering or exiting during the balloting. The Credentials Committee is called upon to give the number of Grand Lodge members present and eligible to vote.

Balloting may be handled by paper ballots or with electronic voting. If paper ballots are used, **tellers** are appointed to superintend the vote-counting in conformity with the procedure given in the constitution and by-laws of the jurisdiction, which will often include allowing each candidate to appoint a teller.

Whatever method is used for voting, if a candidate achieves a majority of votes in the first round, that candidate is declared elected. Should no candidate receive a majority, then the candidate with the lowest vote total is dropped and the ballot is repeated. This process continues until a candidate receives a majority of the votes. Should there be but two candidates and a tie occurs, then the ballot is repeated until a winner emerges. In cases where a candidate is running unopposed, the election may be conducted by acclamation collectively.

## OF IMPEACHMENT AND FILLING OF VACANCIES

Should it become necessary to remove a Grand Lodge officer from their office due to malfeasance, nonfeasance, or misconduct, procedures for this are supplied in the Odd Fellows codes of law. An officer of a Grand Lodge may be impeached and removed from office for cause. An officer, representative, or member may also be suspended or expelled from membership in the Grand Lodge entirely.

First, **charges** must be filed with the Grand Secretary, and the accused must receive a minimum of three days' written notice prior to the Grand Lodge acting on the charges. The motion to impeach requires a simple majority to pass. Following that, the accused is entitled to receive a hearing per the laws of the Order and may present evidence at that time. After the hearing, the vote to convict requires a two-thirds majority vote. Should the Grand Master be the officer impeached, they are required to surrender the chair during the proceedings.

When a vacancy occurs in the middle of the term due to impeachment, resignation, incapacitation, or death in the office of Grand Master, the Deputy Grand Master assumes the office of Grand Master, subject to approval from the Executive Committee or Board of Directors. If that officer serves the majority of the term through its end, they are to be accorded the rank of Past Grand Master. They may still stand for election to a full term as Grand Master if they wish to do so.

Similarly if there is a vacancy in the office of Deputy Grand Master, the Grand Warden assumes that office, also subject to approval from the Executive Committee or Board of Directors and with the same additional conditions. If the office of Grand Warden, Grand Secretary, or Grand Treasurer becomes vacant, then the office is filled by appointment by the Grand Master, subject to approval from the Executive Committee or Board of Directors, and handled similarly to the aforementioned offices.

A vacancy in Grand Representative is filled by the Alternate Grand Representative if there be one; otherwise the same procedure is followed as with other elected offices. Should a Director position become vacant, the Board of Directors selects the replacement, but the replacement only serves the remainder of the current term until a new Director can be elected at sessions, even if replacing a Director who was serving a multi-year term of office. Individual Grand Lodges may provide further specificity on the laws regarding the filling of vacancies in their constitution and by-laws.

## THEIR EXECUTIVE COMMITTEES AND BOARDS

Considering that a Grand Lodge is only in session several days out of the year, it is necessary to provide for decision making during the rest of the year. The solution supplied for this is an Executive Committee, or in the case of a Grand lodge that opts for a Grand Lodge Board of Directors, the board serves the equivalent role.

By default, an Executive Committee or Board of Directors is composed of the Grand Master, Deputy Grand Master, Grand Warden, Grand Secretary, and Grand Treasurer, though Grand Lodges are permitted to also include the Grand Representatives and the immediate Past Grand Master if desired. In the case of a Board of Directors, any Term Directors elected are also included. The Executive Committee or Board of Directors is authorized to continue the operations of the Grand Lodge during the interim period in accordance with the laws of the jurisdiction, but is not permitted to perform any legislative function.

If an Executive Committee is utilized, it is to be chaired by the Grand Master, but in the case of a Board of Directors, a chairperson and vice-chairperson may be elected from among the members of the board. A Board of Directors is entitled to appoint committees of the board to address specific needs of the Grand Lodge during the period between sessions. Examples of possible committees include an Investments Committee, Properties Committee, and Programs Committee, though the jurisdiction or Board may define any committees it wishes for the Good of the Order.

In addition to a Grand Lodge Board of Directors, a Grand Lodge is also permitted to establish additional corporate boards with elected directors. These are frequently used for Odd Fellows homes, camps, and charitable foundations.

# CHAPTER XVIII

## ON SOVEREIGN GRAND LODGE

### *THEIR COMPOSITION AND PURPOSE*

Sovereign Grand Lodge is the highest authority in the Independent Order of Odd Fellows worldwide. It is composed of the elected Grand Representatives from among the diverse grand bodies which pay dues to Sovereign Grand Lodge, namely the Grand Lodges and Grand Encampments. In addition to the Grand Representatives chosen from these bodies, one additional Grand Representative is allocated to the General Military Council and the International Association of Rebekah Assemblies. Elected and appointed officers of Sovereign Grand Lodge, Past Sovereign Grand Masters, District Deputy Sovereign Grand Masters, **Special Deputy** Sovereign Grand Masters, and Representatives from independent grand lodges are non-voting members, but nevertheless possess the right to make **motions** and debate questions. District Deputy Grand Masters from outside of North America may also serve as or select Grand Representatives from their **jurisdictions** if they have more than 100 dues-paying members.

Like a Grand Lodge, it meets annually to pass legislation and elect its own officers. The Sovereign Grand Lodge has sole authority over the Order's Ritual, including all the degree rituals, which may be revised from time to time through resolution. Sovereign Grand Lodge also has ultimate authority over the Order's official appendant bodies, such as the Encampment and Patriarchs Militant. Sovereign Grand Lodge also exercises limited authority over the Quasi Independent Jurisdictions, having charge over Latin America, Europe, and Australasia. It has committees composed of Grand Representatives and other members of the Order.

## THEIR ELECTED AND APPOINTED OFFICERS

The elected officers of Sovereign Grand Lodge are parallel to those of a Grand Lodge, including the Sovereign Grand Master, Deputy Sovereign Grand Master, Sovereign Grand Warden, Sovereign Grand Secretary, and Sovereign Grand Treasurer. The principal officer is the Sovereign Grand Master, who has supervision over all of Odd Fellowship under the jurisdiction of Sovereign Grand Lodge. Correspondingly to a Grand Lodge, the Sovereign Grand Master is assisted by the Deputy Sovereign Grand Master and the Sovereign Grand Warden, who form a **progressive line**. The Sovereign Grand Secretary and Sovereign Grand Treasurer are responsible for recording keeping and financial functions for Sovereign Grand Lodge.

The appointed officers selected by the Sovereign Grand Master are directly equivalent to the officers of a Grand Lodge. They are similarly named, except for the Sovereign Grand Messenger, who is analogous to the Grand Herald. The

"SGM Jewel"

complete set of appointed officers are the Sovereign Grand Marshal, Sovereign Grand Conductor, Sovereign Grand Chaplain, Sovereign Grand Guardian, Sovereign Grand Messenger, and Sovereign Grand Musician. The Sovereign Grand Master also appoints all District Deputy Sovereign Grand Masters and Special Deputy Sovereign Grand Masters. The Sovereign Grand Secretary appoints an Assistant Sovereign Grand Secretary to assist in their duties.

As in a Grand Lodge, the Sovereign Grand Master is responsible for presiding over annual sessions. The Sovereign Grand Master appoints standing and special committees with only

Grand Representatives eligible to serve on standing committees, though any Past Grand may serve on special committees. The Sovereign Grand Master only casts a vote on **propositions** in the case of a tie. Each year, the Sovereign Grand Master selects the **Annual Traveling Password** for the entire Order. The Sovereign Grand Master issues **dispensations** for new units of the Order under the direct jurisdiction of Sovereign Grand Lodge. The Sovereign Grand Master is also the penultimate legal decisor for the Order. Only Sovereign Grand Lodge has the authority to overturn the interpretations of the Sovereign Grand Master.

## *THEIR SESSIONS*

The annual session for Sovereign Grand Lodge occurs in August. It takes place in a different host city each year, as determined by a vote of the Representatives. If it is impracticable to meet in the location so designated due to contagious disease, the Sovereign Grand Master is empowered to alter the location and date of the session, subject to the concurrence of the Sovereign Grand Lodge Executive Committee. If due to war, pandemic, or other calamity, the session may not be held at all, but dispensed with entirely, with all officers retaining their positions until a session may be held.

To attend a regular or special session as an observer with no voice or vote, a brother or sister must be a member in **good standing** of an Odd Fellows Lodge, an encampment, a canton, and a Rebekah lodge. To demonstrate this, they may present **dues cards** from all four bodies or may be vouched for by a Grand Representative from their jurisdiction.

Special sessions may be called by the Sovereign Grand Master or by a majority of Grand Representatives. Sixty days' notice must be given to the Sovereign Grand Lodge officers and Grand Representatives. The special session's purpose must be delineated in the call, and no other business may be transacted unless by **unanimous consent** and adopted on roll call. If the majority of Grand Representatives concur, a special session may further be called with less than sixty days' notice.

The **quorum** for conducting business at a session is the majority of Grand Representatives elected. For most matters to come before Sovereign Grand Lodge, business is conducted in a like manner to the Grand Lodge level regarding legislation and rules of order. Any bills or resolutions must be submitted to the Sovereign Grand Secretary at least forty-five days before the start of the annual session. Other bills may be introduced at sessions, but these require a two-thirds majority of the voting members to concur. Holdover and pre-filed bills must lay over one day before being voted on. Any bill filed at the session must hold over two days. A bill may be considered as an emergency bill and bypass the two-day requirement if a three-quarters majority votes to bring them to the **floor**. Resolutions involving the appropriation of funds must lay over for two days unless brought to the floor by unanimous consent. Any other resolution only need lay over for one day and may be brought immediately by a three-quarters vote. All regular votes on passing bills require a two-thirds majority vote and take effect on the following January 1st. In the case of an emergency, however, an emergency clause may be added to the bill by a three-quarters majority. If so designated, the bill takes effect immediately on passage. Unless otherwise specified, resolutions require a simple majority for passage. Unlike bills, they usually take effect at the end of sessions, but if an emergency clause is attached and approved by a three-quarters majority, they too take effect immediately.

Sovereign Grand Lodge possesses the unique power to amend the Order's Ritual by resolution and, when considering such alterations, must resolve itself into a closed session. To be present during a closed session, a brother or sister must have received the **Third Degree, Royal Purple Degree, Rebekah Degree**, and **Patriarchs Militant Degree**. Such a resolution must lay over for one year and then requires a three-quarters majority for passage.

## THEIR EXECUTIVE COMMITTEE

The Executive Committee of Sovereign Grand Lodge consists of the elected officers and the immediate Past Sovereign Grand Master. When Sovereign Grand Lodge is not in session, the Executive Committee has charge over the Sovereign Grand Lodge's affairs, playing a similar role to that of the Executive Committee or Board of Directors of a Grand Lodge. They meet periodically and direct Sovereign Grand Lodge's operations, promoting the development and expansion of the Odd Fellowship. As with other Executive Committees, their actions are subject to the whole body's ratification at the following annual session.

## THEIR STANDING COMMITTEES

Like a Grand Lodge, Sovereign Grand Lodge has established multiple types of committees, standing and special. Standing committees are appointed at the start of the term. Only Grand Representatives may be appointed to standing committees, and no Grand Representative may chair more than one standing committee at a time.

Additionally, due to the greater complexity of the work done by some of the standing committees, **subcommittees** are assigned from a subset of the committee members. These are charged with more specific tasks than the committee as a whole. However, these are beyond the scope of the present descriptions. The committees and subcommittees are officially defined in the Code of General Laws.[24]

Among the standing committees of Sovereign Grand Lodge, several are primarily involved in the disposition of legislation. The Committee on Distribution of Officer Reports handles referrals of recommendations made by Sovereign Grand Lodge officers in their reports to appropriate committees for consideration. This is similar to part of the role of an assignments committee at the Grand Lodge level. The Committee on Legislation is responsible for examining all proposed bills to come before Sovereign Grand Lodge and making recommendations, making editorial changes, and consolidating duplicate bills. The Committee may also draft and submit legislation to implement accepted recommendations of the Sovereign Grand Master at the Sovereign Grand Lodge Executive Committee's request or at the direction of Sovereign Grand Lodge.

The Committee on State of the Order weighs in on all matters or questions related to the Order's general welfare and activities. As at a Grand Lodge, State of the Order also submits a report on the Order's current state, which in this case is worldwide in scope. The Committee on Ritualistic Work reviews all resolutions containing revisions to the Ritual or other ceremonies. In the case of revisions to Rebekah or Theta Rho rituals and ceremonies, the Committee on Ritualistic Work formulates a joint report with the Committee on Rebekah Matters.

There are also standing committees with responsibilities specific to different branches of the Order. This includes the Committee on Patriarchal Degrees, which makes recommendations concerning anything related to the Encampment branch of Odd Fellowship or Ladies Encampment Auxiliaries and the Committee on Patriarchs Militant, which plays a similar role for anything related to Patriarchs Militant and Ladies Auxiliary Patriarchs Militant. Also included is the Committee on Youth Activities, which works on anything related to the youth branches, namely Junior Lodge, Theta Rho, and United Youth Group.

Some standing committees of Sovereign Grand Lodge have a specific focus on the body's legalistic functions, such as interpretation of law and the fair disposition of appeals. The Committee on Judiciary reviews the Sovereign Grand Master's decisions for compliance with the legal **codes**, reporting back to the body for final approval. They may also be consulted for interpretations of the laws during sessions. The Committee on Appeals and Petitions considers any appeals on decisions from the Grand Master after those appeals have been reviewed by the Committee on Judiciary. That Committee also reviews appeals from the decisions of grand bodies. It considers petitions for **charter** for new units for which the Sovereign Grand Master has issued dispensations.

The Committee on Investigation of Grievances acts when such a situation arises that may be detrimental to the welfare of the Order. At least one member of that Committee should be a practicing attorney, but if none is available, then Sovereign Grand Lodge's legal counsel may be appointed in an advisory capacity. The Committee on Constitutions reviews all **constitutions**, by-laws, and amendments thereto submitted by each grand body under Sovereign Grand Lodge's authority. They review the full constitution and by-laws of each on a rotating twelve-year basis.

Three standing committees have functions related to the attendance of Grand Representatives and officers at the session. The Committee on Drawing of Seats arranges the meeting space for Sovereign Grand Lodge before each daily session. It is responsible for ensuring that the seating for jurisdictions is assigned impartially. The Committee on Credentials considers all matters which may arise in the course of reviewing and accepting the credentials of individual Grand Representatives. The Committee on Mileage and Per Diem makes any necessary corrections to the table of mileage and per diem of the Grand Representatives, officers, and past sovereign grand masters. The mileage and per diem rates are set by the Committee on Finance and approved by the Grand Representatives in the annual budget resolution. Mileage is only computed within the North American continent.

The Committee on Finance produces the annual budget for Sovereign Grand Lodge, including expected revenues and expenditures, subject to approval by the entire body. It is also responsible for any other matters which may arise related to finance and appropriations, including examining the books and records from the Sovereign Grand Secretary and Sovereign

Grand Treasurer and arranging audits at the close of the fiscal year or when otherwise necessary.

The remaining standing committees address matters related to their specific commissions. The Committee on International Issues addresses any topic or question that might put Sovereign Grand Lodge in conflict with any nation's laws. The Committee may also make recommendations related to monetary exchange rates, customs, and excises, and any other international concerns, such as disasters. The Committee on Property attends to the subject of Odd Fellows homes, camps, and cemeteries. The Committee on Relief superintends programs related to mutual relief, including disaster relief. The Committee on Miscellaneous Business is responsible for any matters that do not have another committee designated to oversee.

## THEIR OTHER COMMITTEES

During annual sessions of Sovereign Grand Lodge, several other committees also play significant roles. The Legislative Council consists of two members charged with assisting Grand Representatives in preparing bills to amend the Code of General Laws.

The Committee on Memorials prepares solemn and dignified memorial services to remember past officers and members who passed during the previous year.

The Committee on Courtesies Extended ensures that all proper courtesies are extended to those entitled to receive them. The members of this committee may engage in tasks such as making sure the needs of visiting dignitaries are taken care of at the hotel and elsewhere during their visit to the body, potentially including running errands if needed. While this may sound like a menial role on its face, it nevertheless presents a unique opportunity to get to know highly ranked members of the Order, which can be the first step towards the attainment of higher office in the future.

Two of the committees have larger roles during the year than at sessions. The Committee on Communications is the prime authority for Sovereign Grand Lodge's online communications, including guidelines for the official website, blogs, and social media. The Committee also develops guidelines for use by individual jurisdictions for their own web and online presence. The Committee on Membership promotes membership in the Order by providing plans and procedures for jurisdictions and lodges to gain and retain new members.

Some committees are joint efforts of Sovereign Grand Lodge and the International Association of Rebekah Assemblies, with members originating from both bodies. The Committee on Rebekah Matters reviews all matters related to the Rebekah Degree or the Rebekah branch of Odd Fellowship. The Joint Youth Committee supports the activities of the Order's youth branches, including Junior Lodge, Theta Rho, and the United Youth Group.

## THEIR BOARDS AND FOUNDATIONS

The work of Sovereign Grand Lodge is often specialized enough that a separate Board of Directors or foundation is established to govern a particular program. The Educational Foundation focuses on aiding Odd Fellows and their family members in securing a higher education. This aid can take the form of scholarships, loans, or other awards. The Foundation is managed by trustees from both Sovereign Grand Lodge and the International Association of Rebekah Assemblies.

The Independent Order of Odd Fellows Pilgrimage for Youth governs the annual trip, which brings students to governmental and historical sites to learn about the government's functioning and exchange viewpoints with the other participants. The Board of Directors includes Sovereign Grand Lodge and International Rebekah Assembly officers and members. Also, it employs an Executive Director to manage the program. The Board oversees the application process for participants as well as the planning of the tours. Individual jurisdictions may also have their own committees to help guide the program within that jurisdiction.

The Odd Fellows and Rebekah Arthritis Advisory Board supports raising funds by Odd Fellows across the various jurisdictions in raising money for arthritis research and treatment under the auspices of the National Arthritis Foundation in the United States and the Arthritis Society in Canada. The Board is composed of both Odd Fellows and Rebekahs from the United States and Canada. Jurisdictions also have their own respective Arthritis Committees, which govern local fundraising in cooperation with the Board.

The Odd Fellows and Rebekahs Visual Research Foundation exists for the purpose of aiding and restoring eyesight. The Foundation accomplishes this by funding related research through scholarships, fellowships, loans, grants, and other financial assistance. The Foundation also assists persons experiencing difficulty with vision by purchasing lenses or other devices for improving vision. It is composed of members from both the Odd Fellows and the Rebekahs.

# CHAPTER XIX

## ON THE FORMATION OF A LODGE

### *OF REASONS TO INSTITUTE A LODGE*

Not every aspiring initiate of Odd Fellowship lives within an agreeable distance from an existing lodge. Likewise, a dedicated Odd Fellow may have relocated to a new locale where no lodge is available to join. In either scenario, the best course of action is likely to work to establish a new lodge. Brothers and sisters also found new lodges in cases where they wish to go in a different direction or assume a different focus than the existing lodge they may already be a part of. In these circumstances, the preferred option may also be to institute a new lodge. However, when dividing from an existing lodge, one should always be sure that the two resulting bodies remain large enough to be fully viable.

## OF REQUIREMENTS FOR INSTITUTION

The basic requirement handed down by Sovereign Grand Lodge is that the institution of a new Odd Fellows lodge should have either five or more Odd Fellows who have already achieved the **Third Degree** or fifteen or more persons who are eligible to join the Order if they have not already become members.[25] No more than two-fifths may be **associate members** in either case.[26] These prerequisites may be further added to in the laws of the specific **jurisdiction** the new lodge aspires to unite with, so those must be consulted with as well. A superior approach is to contact the Grand Lodge directly to inquire, as this will allow the Grand Lodge to offer assistance in the process immediately.

## REGARDING HOW TO BEGIN

The first order of business in the creation of a new lodge is to determine who will serve as the **charter members**. Generally, one prospective charter member will take the lead on organizing during the formative stages, taking responsibility for calling everyone together and facilitating meetings and discussion. However, there may be a slightly larger core group of founders in some cases who share this role. It is highly recommended to get a consensus as early as possible on what the meeting night and location for the fledgling group will be, so that all future members who are approached can be informed up front about scheduling, preventing any misunderstandings or disagreements later. Having organizational meetings on the same days, which will later become the regular meetings, is an effective way to keep the desired time open for the prospective charter members and build momentum for the group.

Scheduling for lodge meetings also presents a set of choices. While lodges of the past would often meet once a week, the customary cadence now is twice a month based on a set day of the week. For example, a lodge may opt to meet on the first and third Mondays or the second and fourth Tuesdays.

Having a determined day of the week makes it easier for lodge members to remember the meeting nights and provides greater compatibility with the scheduling of lodges and many external organizations. A lodge may meet for business as infrequently as once a month if it opts to make one of the two required meetings a month a social meeting. If business is only conducted once a month, though, the lodge should consider establishing an Executive Committee or otherwise empowering the **desk officers** to pay bills that might arrive at inopportune times when the due date would arise before the next regular meeting night. The term of office for lodge officers must be annual if the lodge meets twice a month but can alternatively be shortened to six months for weekly lodges if desired.

Selecting an optimal time of day to meet is a necessity. The most common meeting time among lodges is eight o'clock in the evening, though some lodges choose to meet earlier. The prospective lodge should consider membership factors when selecting a time. If the majority of members are working until later in the day, the best time to meet could be on the later side, but if the membership is primarily of retirement age and this is the demographic being targeted, meeting earlier may help address concerns some members may have about traveling after dark. Rarely lodges will meet during the daytime or perhaps on Saturdays. Still, in these instances, it may be more difficult to recruit members who are interested in meeting at those times.

Where the new lodge can meet will depend on what resources are available in the area. If there is already another Odd Fellows lodge nearby, it may be an ideal meeting place, as lodges will often give each other very favorable rental terms for the Good of the Order. If no such opportunity exists, other fraternal orders may have a hall in the vicinity that will have a **lodge room** configuration largely compatible with Odd Fellows ritual, which could also be rented. A lodge can also use a commercial or community space. However, this may be prohibitively expensive or may present challenges regarding lodge room arrangement. A less desirable option may be to initially hold meetings in a member's personal residence. This has the advantage of reducing costs but is non-ideal. It can feel less official and may make the lodge unduly dependent on a particular member. Depending on local economic factors, the lodge may be able to realistically start saving money to purchase a property in the medium to long term, but this could require the lodge to charge unusually high dues and will almost certainly not be the initial meeting place.

There are a few vital decisions to be made in addition to the meeting time and place. The selection of a name for the lodge is chief among them, as it will set the tone for the overall branding and marketing of the new lodge. One time-tested approach is to revive the name and number of a defunct lodge. This provides the nascent lodge with an immediate history and connection to the community in which the lodge is situated. Another approach is to name the lodge after the community, such as the name of the town or county in which the lodge will meet. It can also be desirable to select a more historical, poetic, or evocative name for the locality if one is available, even if this is not the current official place name. Lodges may also be named after historical persons, typically deceased, who were local celebrities or were Odd Fellows of renown. The final commonly adopted approach is to name the lodge after a symbol of Odd Fellowship or an aspirational virtue or principle such as "Three Links Lodge" or "Friendship Lodge." In all cases, it should be borne in mind that the choice made can profoundly impact how the lodge develops and what sorts of members it attracts. One should certainly steer clear of any names that may have political or sectarian implications.

After the meeting time and place and the lodge's name have been chosen, the next determination to be made is the initial officers for the lodge. This, like the preceding decisions, may be handled through a vote of the charter members, though it need not initially be done with the formality that lodge voting generally consists of. The most important thing to consider is that all members perceive that their viewpoints are being heard and considered and that a fair decision-making process is conducted. Regardless of whether the lodge has previously determined who will be the initial officers or not, it will be necessary to hold a formal election after the institution is

"First Meeting at the Seven Stars"

performed before the instituting officers proceed to perform the lodge's inaugural installation.

Often, the lead organizer will assume the role of **charter** Noble Grand or charter Secretary. When pondering candidates for charter positions in the lodge, it is worth taking into consideration past offices the individual may have already held in Odd Fellows lodges or even other organizations entirely, as it is crucial that the initial officers of the lodge are as well-versed in the duties of their offices as possible. Even in cases where all the charter members are new to Odd Fellowship, there are still plenty of opportunities for receiving mentorship from other nearby lodges, the District Deputy Grand Master, and the Grand Lodge officers.

## OF THE FORMAL PROCESS

To become a legitimate lodge, it is necessary to apply for a charter from the authoritative body having jurisdiction over the region. This instrument names the new lodge and provides it with all the rights and privileges legally and customarily belonging to Odd Fellows lodges. No lodge may function without a charter. It must be displayed at the meeting location to have a valid meeting.

Which jurisdiction the new lodge is to be instituted in will determine to whom the application for charter is submitted. In most cases, this will be a Grand Lodge. For those living in nations or provinces under Sovereign Grand Lodge's jurisdiction or who do not have any lodges in them at all, however, the application will be handled directly by Sovereign Grand Lodge.

The application for a charter for a nascent lodge within an existing jurisdiction is conveyed to the Grand Secretary along with the application fee. It must include the names, ranks, and any existing home lodge affiliations of the intended charter members and the desired name for the new lodge. If reviving an extinct lodge, the proposed lodge number should be included as well.

In some jurisdictions, special provisions exist requiring that if there is already an existing lodge in the same city that lodge must provide a letter supporting the new lodge's establishment before permission may be granted. When the Grand Lodge is not in session, the Grand Master will receive and act on the application. In contrast, during sessions, it may be taken up directly by the full body.

When working directly under Sovereign Grand Lodge's auspices, the application for charter the application for charter, together with the application fee, is to be delivered to the Sovereign Grand Secretary, who then provides it to the Sovereign Grand Master for action. The Sovereign Grand Master decides whether to grant the charter or alternatively to hold it to be decided on at the next Sovereign Grand Lodge session.

The day of the institution is decided in coordination with the Grand Lodge or Sovereign Grand Lodge officers performing the ceremony. It is imperative that all the **charter members** be present on that day to retain their official status. The Grand Master or Sovereign Grand Master customarily leads the institution themselves, but if necessary, this role may be delegated to a District Deputy Grand Master, District Deputy Sovereign Grand Master, or a **Special Deputy** appointed for this explicit purpose. This officer's responsibility is to verify that everything is in order and all charter members are eligible for this honor. Should there not be a sufficient number of qualified petitioners present, the ceremony may not proceed. The **charter** is to be presented to the new lodge at the conclusion of the ceremony. Most often, the initial installation of officers takes place directly following the institution. The organization of a new lodge is a major cause for celebration and can be accompanied by a festive meal or other social function.

"Example of Modern Charter"

## AFTER THE INSTITUTION

By-Laws must be written for the new lodge within the first year in most cases. However, some jurisdictions may have other requirements, potentially even mandating them in advance of the institution. The charter granting body may furnish model by-laws to work from. In the absence of this, the most expedient path is to request copies of by-laws from other lodges under the same jurisdiction to use as a guide. Several of the decisions to be enshrined in the by-laws, such as the name of the lodge and its meeting time, should have already been determined, but there are additional choices to be made at this time as well.

The lodge should determine its annual dues and sundry fees, subject to the jurisdiction's minimum required amounts. The lodge may wish to keep these as low as possible to encourage more individuals to join and to be sensitive to the needs of those who are of limited means. However, it may also want to set dues well above the **per capita** amount required, to begin to build up cash reserves for the fledgling lodge, enable the purchase of lodge paraphernalia, or allow for higher-quality events. There is also the possibility of a middle ground, permitting lower dues for those members experiencing financial hardship.

In cases where the lodge is to be the only Odd Fellows body for a large region, the dues can also vary based on distance from the lodge's meeting location, with members living over a certain distance away paying a lower rate, as they will not be able to attend and participate as frequently but might nevertheless want to establish an affiliation with the Order. The standing committees which are to be appointed each term are also defined at this time.

One of the challenges a new lodge faces is the acquisition of lodge furniture and paraphernalia for the meetings and degrees. This need not be onerous because there are often options available to acquire effects from defunct lodges or lodges that have consolidated and have surplus items. Some Grand Lodges hold these extra furnishings in reserve for precisely such a scenario. There are also vendors who sell Odd Fellows supplies, and an enterprising lodge with talented artisans can even craft their own **collars**, robes, or props based on the official specifications.

A new lodge should put a plan in place immediately to begin recruiting new members. A degree team should be established expeditiously to better accommodate incoming candidates and because it draws the charter members further into Odd Fellowship and reinforces the philosophy and principles of the Order while providing an aspirational project to rally around. A new lodge, in particular, should always be working towards one goal or another to build momentum and keep the members engaged.

# CHAPTER XX

## ON THE SYMBOLS OF ODD FELLOWSHIP

### *THEIR PURPOSE AND NATURE*

Throughout the years, Odd Fellows have adopted various symbols to teach the lessons of Odd Fellowship and express the values and principles of the Order. Many of these symbols originated before the advent of fraternalism. They have held disparate meanings at different times or amongst different cultures.

Other symbols are more exclusive to Odd Fellowship, but they, too, have often been accorded diverging meanings or purposes periodically. It is incumbent upon the Odd Fellow who wishes to mature in their knowledge and understanding to formulate a personal relationship with these symbols through study and contemplation.

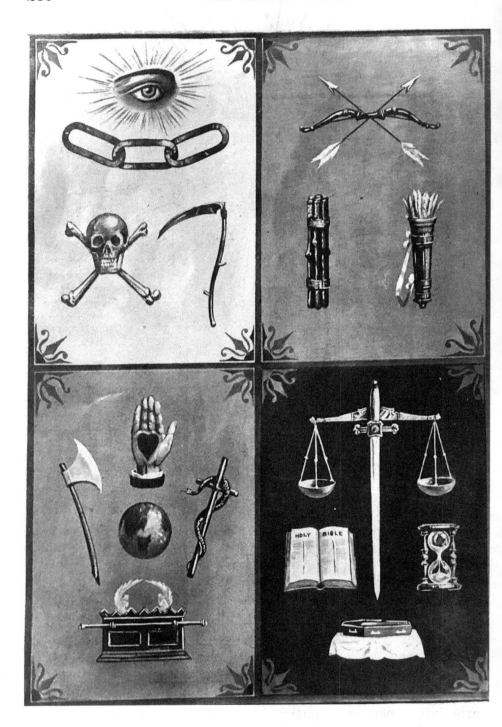

It should be borne in mind that symbolism is inherently subjective, with the viewer's ideas and experience playing a role in how the symbol is interpreted. Nevertheless, symbolism draws from a repository of shared culture, including art, literature, philosophy, and religion. Interpretations inevitably change over the years as the march of societal change proceeds. All of this comes into play in the understanding of Odd Fellows symbols, just as with any other.

## OF CURRENT SYMBOLS

The **All-Seeing Eye** represents the watchful eye of Deity observing the actions of all created beings. The Eye sees who a human being portrays themselves to be, who they strive to be, and who they truly are. Any action, word, or thought is marked indelibly on the fabric of the universe and emanates a cascade of consequences, seen and unseen. The All-Seeing Eye neither slumbers nor sleeps. It reminds all Odd Fellows that they should be mindful that individual choices are significant whether they occur in the dark of night or the broad light of day. When superimposed in the center of the Sun, this symbol indicates blessings descending on the world from on high, but when superimposed on a cloud, the allusion is to the suffering of humanity, prompting Odd Fellows to seek to alleviate trouble and woe. This symbol further reminds Odd Fellows to watch over each other's life and conduct, rendering assistance as needed.

The **Three Links**, also referred to as the "Triple Links," represent the fundamental principles of Odd Fellowship: Friendship, Love, and Truth. So long as these links remain strong, they present a cohesive set of virtues, allowing them to work in concert for the good of the individual, the lodge, and all humankind. Should one of the links weaken or fail, the adherence to Odd Fellowship's purpose would crumble, and the Order could not adequately perform its function in the world. Before uniting with Odd Fellowship, the initiate is instructed to forgo the chains forged from ignorance and vice, which constrain them, replacing them with chains formed from virtue. All Odd Fellows should examine their actions to discern whether they strengthen Friendship, Love, and Truth or diminish the links. The Three Links are often represented with the letters F, L, and T within the links. In this form, the letters are sometimes read backward to spell out "Three Link Fraternity."

The **Skull and Crossbones** are a nearly universal symbol for death. They are associated with the Latin phrase "Memento Mori," translated as "Remember your end," which instructs the hearer to consider their final fate and live their life accordingly. Death is the universal fate of all living things. Although an individual may take many roads in life, they will all ultimately reach the same destination. Once this destination has been reached, all that is left is bones and dust. The crossed femur bones, which come from the legs, allude to this final journey. Simultaneously, the skull that houses the brain is the seat of the personality which also vanishes from the world when the mortal coil is left behind. The femur bones are crossed in reference to the ancient posture of meditation, representing the enlightenment that may be attained through the embrace and acceptance of death. In Odd Fellowship, this symbol also reinforces the age-old command to bury the dead, remembering the deceased's virtues while burying their imperfections together with their physical remains.

The **Scythe** is an ancient symbol referring to the ongoing cycle of nature. All living things and indeed everything in the world is transient and impermanent. A scythe is an agricultural tool that is used to reap crops that are ripe for harvest. So too, the Grim Reaper harvests souls when they have reached their allotted time on the earth. As the scythe brings down the weed and the useful herb alike, all must fall to the cut of the scythe. This is equally true whether their time on the earth has been well-lived or whether it has been wasted without value. When the time of reaping is at hand, lives will be measured by what they have produced in the world.

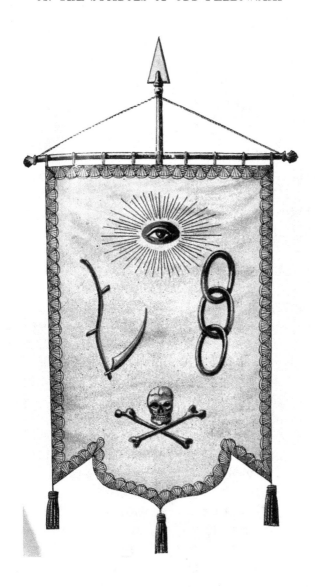

The **Bow and Arrows** symbol is used across many different cultures. Its meaning encompasses both peace and war, as the bow may be used in hunting for sustenance or as a weapon of conflict, either offensively or defensively. When crossed, the arrows may also indicate friendship. Within Odd Fellowship, this emblem further alludes to David and Jonathan's friendship, reminding us of the duty Odd Fellows have to support each other through trials and tribulations. It also refers to battling for the cause of righteousness. Attention should also be paid to the nature of the arrow itself. To fly straight and true, an arrow must be free of imperfections and imbalances. Likewise, an Odd Fellow should strive to live a life of balance and moral integrity to hit the mark.

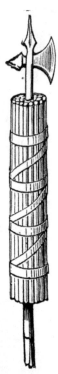

The **Bundle of Sticks**, also called a "fasces," from the Latin *fascis*, meaning "bundle," is an item used by ancient Roman magistrates as a badge of their authority.[27] The Roman version included an axe blade, but it is frequently depicted without the axe when referring to the power of the collective. It teaches the power of unity, demonstrating how a single person can be easily overpowered. But when many people band together, their combined power may not be easily broken. In Odd Fellowship's symbolism, the bond tying the sticks together refers to the oath that unites the members of our order. Should Odd Fellows remain united, there is no dominion which cannot be vanquished. The sticks in the emblem should be depicted as varied individuals rather than as uniform rods. This references Odd Fellowship's role in uniting disparate brothers and sisters into a cohesive whole without sacrificing their individuality.

The **Axe** is a tool that has been used by humankind since the dawn of civilization for harnessing productive labor. It represents the principle of progress, based on the image of pioneers clearing forests to establish human habitation and industry. This macrocosmic meaning is further accompanied by a microcosmic meaning for the individual. On the individual level it encourages Odd Fellows to cut away those parts of their personalities that do not bear good fruit. As an institution should strive to improve itself for its members' benefit, so too should each Odd Fellow be focused on personal growth. The notion of progress and expansion may also be applied to Odd Fellowship's growth through the institution of new lodges throughout the world.

The **Heart in Hand** is one of the symbols most unique to Odd Fellowship, together with the Three Links. It teaches how Odd Fellows should relate one to another, always extending their hearts together with their hand when greeting a brother or sister. It also alludes to the way charity should be rightly performed, cheerfully and not begrudgingly. While charity is always a positive virtue, when this obligation is discharged begrudgingly, it can result in shame or discomfort on the part of the recipient. The hand in this symbol is open, betokening the openness an Odd Fellow should always have when meeting or interacting with brothers and sisters. This is in contrast to the guardedness one would usually expect when relating to a stranger.

The **Globe** is a common motif used in art, worldwide, and throughout history. Although literally depicting only the earth, it often refers to the entire cosmos or created world. It may refer to the perfected universe wherein order pervades. It may also allude to the material realm and temporal power or secular authority. Within Odd Fellowship, the Globe indicates the field of concern of Odd Fellows who seek to bring about a perfected world through universal brotherhood and sisterhood, transcending nations and provincial concerns. Odd Fellowship looks forward to a time when all of humanity can unite in harmony, recognizing that all people are brothers and sisters, the offspring of a mutual Parent. This may be considered the ultimate goal of Odd Fellowship. It also has meaning for the individual Odd Fellow who seeks to unify the disparate forces comprising their own self into an integrated whole.

The **Ark** refers to the Ark of the Covenant, which the Israelites carried with them through the wilderness. It later found its resting place in the ancient Israelite Temple in Jerusalem. The Ark housed several sacred relics: the original tablets of stone bearing the Ten Commandments, the blossoming staff of Aaron the first High Priest, and a jar of the manna which fed the Israelites during the Exodus from Egypt.[28] The final fate of the Ark has been lost to history. In Odd Fellowship, the Ark is primarily representative of the receptacle of tablets of law. It indicates that Odd Fellows should consider law to be sacred, as it forms the basis for a just society. On the individual level, it may also be viewed as representing the body as the seat of the soul. Without caring for and protecting the body, an Odd Fellow will not be able to achieve their lofty spiritual aims.

The **Serpent** has a dichotomous meaning in symbolism, frequently used positively, as in medicine, but in other cases representing evil, relating to the poisonous venom of various snakes. It can be a symbol of fertility or creative force, as in the coiled serpent of Kundalini. It can also refer to rebirth or transformation, due to the process of shedding the skin. When formed into a circle with the head of the serpent eating its tail, it is referred to as an "Oroboros" and represents eternity or everlasting life. In Odd Fellowship, the serpent specifically alludes to wisdom. Odd Fellows should be advised to cultivate the wisdom necessary to discern good from evil and always strive to act for the greater good.

The **Scales and Sword** are derived from the Ancient Roman personification of justice, Iustitia, better known in modern times as "Lady Justice." In this form, she is typically depicted as being blindfolded to signify that justice is impartial and should not be influenced by the power or status of the individual being judged. The scales represent the weighing of evidence with the two pans alluding to mercy and severe judgement. The sword is a symbol of authority which further suggests that justice is both swift and final. Congruent with the notion of impartiality, Odd Fellows too meet as equals within the **lodge room**, without regard to their wealth or influence in the outside world. The scales are not static, but rather in a state of equilibrium. Any action may potentially disrupt their balance if unwisely put into effect. The balancing of contending forces with the scales contains an essential lesson for the aspiring Odd Fellow. While balancing severity and mercy is a necessity in fair judgment, so, too, it is integral to guiding one's individual actions to maintain stability and sound decision-making. The combination of the Scales with

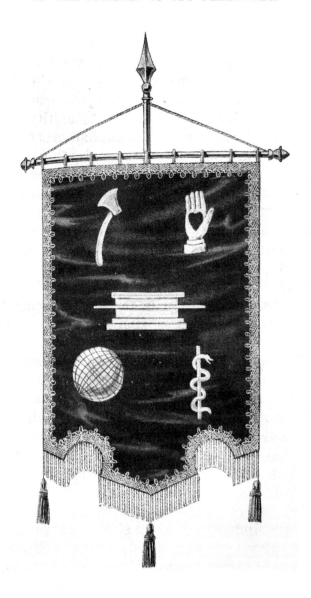

the Sword indicates that justice is an empty promise unless combined with the resolve needed to enforce it. An Odd Fellow should always ensure that they stand up for their beliefs and only use force when it is demanded by justice.

The **Bible** is symbolic of all sacred scripture regardless of what religious tradition it derives from. Therefore, Odd Fellows are bound to respect all persons of faith, even if they hold to a different spiritual path. Moral law serves as the foundation of a just society. It provides the basis for the doctrines and practices of Odd Fellowship. Humanity is separated from the remainder of the animal kingdom by its ability to formulate general principles of behavior to accomplish benevolence in word and deed. These fundamental moral and ethical precepts are unchanging, even as society progresses and takes on new forms which may be unrecognizable to people from earlier epochs. It is essential to distinguish between eternal, unchanging moral law and the pale imitation of it, which is produced by the imperfect human mind. Thus, over time, humanity may strive to bring its actions and principles ever closer to that which is truly right and good. By studying and grappling with the founts of moral law, an Odd Fellow can learn how to bring benevolence to bear in all their intercourse with the world at large.

The **Hourglass** represents the never-ending progress of time, providing a needful reminder of the transience and impermanence of all earthly creation. As the sands silently pass through the hourglass, the allotted time for all living beings marches ever onwards until the last grains of sand have come to rest. In contrast with the literal hourglass, the ineffable hourglass which marks the passing of time for a human being does not inform the bearer how much sand remains. An Odd Fellow should always maintain the awareness that their hours on the earth are limited, and they should guard their precious moments, not knowing which will be the last. Thus, every day matters, and every action counts. Those who have mastered the secret of the hourglass spend their time wisely, balancing the need for refreshment and enjoyment with the desire to have a lasting impact on the world for the greater good. Whether Odd Fellows or otherwise, these individuals are often the best and most productive members of society.

The **Coffin**, also referred to as the "narrow house," is the weary traveler's last resting place. If depicted as open, it represents a fate that has not yet been accepted, but if depicted

as closed, it signifies finality and acceptance. This gloomy emblem reminds Odd Fellows that in the end, all are united in the same fate no matter the heights they may have risen to in a life well-lived. It should bestow a sense of modesty, precluding one from thinking they are better than their fellows. Lest one conclude that all endeavors are futile, the Odd Fellow is reminded that what is accomplished in this life lives on after them, even as they are returned to the dust from which they so lately sprang.

## OF HISTORICAL SYMBOLS

As with the degrees, ceremonies, laws, and practices of Odd Fellowship, the symbols too have been adapted to the changing needs of the membership and the state of the world. In some cases, symbols have been added or dropped altogether. In others, multiple symbols have been combined or split apart to allow for greater nuance in the meanings. While the historical symbols of Odd Fellowship are not directly relevant to an Odd Fellows lodge today, there is still much to be gained by studying these emblems and what they taught. These symbols can continue to teach the brothers and sisters about personal development and the practice of Odd Fellowship.

The **Globe in Clouds** is one of two older variations on the Globe emblem, which is in use today. It represents the imperfect material realm in which humanity dwells. In this world, it is not possible to achieve perfect knowledge, but as the light of the Sun pierces the clouds, emanating down to the created world, so too do seekers after the truth catch glimpses of the infinite realm of the spirit. In Odd Fellowship, the Globe in Clouds is the field of our endeavors. The world needs Odd Fellowship specifically because of the imperfections inherent in the world. If there were no hungry, needy, or afflicted, then the mission of assuaging these ills of society would not be necessary. Should humankind band together to overcome these challenges under the leadership of Odd Fellows and others, the Globe in Clouds may be transformed into the Globe in Full Light.

The **Bow and Quiver** includes the modern-day symbolism of the bow, but in this earlier incarnation, the bow was combined with the quiver rather than the arrow. As in the current era, it relates to David and Jonathan's friendship in particular and the principle of Friendship in general. The difference is that quiver alludes specifically to the notion

of preparation, as this is where the arrows are housed before being loosed on their flight. The quiver is depicted as full, indicating a readiness to take up arms to render protection and aid to another Odd Fellow. If depicted as unstrung, the bow demonstrates a state of relaxation, indicating that, when not called to action, Odd Fellows should take the opportunity to refresh their minds and bodies, that they may be prepared to act when needed.

The **Three Arrows** were originally distinct from the bow in their symbolism, being depicted as crossed with the points downwards in conformity with heraldry's customs. In this form, they are referred to as a "sheaf" and are generally considered an emblem of war. Within Odd Fellowship, the Three Arrows also reference war, but not a literal war to be fought with physical armaments. Instead, the symbol references the war against vice in all its forms that an Odd Fellow should be party to. This war may be battled in the world, but

more significantly, it is the individual's struggle against their iniquitous nature, which presents a stumbling block of temptation even to those who already have a well‑developed sense of right and wrong. There are three arrows specifically to reference the Odd Fellow's

three principal weapons, namely Friendship, Love, and Truth. The distinction from the Three Links is that in this form, they represent the active efforts taken by the Odd Fellow to rectify their conduct through the application of these principles in isolation.

The **Lamb** is a symbol that comes to Odd Fellowship primarily from Christianity. In earlier religions, lambs were supplied as sacrifices in burnt offerings for the remission of guilt or sin and were generally required to be physically unblemished. In Christianity, the sheep has been replaced symbolically with Jesus, who is considered the perfect sacrifice within that religion. This further relates to the metaphor of humankind as a flock under the care of God as the divine shepherd. In Odd Fellowship's symbolism, the Lamb represents innocence and gentleness, reminding Odd Fellows to embody these characteristics as part of the flock of humanity. Only by retaining a child-like state of receptivity can an Odd Fellow achieve spiritual enlightenment and respond to the vicissitudes of the world without judgment or bias. This form of disconnection from the ego and goal-oriented action allows for an objective consciousness that takes in each moment as it comes and is the goal of many religious or spiritual philosophies.

The **Sun** is of such profound importance to all life on earth that it should not be surprising to see it in use as a symbol in nearly every culture. It is depicted in various ways, ranging from the simplest disc through more intricate designs incorporating a face and rays. Its emblematic meaning includes attributes such as health, vitality, power, strength, royalty, and the self. Historically, it has also been used as a masculine symbol, with the Moon correspondingly referring to the feminine. When referring to the self, the Sun often represents the ego or the rational part of the personality, which keeps the more child-like, instinctual, or emotional parts in check. The Sun can refer to self-actualization or achieving one's highest aims. In the context of Odd Fellowship, it represents benevolence and life emanating from Deity for the blessing of all created beings,  regardless of whether they are deserving or not. A parallel is also drawn with the human soul, indicating that its light always shines brightly, even when challenges and difficulties beset the body and mind.

The **Rainbow** is also an emblem used in a plethora of ways throughout history. It may be considered a bridge to the heavens, as a divine messenger, or a sign of the covenant between God and humanity after the Flood. More recently, rainbows have also been used as a symbol of diversity, particularly for social movements involving sexuality and gender identity. The meaning within Odd Fellowship hearkens back to the Judeo-Christian notion of the rainbow as a symbol of God's promise never again to destroy the world through a flood. The Biblical covenant sealed by the rainbow refers to God's promise and the reciprocal promise made by humanity to establish just societies and treat their fellows with love and respect. This symbol should remind Odd Fellows of their obligation to care for and protect their brethren just as they wish for their brethren's support in their hour of need. This is also the essence of the

Covenant of Friendship as illustrated in the **First Degree** of Odd Fellowship.

**Moses' Rod** represents authority and self-sacrifice. In the well-known Biblical story, Moses left behind a life of comfort and honor in Pharaoh's household to unite with his persecuted brethren and lead them through many hardships to freedom. As a leader, Moses' role was two-fold. In addition to protecting and tending to his people, Moses was also responsible for chastising them and setting them back on the right path when they went astray. The rod itself was likely in the form of a walking stick, which travelers would have used to ease their progress through rugged terrain. However, Moses is also thought to have used it to shepherd sheep when he dwelled in Midian before returning to Egypt to retrieve his people. The Odd Fellow should interpret this symbol as a reminder on their journey of life to bestow brotherly love upon the afflicted and to lead them towards a better future when possible.

**Noah's Ark** comes from the Biblical story of the Flood. Noah was warned in advance of the coming calamity and prepared for it by constructing the Ark in response to divine decree. Within the Ark were preserved Noah and his family and two of each species of animal so that the world could be repopulated after the waters

receded. The Ark was constructed in three levels, representing the world's three parts: the earth, the heavens, and the underworld.[29] It served as a microcosm of the world, befitting a vessel that served as the habitation for life's continuation in the world. Within Odd Fellowship, the emblem of Noah's Ark represents preservation. Like Noah preserved a sampling of each species, so too should an Odd Fellow strive to preserve those in need of shelter within their lodge and their community. The diversity of species that were rescued further reminds the Odd Fellow to value diversity in the lodge and in the traditions of the Order.

The **Cornucopia** is a symbol derived from ancient Greek myth. The word literally translates to "horn of plenty." According to the myth, the infant Zeus was nursed by the goat Amaltheia while being hidden from his father Kronos. Due to his great strength he accidentally broke off one of her horns, which he subsequently gave the power of filling up with whatever the owner desired. The symbol takes the form of a horn-shaped basket used in the ancient world to carry produce, often slung over the back to leave the hands free. Often it is depicted as being overflowing with fruit, vegetables, flowers, or other produce. It represents abundance or the bounty of the earth. Within Odd Fellowship, the cornucopia was originally the symbol of the old Fourth Degree or Remembrance Degree. In that usage it was considered to represent the vast stores of knowledge and wisdom collected in memory. Having acquired a bounty of experience, an Odd Fellow is encouraged to share this bounty with those who are newer to the path. The initiate is further reminded that, should they be faithful to their duties as an Odd Fellow, the Order will provide for them in their own hour of need.

**Aaron's Budded Rod** also derives from the story of the Exodus from Egypt. Aaron was the brother of Moses and a prophet in his own right. He served as Moses' spokesman due to Moses' difficulty with speech. He was selected to

be the first **High Priest** of Israel due to his deep and abiding love for Israel, giving him particular relevance for the current **Third Degree** of Odd Fellowship, which is considered the "priestly" degree. As a spokesman for Moses, Aaron provided education and guidance for his brethren. Like Moses, Aaron carried a rod or staff, which was involved in some of the drama which transpired. There was opposition to Aaron's Tribe of Levi serving as the exclusive priesthood, so a challenge was declared. One leader from each of the twelve tribes presented a rod, with the rod that sprouted overnight to determine which tribe would serve the priestly function. Ultimately, Aaron's rod budded, blossomed, and bore almonds, indicating that the Tribe of Levi was destined for the priesthood. In Odd Fellowship, this emblem pertains to the vitalizing nature of Truth. All brothers and sisters of the highest degree of an Odd Fellow's lodge should emulate Aaron, training and advising those who come after them in the life-giving tenets of Odd Fellowship. Like Aaron, they should teach both explicitly as well as by example.

# CHAPTER XXI

## ON APPENDANT AND

## ASSOCIATED BODIES

### *THEIR PURPOSE AND NATURE*

During the 19th century, the lodges were hives of activity, with meetings and degree work held as frequently as every week. This was not enough to meet the demand of members who wanted more fellowship, more degrees, and more positions of responsibility to serve the Order. The solution was to create appendant or "side" bodies that a brother or sister can join after having completed the basic work of an Odd Fellows lodge. Some bodies are official, coming under the full authority and direction of Sovereign Grand Lodge, while others are unofficial, acting independently while still requiring being an Odd Fellow

STRUCTURE OF THE
Independent Order of Odd Fellows

in **good standing** within a <u>local lodge</u> to allow participation. In all cases, these bodies are recommended to the Odd Fellow who wishes to learn more and expand their participation in Odd Fellowship. However, they should never be used to detract from participation in the member's Odd Fellows lodge, nor should they advance any viewpoints or usages that violate the Order's tenets.

## *OF THE REBEKAHS*

The Rebekahs, also known as "The Daughters of Rebekah," are not an appendant body per se but actually an independent degree that may be bestowed upon any eligible woman or man regardless of whether they are already affiliated with an Odd Fellows Lodge. It began in 1851 as an auxiliary degree for women who were associated with Odd Fellowship through a male relation such as a husband or

father.[30] It presents a single degree originally written by the 17th Vice President of the United States, Schuyler Colfax, which promotes teachings based on prominent women from biblical history. By 1868 it had become so popular that it was spun off into a distinctive body with its own lodges, officers, and ultimately its own customs and traditions.[31]

The **Rebekah Degree** contains lessons drawn from the lives and accomplishments of the mother of Samson who gave her firstborn up to the service of God, the prophetess Deborah who led the Israelites during the period of Judges, Esther who saved the Jewish People during the reign of Xerxes I in Persia, Ruth the Moabite who left her country and people behind to unite with the Israelites, the matriarch Sarah who had the faith to give birth to a nation, the prophetess Miriam who lead the women of Israel in the wilderness, and, of course, the matriarch Rebekah who went above and beyond in her practice of hospitality to weary travelers. These eminent women exemplify admirable traits that any contemporary woman or man would do well to emulate. The Rebekah Degree also advances four symbols that have been a part of Odd Fellowship's corpus far longer than this degree has been in existence but have fallen away from usage within the Odd Fellows lodge. The Rebekah Degree symbols are the Beehive, the Moon and Seven Stars, the Dove, and the Lily.

The **Beehive** has been used as a symbol since time immemorial, including among the ancient Romans and in medieval heraldry. It has also been used by numerous fraternal orders and friendly societies. Bees form a collective society in which every individual plays a role integral to the success of the community. The hive includes countless workers who gather nectar from plants and, through their labor, transform it into sustenance for the colony. Thus, the Beehive is a symbol of industry, providing a reminder that, without labor, none may eat, and also demonstrating the importance of collective effort. A lodge, household, or entire society, like a hive, must be well-ordered, with each participant playing their respective role for the betterment of all. The Rebekah or Odd Fellow should be inspired by this symbol to make their own unique contributions to their lodge's workings, the sustenance of their families, and the advancement of human civilization. Though the bees of a hive are large in number, it should be remembered that each individual's contribution is important and valuable. The Beehive also reminds Rebekahs and Odd Fellows to prepare for the future, just as bees toil ceaselessly while the flowers are in bloom to prepare provisions for the winter. The hive itself may be considered representative of the lodge, the central location that all return to for communal life and efforts. Rebekahs and Odd Fellows should strive to ensure that they are building strong communities able to care for and protect their brethren, from the most able to the most vulnerable.

The **Moon and Seven Stars** is also of venerable origin, though two principal explanations are given for what it represents celestially. In some traditions, the Seven Stars represent the Pleiades, a star cluster in the constellation of Taurus, also known as the "Seven Sisters." In classical Greek mythology, the Seven Sisters were the seven daughters of Atlas who served as the companions of Artemis. The other explanation is that the Seven Stars are the seven wandering stars of antiquity. These were not, in fact, stars, but rather the seven planets that were visible to the ancients: the Sun, Mercury, Venus, the Moon, Mars, Jupiter, and Saturn. They possess numerous correspondences throughout history, ranging from the seven archangels and the seven days of the week to the seven alchemical metals, namely gold, quicksilver or mercury, copper or bronze, silver, iron, tin, and lead. The problem with the latter explanation, though, is that the Moon is then included twice, because it is considered an independent part of the Moon and Seven Stars in addition to being one of the stars. Although this is rather unsatisfactory as a result, the interpretation has persisted for hundreds of years.

Within the context of Odd Fellowship, the Moon and Seven Stars represents the orderly workings of the created universe. The stars and planets occupy their own designated orbits, each independent of the others. As these empyrean bodies do not interfere with each other, likewise, Rebekahs and Odd Fellows should not interfere with the rights or happiness of others. All Rebekahs and Odd Fellows may further interpret this symbol to indicate the necessity of being systematic and precise in collective and individual efforts. Thus, this symbol overlaps somewhat with the Beehive. The distinction is that the Beehive is more focused on developing a healthy work ethic. Simultaneously, the Moon and Seven Stars address the need for organization and process in the endeavor. The Odd Fellow or Rebekah should adhere to the principles of order and regularity so that their work is effective and makes a lasting impact. The juxtaposition of the Moon, which is a singular luminary, with the stars in their multiplicity, may further allude to the tension between unity and plurality. On the one hand, Odd Fellowship is unified, with shared values and modes of working. On the other, it allows for diverse expression across the multiform possibilities that the framework of Odd Fellowship offers.

The **Dove** is a well-known symbol in many cultures, emblematic of love, innocence, or peace. There is also the well-known story involving a dove, common to many Near Eastern cultures, including both the Epic of Gilgamesh and the biblical Book of Noah, in which a dove is sent forth to determine whether the floodwaters have receded sufficiently for dry land to appear, ultimately returning bearing an olive branch. The Spirit of God is compared to a dove in both Jewish and Christian teachings, with a descending dove depicting the Holy Spirit's descent in the latter. The primary meaning in Odd Fellowship stems from the flood story, encompassing both the peace and innocence meanings. Like the dove, the Rebekah or Odd Fellow should go forth into the world, spreading love and comfort wherever they go. Like the dove navigating the flooded terrain, this may involve crossing obstacles and piloting through troubles, but if they are pure of heart, they will merit to return, bearing the olive branch of peace.

The **Lily** is frequently representative of purity, virtue, or devotion, particularly when the white varieties of lilies are referred to. A Rebekah or Odd Fellow should always be reminded by this emblem to be pure of heart and virtuous in all their thoughts, words, and deeds. Being innocent or pure doesn't mean that one cannot be worldly or benefit from the experience. Rather, one should cultivate a childlike wonder at the beauty and magnificence of the world and always retain an open mind and an open heart. If this is begun on the level of feelings and perceptions, it will naturally flow into one's actions and relationships with others, allowing one to express one's deepest self and intrinsic values.

## *OF THE ENCAMPMENT*

The first encampment was **chartered** in 1827.[32] Encampment provides an Odd Fellow who has completed the degrees of an Odd Fellows lodge with the opportunity to take three further degrees.

The earliest history of the Encampment degrees is shrouded in mystery. The **Golden Rule Degree** is the first to enter the historical record in 1821, when it was conferred by one Past Grand on five other Past Grands, including Thomas Wildey.[33] This degree, which teaches toleration of differences, is thought to have been authored by American Odd Fellow John Entwisle, who authored the Covenant and Remembrance Degrees, which later formed part of the basis of the present **First** and **Second Degrees**. However, other sources propose an English origin by way of the first Grand Conductor of the Grand Lodge of the United States, William Larkin, who was present at its initial conferral within America.[34]

The **Patriarchal Degree**, which focuses on the lesson of hospitality to the stranger and to the brother or sister alike, demonstrably came from England, where it was written by a Past Deputy Grand Master named Smith, adopted by the Manchester United in 1825, and subsequently brought to the United States in the hands of Past Grand McCormick of Maryland.[35]

The final degree of the Encampment, the **Royal Purple Degree**, which conveys the idea of the journey of life and rest from that journey, is also of somewhat unclear parentage and is thought to most likely have been written in the United States by one or more of the early founders of American Odd Fellowship.[36]

As with most of the original degrees of Odd Fellowship, these were initially presented entirely in lecture form when they were compiled by the Grand Lodge of the United States in 1835, but beginning in 1845, they were expanded to include fully immersive drama, setting the stage for the later expansion of all the degrees of Odd Fellowship into dramatic form after this format became extremely popular with the members.[37]

Encampments provide a forum for experienced Odd Fellows, usually from across multiple lodges, to gather to exchange ideas and make connections with other Odd Fellows. There is often a specific focus on delving further into the symbolism of Odd Fellowship and in training new leaders for the Order based on the experience of those who have come before. In some **jurisdictions**, particularly in Europe, membership in Encampment is by invitation only.

The **Tent** is the symbol most strongly associated with the Encampment branch of Odd Fellowship. Within Odd Fellowship, the Tent represents hospitality. It is said that the tent of Abraham the Patriarch had a doorway in each of the four cardinal directions to facilitate spotting and welcoming guests, no matter what direction they approached from. All Patriarchs and Matriarchs should be reminded by this emblem to always be welcoming to the stranger as well as the brother or sister. The Tent is inherently a temporary dwelling that can be packed up and moved to another location when desired. It also does not afford the same measure of protection from the elements as a permanent structure, emphasizing humanity's transient and fragile nature. Meditating on this impermanence should further highlight the importance of hospitality, as any person might unexpectedly find themselves in need of shelter and nourishment.

The **Crook** is a staff traditionally used by shepherds in the guiding of their flocks. The crook has a curved head specifically for pulling the sheep or other livestock back should they wander in the wrong direction. It is also often used in ecclesiastical regalia, art, or heraldry to emphasize the role of a bishop or other leader in spiritually guiding their congregation. The Patriarch or Matriarch should be inspired by this symbol to exert themselves in guidance towards all Odd Fellows who seek their aid, not only in worldly matters but also in the realm of the sacred. So too, should they look to the Shepherd of All for guidance in their own affairs.

The **Three Pillars** represented in the symbology of Encampment are Faith, Hope, and Charity. They originate from the "theological virtues" expressed in Christian thought and are said to be the guide to living a moral life. Faith pertains to the intellect, allowing an individual to subscribe to the truth of divine revelation even when not comprehensible to the mortal mind. Hope pertains to the will, allowing one to act righteously with the expectation of future reward in this world or the next. Charity pertains to the emotions, bestowing a love of God and a love for one's neighbor as much as one loves one's own self. In the context of Encampment, which builds atop the Odd Fellows Lodge lessons, the **Three Links** may be considered the foundation of the edifice, while the Three Pillars represent the next level of the superstructure erected by Odd Fellowship. The Patriarch or Matriarch should be ever mindful of taking the pillars as their guide as much as they hew to the lessons taught by the links.

The **Altar of Incense**, also known as the "Golden Altar," is a symbol stemming from the Israelite Holy Temple in Jerusalem. Historically, it was constructed of wood covered in gold and was used only for the burning of incense in accordance with precise instructions given in the Book of Exodus and in the Talmud, or compendium of Jewish law, interpretation, and customs. The incense formula consisted of eleven specific ingredients, but the precise method for preparing it was a closely guarded secret, attended to by a specific family. Within Encampment, the Altar emblem embodies the pervasiveness of the impulse to spirituality and religion among all peoples of the earth. A major theme of Encampment Odd Fellowship is religious toleration. No one faith possesses a monopoly on truth, so a Patriarch or Matriarch should always take the Altar of Incense as a reminder to respect the sincerely held beliefs of others, even if they are foreign or unfamiliar. The eleven spices comprising the incense, one of which was the foul-smelling galbanum, are said to allude to the necessity of unity amongst the Israelites, including even the unrighteous. If any ingredients were missing, the incense so prepared was invalid, demonstrating to Patriarchs and Matriarchs that the piety of all seekers is important in the world, regardless of what tribe they hail from or what sect they adhere to.

The **Tablets of Law** are an emblem originally from Judaism, but also adopted by Christianity, which are also known as the "Tablets of Stone" or "Tablets of Testimony." According to the story in the Book of Exodus, they were hand-carved by Moses after the original tablets made of sapphire or lapis lazuli were smashed following the incident with the Golden Calf. The two tablets were carved with the Ten Commandments. Although most commonly depicted as having rounded tops, Jewish sources note that the tablets were in actuality rectangles with square corners.[38] The tablets are said to have been deposited within the Ark of the Covenant. The symbolic meaning provided by Encampment is that of divine law. Within the Western cultural tradition, the Ten Commandments are considered part of a shared ethical heritage. However, they are not explicitly part of Islam, which has its own variations of the laws contained therein. Patriarchs and Matriarchs are instructed to focus on this shared vision of moral law and to work together to promote these common principles while acknowledging and respecting doctrinal differences. A Patriarch or Matriarch should always be mindful to follow their own conscience and personal beliefs to promote society's general welfare.

The **Globe in Full Light** represents the world in a state of perfection, with all humanity working together for the common good of all. Achieving this ideal requires all men and women to cast aside their own peculiar views and

EMBLEMS OF THE SUBORDINATE ENCAMPMENTS.

prejudices to perceive the potential of heaven on earth, which may be brought about through cooperation and concern for all living creatures. This emblem was originally assigned to the Royal Purple Degree, making it one of the Encampment branch's capstone symbols. After receiving the full measure of wisdom within the Encampment, the Patriarch or Matriarch has completed their journey to enlightenment and is urged to spread that wisdom far and wide within the Order and into the world beyond. The pinnacle of human civilization so depicted requires the participation of all, so the brothers and sisters should never cease from their attempts at outreach and expansion for Odd Fellowship and its principles.

## OF THE PATRIARCHS MILITANT

After the Civil War, there was a demand for a uniformed, marching branch of Odd Fellowship among military veterans and others. Initially, this took the form of uniformed Encampment units, but in 1885, Patriarchs Militant was established as a full, new branch.[39] Originally to join required being a Patriarch of the Royal Purple Degree, but as of 2018, Patriarchs Militant is now open to any Odd Fellow of the **Third Degree**. There is only one degree in Patriarchs Militant, the **Chevalier Degree**, which reenacts the story of the Battle of the Vale of Siddim, also known as the "War of Nine Kings," in which Abraham joined forces with the southern kings and rescued his nephew Lot. The degree illustrates the principle of universal justice and urges Chevaliers to symbolically take up arms when necessary to protect the innocent and restore justice. It grants admission to the local body for Patriarchs Militant, known as a "canton." Patriarchs Militant are known for their quasi-military uniforms, which were originally in a 19th-century style complete

with a plumed hat but more recently were redesigned to reflect a more contemporary military style. Cantons march in parades as a showpiece for the Order and train in sword drills, with awards bestowed for proficiency.

The Patriarchs Militant symbol consists of a crown with a crossed shepherd's crook and sword extending through it and the Three Links connecting the two implements at the base. The crown is used extensively in heraldry and other forms of symbolism relating to royalty, power, or victory. It is appropriate for the Chevalier, as the degree is generally considered the highest within Odd Fellowship. The crook and the sword represent peace and war, respectively, relating to the Patriarchs Militant battle cry of "Pax aut Bellum," which translates to "Peace or War," and emphasizes that the Chevalier should serve the cause of chivalry in both times of peace and times of war.

## OF THE YOUTH BRANCHES

As with the creation of Rebekahs, originally for the female family members of Odd Fellows, Sovereign Grand Lodge has chartered youth branches to foster engagement with younger individuals in the families of members and in the surrounding community. There are three major youth branches, Junior Lodge for boys ages eight to twenty-one, Theta Rho for girls ages eight to twenty-one, United Youth Group for all children ages eight to eighteen, and the Cadet Corps uniformed youth branch of the Patriarchs Militant.

Junior Lodge was formed by Sovereign Grand Lodge in 1923.[40] However, earlier Odd Fellows youth groups for boys existed in specific jurisdictions or informally but did not persist. Originally the branch was referred to as the "Junior branch," with the individual units referred to as "firesides." In 1929, a new ritual for the branch was adopted based on the story of Daniel as recorded in the Bible, and the name was changed to "Junior Lodge."[41] The watchwords of Junior Lodge are Honor, Fidelity, and Loyalty, though originally they

consisted solely of Honor and Fidelity. Its official colors are silver and dark blue. Its emblem is a heraldic shield containing the Three Links, an eye, and a goblet, and surmounted by a pyramid. Although boys may belong to Junior Lodge until the age of twenty-one, they must be between eight and eighteen years of age to join.

Theta Rho stands for "θυγατέρα Ρεβέκκα" ("Thugatera Rebekah") in Greek, which translates to "Daughters of Rebekah." It was founded in 1929.[42] The Theta Rho motto is "Happiness through Service," and its official colors are peach and Yale blue. Its emblem is a seal with the Three Links and the Greek letters theta and rho.

Although girls may belong to Theta Rho until the age of twenty-one, they must be between eight and eighteen years of age to join.

United Youth Group was formally established as a multi-gendered youth branch in 2002,[43] with a brief initiation ritual touching on the principles of Friendship, Love, and Truth. It was established due to the difficulty in getting a

sufficient number of boys or girls in many jurisdictions to support Junior Lodges or Theta Rho Clubs. However, it has not caught on in most jurisdictions. Its emblem is a yellow seal bearing a Triquetra composed of red, white, and blue in a form reminiscent of the Three Links. The units may consist of both boys and girls, though initiations are performed separately by gender.

## OF THE ANCIENT MYSTIC ORDER OF SAMARITANS

The Ancient Mystic Order of Samaritans is an unofficial appendant body for Odd Fellows, open only to men. It works closely together with the Ladies of the Orient, which is for women, and the two often share joint events and projects. Both organizations are dedicated to the lighter side of fraternity, putting on events for entertainment purposes, often with a strong element of humor and parody present. In its current form, the Ancient Mystic Order of Samaritans began in 1925, but it has an unusual and complicated history dating back to the late 19th century through the various predecessor bodies which merged to form the present body. There was such a strong demand

for a light-hearted, fun body as a supplement to the serious work done by Odd Fellows that different regional bodies formed over time independently. The first of these was the Oriental Order of Humility, which had a Middle Eastern theme. Contradictory accounts of its origin have been put forward, but according to some which appear most credible, it was first founded in New York in 1878 and Canada in 1879.[44] According to the initial supreme leader of the Oriental Order of Humility and Perfection, John A. MacDonald, the Oriental Order of Humility was initially a loose and informal group like many other side bodies at the time, consisting of "A SOLITARY CHARGE, WRITTEN ON A SHEET OF FOOLSCAP PAPER, CRUDE IN FORM, YET WITH A 'STRIKING' IDEA, WHICH GAVE IT THE 'ZIP' THAT MADE IT INSTANTLY POPULAR WITH ALL THOSE WHO WERE 'ELEVATED' TO ITS CHARMED CIRCLE."[45] By 1901, it was expanded to a full, fraternal body. A second degree was written, resulting in the organization being renamed the Oriental Order of Humility and Perfection.[46] This body primarily served the northeastern United States and Canada.

Meanwhile, the Imperial Order of Muscovites was established in 1894 in Cincinnati, Ohio, with a Czarist Russian theme.[47] The other major Odd Fellows playground orders were the Pilgrim Knights of Oriental Splendor founded in 1915 in Atlanta, Georgia,[48] the Ancient and Mystic Order of Cabirians which began in Oakland, California, circa 1920,[49] and the Veiled Prophets of Baghdad which began in 1921 in St. Joseph, Missouri.[50] Eventually, a  movement developed to merge all the Odd Fellows playground orders into a single unified body, initially resulting in the United Order of Splendor and Perfection in 1924 and finally the Ancient Mystic Order of Samaritans in 1925.[51] The final group to unite with the collective in 1927 was the Improved Order of Muscovites, an offshoot from the Imperial Order of Muscovites which had splintered from the main body in 1908 and was located primarily on the West Coast of the United States.[52]

As a fully independent order, not under the jurisdiction of Sovereign Grand Lodge, the Ancient Mystic Order of Samaritansis governed by its own parent body, Supreme Sanctorum, which was originally styled the "Supreme Orient," established in 1901.[53] The current ceremonial consists of two degrees, the Humility Degree conferred by local sanctorums and the Perfection Degree which is only bestowed at regional or international conventions. Odd Fellows who have received these degrees are known as "Samaritans" and "Sheiks," respectively. The Ancient Mystic Order of Samaritans has generally limited its operations to the United States and Canada. However, there was a presence established in Cuba and the Panama Canal Zone at one time.[54] Like many other social side bodies which wear fezzes and focus on the lighter side of fraternity, the degrees and other rituals are a composite of many different Near Eastern cultural influences, ranging from Persian to Egyptian and Arabian. The Ancient Mystic Order of Samaritans has a charitable focus on cognitive disabilities in particular.

The standard **regalia** for the Ancient Mystic Order of Samaritans is the fez, an item of headgear originating from the Ottoman Empire and at one time also worn commonly by the Muslims, Christians, and Jews who were subjects of that empire. Beginning with the Shriners, which were formed in 1872,[55] the fez was increasingly adopted by fraternal organizations, including a hanging tassel. Most fraternal organizations opted for a single fez and tassel color, but the Ancient Mystic Order of Samaritans possesses a complex fez and tassel color system indicating rank. At the local sanctorum level, the fez is red with a yellow tassel denoting the rank of Samaritan and a red tassel indicating the rank of Sheik. Blue is interwoven with these colors to mark a Past Grand Monarch, the principal officer of a sanctorum. At the District, Divisional, and Supreme Sanctorum levels, the colors are further altered, including blue fezzes for Divisional officers and purple fezzes for the Supreme Monarchos and Past Supreme Monarchii, and a variety of accompanying tassel colors.

The primary symbols for the Ancient Mystic Order of Samaritans include the Owl, the Pyramid, the Scimitar, and the Crescent Moon. The emblem of the Owl represents wisdom in its association with the Greek goddess Athena and vigilance or watchfulness due to the nocturnal nature of the distinctive bird. The meaning intended within the Ancient Mystic Order of Samaritans is that of nocturnality. Fittingly, the group's motto is "We never sleep," referring to their penchant for hosting elaborate parties that ran up through the break of day, such as the much-acclaimed Moon Feast.

The **Pyramid** symbol refers specifically to the Egyptian variety, which generally has a square base and triangular sides, coming to a single point at the apex. These colossal monuments were built following religious and spiritual principles, often serving as tombs for the Pharaohs and other important officials. They were designed to conform to astronomical phenomena and were also crafted in such a way as to reflect the rays of the Sun. For the Samaritan, they represent the impressive attainments of the Middle East's ancient peoples and indeed the nearly limitless potential of human ingenuity. Although the popular view is that the pyramids were constructed primarily with slave labor, this is no longer thought to be the case, with skilled artisans now considered to be the driving force behind their construction.[56] The pyramids were designed and erected by countless individuals, most of whom are unknown in modern times, demonstrating the power of a well-ordered and harmonious team effort to achieve what might otherwise be regarded as impossible.

The **Scimitar** is an extremely popular symbol used by various fraternal organizations, particularly of the fez-wearing persuasion. It originates from a large class of curved swords popular within Middle Eastern nations. Curved swords were also employed throughout Europe, though these designs are typically assigned the more general term "saber." The shape used for a scimitar by fraternal organizations usually only bears a passing resemblance to the actual weapons used for combat. As it is a slicing weapon specifically, a Samaritan may interpret the scimitar as emblematic of the power of good fellowship and a friendly demeanor to cut through resistance. It is a well-known phenomenon that formulating positive interpersonal relationships within a group makes it easier to marshal resources and smooth over any difficulties that may occur when contending opinions arise.

The **Crescent Moon** has had numerous meanings attributed to it throughout the years, including associations with deities worldwide. It was adopted as a symbol of the Ottoman Empire in about 1453[57] and since then has become increasingly popular as a symbol of Islam. It also plays a role in heraldry, though in this case, it is presented with the two points facing upwards. One of the modern meanings of the Moon in general, which also has roots in the ancient world, is that of lunacy, an association with irrationality or absurdity. This is, in fact, a fitting meaning for Samaritans viewing this emblem, due to the Ancient Mystic Order of Samaritans' role as a playground order. The Samaritan should ever remember that not everything in the world should be taken too seriously. In the words of a common proverb quoted in the early materials of the Order, "ALL WORK AND NO PLAY MAKES JACK A DULL BOY." By taking time to relax and engage in the playful or absurd side of life, a Samaritan can become refreshed and better able to steel himself for the serious work that must also be performed.

## *OF THE LADIES OF THE ORIENT*

Ladies of the Orient is a truly unique fraternal appendant body, serving as a playground order for women associated with Odd Fellowship. Unlike most women's fraternal organizations, it

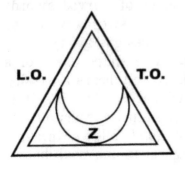

is not a so‑called "auxiliary" body created by men on behalf of women. Rather, the first unit of Ladies of the Orient, Pioneer Zuanna #1, was founded by Emily Voorheis in 1915 together with companions from the Rebekahs for the purposes of having a group dedicated to recreation and amusement.[58] The group, which originally only admitted Rebekahs as members, was incorporated in the State of New York under the name "Supreme Royal Zuanna of the Mystic Degrees of Persecution and Purification Ladies of the Orient of the United States and Canada."[59] There are two degrees, the Persecution Degree, bestowing the title of "Queen," and the Purification Degree, which is conferred at meetings of the Supreme Royal Zuanna, the highest body within Ladies of the Orient. The contents of the Persecution Degree are said to be a parody of traditional notions of femininity, subversively turning them on their head, a feature which may have been considered shocking amongst many at a time when women did not yet even possess the right to vote in the United States. Therefore, Ladies of the Orient could be considered an early feminist organization.

As with the Ancient Mystic Order of Samaritans, the regalia of Ladies of the Orient is a fez. The basic fez of the Zuanna member is white, with blue and purple fezzes reserved for Divisional and Supreme officers. Not to be outdone by the men of the Ancient Mystic Order of Samaritans, Ladies of the Orient possesses a truly dazzling array of tassel colors, with nearly every office in a Zuanna or higher body having its own specific single- or multiple-color tassel. It is possibly the most intricate system of tassel colors ever deployed by a fez-wearing fraternal organization.

The symbols of the Ladies of the Orient include the Crescent Moon and the Sphinx, and the Owl and Scimitar, shared with the Ancient Mystic Order of Samaritans. As distinct from the Ancient Mystic Order of Samaritans, the Crescent Moon is portrayed with the two points facing upwards, and a Z emblazoned on it. This alternative configuration of the Crescent Moon has a somewhat different connotation, relying more heavily on its feminine aspects. Ancient Mediterranean portrayals take this basic form, with the crescent serving as the headdress for the lunar goddess of the hunt, Artemis, and her Roman equivalent, Diana. In Roman Catholicism, it is often used in portrayals of the Virgin Mary. It even appears in many versions of the Tarot, crowning the High Priestess. In the Ladies of the Orient depiction of this symbol, the Z stands for Zuanna, the organization's local unit, which is described as referring to a place where women gather. Thus, the meaning is strongly aligned with the feminine meaning, emphasizing the role of the Zuanna as a space created by and for women.

The **Sphinx** is used in Ladies of the Orient as the emblem for Supreme Royal Zuanna. It originated as an Ancient Egyptian motif, typically depicted as having the body of a lion and a man's head. It was viewed as a guardian and often used at important edifices such as temples or tombs. The most well-known Sphinx and the one depicted in Ladies of the Orient is the Great Sphinx of Giza, situated adjacent to the Great Pyramids. The sphinx was also adopted in Bronze Age Greek culture, but in a different form, with a woman's head and features and the addition of wings from an eagle or other bird. The connotation was also different, having a more threatening or malevolent tone. This is best demonstrated by the sphinx said to guard the city of Thebes and to ask the Riddle of the Sphinx, requiring a correct answer from any traveler who sought to enter the city. The specific riddle asked is not universally agreed upon, but in the story of Oedipus, the riddle was attributed to be "Which creature has one voice and yet becomes four-footed and two-footed and three-footed?"[60] The correct answer given by Oedipus was Man—who crawls on all fours as a baby, then walks on two feet as an adult, and then uses a walking stick in old age. The emblem of the Sphinx in Ladies of the Orient emphasizes the mystery and wisdom of femininity.

# CONCLUSION

I hope you have enjoyed this whirlwind tour through the various facets of our beloved Independent Order of Odd Fellows. As can be seen, Odd Fellowship is a vibrant, living tradition that has changed and grown together with the needs of the brothers and sisters and the world at large.

Certain principles have held the Order in good stead throughout its storied histories, most particularly Friendship, Love, and Truth, as Odd Fellowship has consistently sought to guide its members in personal development and make the world a better place. Education of our members in the venerable traditions and customs remains a profound concern, so I hope this small contribution to the legacy of Odd Fellows instructional manuals, so popular in the 19th century, will find good soil in which to plant the seeds of our future growth and unfolding into the full flower of a knowledgeable and responsible membership. We should always stop to ask what we are doing, why we are doing it, and how it fits into the ongoing conversation of Odd Fellowship stretching back through the long years.

Before I conclude, and we part ways, I issue a challenge to all the new members who have recently united with us and to those who have long been part of this movement. Odd Fellowship is always in need of new leaders to pick up the mantle and continue our march through time. There is no reason why the next leader of a lodge, a Grand Lodge, or even the Sovereign Grand Lodge cannot be you. Leadership and status within the Order are a ladder, the bottom rungs of which have been placed at your feet. Work hard to familiarize yourself with the degrees and the workings of your lodge. Expand your network by building working and social relationships with Odd Fellows in your lodge, district, **jurisdiction**, and worldwide. Deepen your experience by progressing through the chairs in your lodge up through Noble Grand. Broaden your horizons by serving as a District Deputy Grand Master and reaching out to your district and beyond. Make a name for yourself in the Order, and a future Grand Master may appoint you as a Grand Lodge officer. Once you are known throughout your jurisdiction, consider running for Grand Warden, the first step on the path leading to becoming a Grand Master in your own right.

Reach ever upwards and perhaps run for Grand Representative to make your voice known at Sovereign Grand Lodge. Sovereign Grand Lodge needs representatives who truly love and care for this Order and its membership and will work to modernize and improve us while still keeping their feet firmly planted on the solid base laid down by those who came before. Only you know the full extent of your ambition and ability, whether your ultimate aim is to serve on a Sovereign Grand Lodge committee or even hold the office of Sovereign Grand Master itself.

For those who do not wish to lead, there is much else that can be done outside of the spotlight, such as mentoring newer members, writing articles or books, and bringing in new ideas and approaches. The power is in your hands, and Odd Fellowship will become what you and your brothers and sisters make of it. If we all work together and keep our eyes on our lofty principles and values, there is no limit to what can be done to better this world, and to continue the vast story of the Order, which is being written as we speak.

May we ever be faithful to the principles of our beloved Order, and it may it last far beyond our own short lives as an inexhaustible source of life and goodness to be tapped by those with the eyes to see it for what it truly is. Now, the time for your own work is at hand!

Fraternally yours,
Michael Greenzeiger

# ENDNOTES

1. Henry Stillson, *Official History of Odd Fellowship, The Three Link Fraternity.* (Boston: The Fraternity Publishing Company, 1900), 46–47.

2. Stillson, *Official History of Odd Fellowship, The Three Link Fraternity,* 47.

3. Rev. Aaron B. Grosh, *The Odd Fellows Manual: Illustrating the History, Principles, and Government of the Order, and the Instructions and Duties of Every Degree, Station, and Office in Odd Fellowship; With Directions for Laying Corner-Stones; Dedicating Cemeteries, Chapels, Halls, and Other Public Edifices; Marshalling Funeral and Other Processions; Forms for Petitions, Reports, etc.* (Philadelphia: H.C. Peck & Theo Bliss, 1852), 17–18.

4. Grosh, *The Odd Fellows Manual,* 17.

5. James Spry, *The History of Odd-fellowship, Its Origin, Tradition, and Objects; with a General Review of Results Arising from Its Adoption by the Branch Known as the Manchester Unity from the Year 1810 to the Present Time* (Devonport: John R. H. Spry, 1867), 186–188.

6. Daniel Weinbren, *The Oddfellows, 1810–2010* (Lancaster: Carnegie Publishing, 2010), 9.

7. Charles Brooks, *The Official History and Manual of the Grand United Order of Odd Fellows in America: A Chronological Treatise* (Philadelphia: Odd Fellows' Journal Print, 1902), 7–9.

8. Stillson, *Official History of Odd Fellowship,* 51–52.

9. Theodore Ross, *Odd Fellowship: Its History and Manual* (New York: The M.W. Hazen Co., 1888), 11–13.

10. Grosh, *The Odd Fellows Manual,* 28–29.

11. Grosh, *The Odd Fellows Manual,* 31.

12. Grosh, *The Odd Fellows Manual,* 32–33.

13. Grosh, *The Odd Fellows Manual*, 41.

14. Grosh, *The Odd Fellows Manual*, 41.

15. Ross, *Odd Fellowship: Its History and Manual*, 260.

16. Sovereign Grand Lodge, *Journal of Proceedings of the Sovereign Grand Lodge, I.O.O.F* (1968): 485.

17. Henry M. Robert III, Daniel H. Honemann, Thomas J. Balch, Daniel E. Seabold, Shmuel Gerber, *Robert's Rules of Order Newly Revised* (New York: PublicAffairs, 2020), xliii.

18. Robert, *Robert's Rules of Order Newly Revised*, l.

19. Robert, *Robert's Rules of Order Newly Revised*.

20 Sovereign Grand Lodge, *Sovereign Grand Lodge Code of General Laws* (2018), Chapter II. Sec. 14.

21. Sovereign Grand Lodge, *Sovereign Grand Lodge Code of General Laws* (2018), Chapter XXXVIII.

22. Sovereign Grand Lodge, *Sovereign Grand Lodge Code of General Laws* (2018), Chapter XXXVIII. Part II.

23. Sovereign Grand Lodge, *Sovereign Grand Lodge Code of General Laws* (2018), Chapter IV. Sec. 18.

24. Sovereign Grand Lodge, *Sovereign Grand Lodge Code of General Laws* (2018), Chapter II. Sec. 12.

25. Sovereign Grand Lodge, *Sovereign Grand Lodge Code of General Laws* (2018), Chapter IV. Sec. 8. (f)(i)

26. Sovereign Grand Lodge, *Sovereign Grand Lodge Code of General Laws* (2018), Chapter III. Sec. 12. H.

27. *Oxford English Dictionary*, 2nd ed. (Oxford: Oxford University Press, 1989), s.v. "Fasces."

28. Hebrews 9:4

29. Martin Kessler, Karel Adriaan Deurloo, *A commentary on Genesis: The Book of Beginnings* (Maweh, New Jersey: Paulist Press, 2004), 81.

30. Thomas Beharrell, *Odd Fellows Monitor and Guide* (Indianapolis: Robert Douglass, 1882), 17-25.

31. Pascal Donaldson, *The Odd-Fellows Text-Book and Manual* (Philadelphia: Moss & Company, 1878), 291-292.

32. Grosh, *The Odd Fellows Manual*, 33.

33. Stillson, *Official History of Odd Fellowship*, 546–547.

34. Stillson, *Official History of Odd Fellowship*, 547–548.

35. Stillson, *Official History of Odd Fellowship*, 548–549.

36. Stillson, *Official History of Odd Fellowship*, 549–550.

37. Stillson, *Official History of Odd Fellowship*, 552.

38. Adin Steinsaltz, Tzvi Hersh Weinreb, Shalom Zvi Berger,Joshua Schreier. *Koren Talmud Bavli* (Jerusalem: Shefa Foundation, 2016), Volume 27 (Bava Batra Part One, 14A), pp. 76–77.

39. Stillson, *Official History of Odd Fellowship*, 684–688.

40. Sovereign Grand Lodge, *Journal of Proceedings of the Sovereign Grand Lodge, I.O.O.F.* (1923), 345–352.

41. Sovereign Grand Lodge, *Journal of Proceedings of the Sovereign Grand Lodge, I.O.O.F.* (1929), 371–377.

42. Sovereign Grand Lodge, *Journal of Proceedings of the Sovereign Grand Lodge, I.O.O.F.* (1929), 318.

43. Sovereign Grand Lodge, *Journal of Proceedings of the Sovereign Grand Lodge, I.O.O.F.* (2002), 363–369.

44. "Open Convention of Samaritans," *The Ottawa Journal*, May 9, 1936, 23.

45. Arthur Preuss, *A Dictionary of Secret and Other Societies* (St. Louis: B. Herder Book Co., 1924), 386–387.

46. Preuss, *A Dictionary of Secret and Other Societies*, 387–388.

47. Preuss, *A Dictionary of Secret and Other Societies*, 178.

48. "Initiation is Held by Pythian Knights," *The Atlanta Constitution*, March 11, 1916, 10.

49. "Oakland Cabiri and Perfection Orders Combine," *The Oakland Tribune*, April 25, 1925, 6.

50. "Form New I.O.O.F. Order," *The Kansas City Kansan*, September 18, 1921, 1.

51. "Open Convention of Samaritans," *The Ottawa Journal*, May 9, 1936, 23.

52. "Muscovites and Samaritans to Form Alliance," *The Evening Herald*, May 27, 1926, 12.

53. Preuss, *A Dictionary of Secret and Other Societies*, 387.

54. "Samaritans to Hold Annual Convention in California," *Schenectady Gazette*, July 14, 1954, 7.

55. William B. Melish, *The History of the Imperial Council, Ancient Arabic Order, Nobles of the Mystic Shrine for North America, 1872-1921*, 2nd ed. (Cincinnati: The Abingdon Press, 1921), 15.

56. Barbara Watterson, *The Egyptians, The Peoples of Africa* (Oxford: Blackwell Publishers Ltd, 1997), 63.

57. Farrin Chwalkowsi, *Symbols in Arts, Religion and Culture: The Soul of Nature* (Newcastle upon Tyne: Cambridge Scholars Publishing, 2016), 85.

58. "National Royal Zuanna Built by Vision of Syracuse Women," *Syracuse Herald*, August 13, 1925, 4.

59. State of New York, Office of Secretary of State, *Articles of Incorporation, Supreme Royal Zuanna of the Mystic Degrees of Persecution and Purification Ladies of the Orient of the United States and Canada, Inc.* Albany: April 25, 1921.

60. Apollodorus, *Library Apollod*, 3.5.8.

# IMAGE SOURCE CITATIONS

*CHAPTER I*

"Meeting Night of the Club of Odd Fellows," Bentley & Co. etched by Barlow, 1789, *Library of Congress Prints and Drawings Online Catalog, Accessed April 14, 2020,* https://www.loc.gov/item/2006690656/

"Chart Showing the Larger and More Prominent English and American Orders of Odd Fellows." Cyclopaedia of Fraternities, ed. Albert Clark Stevens, Hamilton Printing and Publishing Company, 1899, page 249, Accessed April 14, 2020 https://www.google.com/books/edition/The_Cyclopædia_of_Fraternities/1-KEAAAAIAAJ?hl=en&gbpv=0 (edited, Heilich)

"Seven Stars Tavern," Odd Fellowship: Its History and Manual, Theo Ross, The M.W. Hazen co, New York, 1888, page 13, Accessed April 14, 2020. https://archive.org/details/oddfellowshipit01rossgoog/page/n33/mode/2up

"The Founders of Odd Fellowship in America," The Henderson, Achert, Krebs, Litho Co., 1891, *Library of Congress Prints and Drawings Online Catalog, Accessed April 14, 2020,* https://www.loc.gov/item/2018696007/ (edited, Heilich)

"Charter Washington Lodge No. 1," February 1, 1820, on display in the Sovereign Grand Lodge, IOOF, Winston-Salem, NC.

"Dispensation to Charter the Grand Lodge of US," Odd Fellowship: Its History and Manual, Theo Ross, The M.W. Hazen Co, New York, 1888, page 30.5, Accessed April 14, 2020. https://archive.org/details/oddfellowshipit01rossgoog/page/n55/mode/2up

"The Independent Order of Odd Fellows Arms," John Douglass, 1832, *Library of Congress Prints and Drawings Online Catalog, Accessed April 14, 2020,* https://www.loc.gov/item/2004670518/

"Truth," found ephemera image, unattributed source.

*CHAPTER II*

"Hoodwinks," Henderson-Ames Company, IOOF Catalogue No. 12, page 60

*CHAPTER III*
"Venerable Warden Visits the Widow and Orphans," Odd Fellowship
Illustrated, Tal P Shaffner PGRep KY, Russell Brothers
Publishers, New York, 1877, page 172.
Inside Conductor, M.C. Lilley & Co. Catalog No. 201

*CHAPTER IV*
"Our Emblematic Odd Fellowship," Adams Company, 1907, *Library
of Congress Prints and Drawings Online Catalog*, Accessed
*May 19, 2020*, https://www.loc.gov/item/2018696028/
"An Initiatory Scene in an Odd Fellow's Lodge," Dr. E. Willis, 1846,
unattributed source.
Hoodwinks from Catalog, M.C. Lilley & Co. Catalog No. 201
"The Oddfellows Pictorial Guide. Friendship, Love, Truth," Hildreth,
Young, & Co., 1878, *Library of Congress Prints and Drawings
Online Catalog*, Accessed *May 19, 2020*, https://www.loc.gov/
item/2018696003/

*CHAPTER V*
Application, The Sovereign Grand Lodge, IOOF
Withdrawal Certificate, The Sovereign Grand Lodge, IOOF, 1939,
Western Kentucky University Kentucky Museum Library Special
Collections, Accessed November 27, 2020, https://western
kentuckyuniversity.pastperfectonline.com/archive/ED35D40D
-B57F-45B6-A3B3-137099438865

*CHAPTER VI*
"Washington Lodge no. 1. I.O.O.F. Baltimore, MD," C. W. Sherwood,
Union Lith. Co., Chicago, 1877, Accessed November 27, 2020,
https://www.loc.gov/resource/ppmsca.45338/
Old Illinois Password Cipher, The Grand Lodge of Illinois, IOOF,
1929
Sheet Music, from catalog WM. H. Horstman Co. no. 8
Order of Visitors; Grand Lodge of Illinois Manual of Instruction
Chart of Parliamentary Procedures, Nick Price, Board Effect,
Accessed August 13, 2020, https://www.boardeffect.com/blog/
roberts-rules-of-order-cheat-sheet/
Catalog Degree Team, Henderson-Ames Company, IOOF Catalogue
No. 12, pg. 124
MC Lilley Degree Banner, M.C. Lilley & Co. Catalog No. 201

*CHAPTER VIII*
Chart of Subordinate Lodge Jewels, The Triple Links or Odd
Fellowship Exemplified, B.M. Powell, Moore & Son, Topeka,
KS, 1900, plate page 68.5

## CHAPTER XI
Books and Blanks, Henderson-Ames Company, IOOF Catalogue No. 12, pg.81

## CHAPTER XIII
"Entrance to Odd Fellows Hall, Meriden, Connecticut," Russell Lee, 1939, *Library of Congress Prints and Drawings Online Catalog*, Accessed August 4, 2020, https://www.loc.gov/item/2017741085/

First Odd Fellows Rebekah Rose Float 1908, Odd Fellows-Rebekahs Rose Float Accessed November 23, 2020, http://oddfellows-rebekahs-rosefloat.org/History/1908.html

## CHAPTER XVII
Chart of Grand Lodge Officer Jewels, The Triple Links or Odd Fellowship Exemplified, B.M. Powell, Moore & Son, Topeka, KS, 1900, plate page 248.5

"Grand Lodge Secretaries in the United States IOOF," Henderson-Ames Co., Kalamazoo, MI, 1902, *Library of Congress Prints and Drawings Online Catalog*, Accessed January 19, 2021, https://www.loc.gov/item/2018696848/

## CHAPTER XVIII
Sovereign Grand Master Jewel, The Triple Links or Odd Fellowship Exemplified, B.M. Powell, Moore & Son, Topeka, KS, 1900, plate page 268.5

## CHAPTER XX
M.C. Lilley Full Chart, M.C. Lilley & Co. Catalog No. 201
M.C. Lilley Initiatory Banner, M.C. Lilley & Co. Catalog No. 201
M.C. Lilley First Degree Banner, M.C. Lilley & Co. Catalog No. 201
Fasces, Odd Fellowship Illustrated by Tal P Shaffner, PGRep KY, 1877
M.C. Lilley Second Degree Banner, M.C. Lilley & Co. Catalog No. 201
M.C. Lilley Third Degree Banner, M.C. Lilley & Co. Catalog No. 201
Globe and Clouds, Odd Fellowship Illustrated, Tal P Shaffner PGRep KY, Russell Brothers Publishers, New York, 1877, page 184
Bow and Quiver, Odd Fellowship Illustrated, Tal P Shaffner PGRep KY, Russell Brothers Publishers, New York, 1877, page 193
Three Arrows, Odd Fellowship Illustrated, Tal P Shaffner PGRep KY, Russell Brothers Publishers, New York, 1877, page 193
Lamb, Odd Fellowship Illustrated, Tal P Shaffner PGRep KY, Russell Brothers Publishers, New York, 1877, page 186
The Sun, public domain clipart

Rainbow, Odd Fellowship Illustrated, Tal P Shaffner PGRep KY, Russell Brothers Publishers, New York, 1877, page 191

Moses Rod, Odd Fellowship Illustrated, Tal P Shaffner PGRep KY, Russell Brothers Publishers, New York, 1877, page 205

Noah Ark, public domain clipart

Aaron Rod, Odd Fellowship Illustrated, Tal P Shaffner PGRep KY, Russell Brothers Publishers, New York, 1877, page 226

Cornucopia, public domain clipart

## CHAPTER XXI

"Rebekah Degree of Odd Fellowship," Geo. H. Walker & Co., *Library of Congress Prints and Drawings Online Catalog, Accessed November 24, 2020,* https://www.loc.gov/resource/pga.02989/

Encampment Degree Chart, The Triple Links or Odd Fellowship Exemplified, B.M. Powell, Moore & Son, Topeka, KS, 1900, plate pg 224.5

Patriarchs Militant Uniform, CE Ward, PM and LAPM Catalog from 1950s

All emblems and logos are the property of their respective organizations.

# GLOSSARY

**Alarm:** A signal given at the outer or inner doors of a **lodge room** indicating that a member desires to enter.

**Annual Term Report:** Report filed annually by lodges, typically containing a roster of current lodge members, noting any additions or subtraction, names and contact information for lodge officers, and also providing financial data. Also referred to as an "Annual Per Capita Report."

**Annual Traveling Password:** A password selected each year by the Sovereign Grand Master allowing Odd Fellows traveling between **jurisdictions** to help prove their membership in the Order.

**Anteroom:** The outer room leading into the **lodge room**. It is traditionally guarded by the Outside Guardian and typically contains **regalia** for members to put on before entering the lodge room itself.

**Arrearage:** The state of being behind on the payment of dues. If a member is behind they are said to be "in arrears."

**Arresting a charter:** The process by which a charter-granting body such as a Grand Lodge temporarily or permanently revokes the charter from the subordinate body. Also referred to as "suspending" or "pulling" a charter.

**Associate Membership:** A form of membership allowing a member who already has a **home lodge** to join an additional lodge. Joining a lodge in this manner is referred to as "admission by association."

**Bill:** Legislation drafted to add, strike, or amend parts of the codes of law.

**By-Laws:** A collection of rules and procedures governing how an organization operates. In contrast to a **constitution**, they are often lengthy and specific and may be modified relatively easily. In contrast to **standing rules**, they usually require a two-thirds majority to adopt or modify and may not be suspended.

**Calling up the lodge:** Signaling the members of a lodge to stand during a meeting. This is usually done by the Noble Grand or whomever is **chairing** the meeting.

**Chairperson:** The primary individual responsible for convening a committee and facilitating the flow of decision making on the committee. Typically, the first member named when the committee is appointed is the chair unless otherwise specified.

**Charge:** A speech given by an officer during a degree or other ceremony. Alternatively, accusations of wrongdoing against a member in the course of a trial, the presentation of which is referred to as "bringing charges" or "preferring charges" against the member.

**Charge Book:** The book issued by Sovereign Grand Lodge which includes all the degree work and other ceremonies performed by a lodge. Generally, only the smaller editions are referred to as "charge books."

**Charter:** A document issued by a Grand Lodge or Sovereign Grand Lodge establishing and authorizing a new **local lodge**.

**Charter Member:** A member who has belonged to a new lodge since the time of its institution. This is considered a great honor, as the names of these individuals are usually listed on the **charter** itself.

**Chevalier Degree:** See **Patriarchs Militant Degree**.

**Closed Installation:** An installation of officers held during a closed meeting and only open to members of the lodge. During a closed installation, **signs**, passwords, and other **secret work** are utilized since all present are entitled to make use of them.

**Closing Ode:** A song sung by the members of the lodge during the closing ceremony of a lodge.

**Closing Prayer:** A prayer recited by the Chaplain during the closing ceremony of a lodge.

**Code:** The legal documents governing Odd Fellowship on a Grand Lodge or Sovereign Grand Lodge level. May include **Constitutions, By-Laws,** or any other legal documents issued by these bodies.

**Collar:** **Regalia** traditionally worn in an Odd Fellows lodge, consisting of a ring of cloth draped around the neck. The color and emblems on the collar are indicative of rank within the Order.

**Collation:** A light meal or other refreshments served in conjunction with a meeting or other event.

**Commission:** A document presented by an officer to a deputy indicating delegated authority of the affairs of the Order. The most common example of this is the commission presented by a Grand Master to each of their District Deputy Grand Masters granting authority over the district.

**Constitution:** A legal document outlining the fundamental purpose and basic governing procedures of an organization. In contrast to **by-laws**, they are often concise and general, but more difficult to modify.

**Death Benefit:** A form of pecuniary or financial assistance provided to the heirs of a deceased member to assist with funeral costs or other needs arising as a result of their passing. These benefits were once commonplace among Odd Fellows lodges but are far less so today.

**Degree of Friendship:** The First Degree of Odd Fellowship conferred following the **Initiatory Degree**. It retells the Biblical story of David and Jonathan, setting it forth as an exemplar of the virtue of Friendship.

**Degree of Love:** The Second Degree of Odd Fellowship conferred following the **Initiatory Degree**. It is drawn from the New Testament parable of the Good Samaritan, an exemplar of the virtue of Brotherly Love. In earlier times, this degree told the story of Moses leading the Israelites during the Exodus from Egypt.

**Degree of Truth:** The Third Degree of Odd Fellowship conferred following the **Initiatory Degree**. In it, the candidate is introduced to a series of symbols that betoken the inner nature of what must be grappled with as men, women, and Odd Fellows. This is the highest degree conferred by an Odd Fellows lodge.

**Degree Password:** A password specific to each degree of Odd Fellowship. They are used when opening the lodge in that degree or in **working into the lodge** subsequent to opening.

**Degree Rally:** An event at which multiple degrees are conferred in one day, often on a large class of candidates. Also referred to as a **One-Day Class** or alternatively as a "Three Degree Day" if it only consists of the **Three Degrees**, omitting the **Initiatory Degree**.

**Deposit of Card:** A method of transferring from one lodge to another by receiving a **withdrawal card** from the original lodge and later depositing it with the new lodge.

**Desk Office:** A collective term referring to the officers of a lodge who perform administrative work. In a **local lodge** this includes the Secretary, Financial Secretary, and Treasurer.

**Dinner Installation:** A form of installation used in some **jurisdictions** which takes place seated around a table in the context of a meal.

**Dismissal Certificate:** A document provided to a member indicating their membership in a lodge has terminated. It may be used as proof of rank within the Order but not as proof of being a member **in good standing**.

**Dispensation:** A written communication from a District Deputy Grand Master, **Special Deputy**, Grand Master, or the Sovereign Grand Master allowing a lodge to hold a public installation, install a member who doesn't have the required service in other offices, or perform another designated action which would otherwise not be permitted. No dispensation may be granted unless it is specifically provided for in the legal codes of the Order. Also refers to the document issued prior to a **charter** allowing a new unit to begin operating immediately following institution.

**Dues Card:** An official card showing that the member has paid dues through a specified time period. May be used as proof of being a member **in good standing** as well as of rank within the Order. Also referred to as an "official card or certificate."

**Electioneering:** The prohibited practice of publicly promoting specific candidates for office within the Order. In some **jurisdictions** this term may also be applied to publicly promoting legislation outside of official channels for debate and discussion.

**Escort:** The procedure of formally conducting an officer or member from one place to another during a meeting. In a **local lodge**, it is normally performed by the Warden or Conductor. Also refers to the process of carrying in a flag or flags.

**Examination:** A test in the **secret work** of the Order administered to a visitor to verify what degrees they have attained within Odd Fellowship. Often performed by a committee appointed specifically for this purpose.

**Ex-officio:** A member of a committee "by virtue of their office." An ex-officio member is a member simply due to another office held, such as Noble Grand or Vice Grand, and has all the same rights and privileges as any other member of the committee unless otherwise specified.

**Expulsion:** The removal of an individual from membership within a <u>local lodge</u> or other body of the Order. It requires due process and may only be subsequently revoked by the body which expelled the member.

**First Degree:** See <u>Degree of Friendship</u>.

**Floor:** In a parliamentary sense, whatever proposition is currently on the "floor" is under active consideration by the body. Alternatively, it refers to the physical floor of the <u>lodge room</u>, namely the open space in the center of the room, which is typically surrounded by seating.

**Floorwork:** Prescribed movement around the <u>lodge room</u> occurring during a ceremony or meeting.

**Gavel:** A small mallet used by the presiding officer to call for order or as prescribed in the ceremonies of the Order.

**Golden Rule Degree:** The second degree conferred by an Encampment. It teaches toleration of differences.

**Good Standing:** Free from any indebtedness to the lodge, including being paid up on <u>dues</u>. Being in good standing also requires not being under suspension and that the lodge and <u>jurisdiction</u> the individual belongs to are also in good standing. Only members in good standing may vote, hold office, or visit other lodges.

**Grand Lodge Room:** See <u>lodge room</u>.

**Hall Association:** A separate legal entity formed by one or more lodges to hold and manage a lodge hall. May also be referred to as a "building association," "temple association," or "temple board," depending on the jurisdiction.

**Home Lodge:** The lodge in which a member pays <u>per capita</u>, as opposed to a lodge where they hold <u>associate membership</u>. Also referred to as the member's "primary lodge."

**Honors of the Order:** A ceremonial procedure used to honor elected and past elected officers of grand bodies. When given to a District Deputy Grand Master, that officer is only entitled to receive them by virtue of the fact that they are the Grand Master's officially delegated representative. The procedure is considered part of the <u>secret work</u> of the Order and therefore may not be revealed publicly.

**Initiatory Degree:** The first degree conferred within an Odd Fellows lodge, by which a candidate becomes a member. It communicates the fundamentals of what it means to be an Odd Fellow.

**Initiatory Ode:** A song sung by the members during the **Initiatory Degree** to welcome the new initiates.

**Inner Door:** The door leading directly from the **anteroom** into the **lodge room**. It is guarded by the Inside Guardian under the direction of the Vice Grand.

**Installing Officer:** An individual playing a role in performing an installation. The officer parts correspond to the offices of a district or Grand Lodge and are most frequently performed by the District Deputy Grand Master and their staff.

**Interviewing Committee:** A committee selected to interview candidates for membership in the lodge and report back with a recommendation on whether to accept or reject the prospective member.

**Jewel:** A metal emblem worn to indicate office, rank, or achievement within the Order. May include emblems worn on **collars** as well as **pocket jewels**. When worn it constitutes official **regalia** and may be worn in lieu of a regular collar during a meeting when not occupying an official station.

**Joint Public Installation:** An installation which is open to the public in which more than one lodge is installed simultaneously, most frequently an Odd Fellows Lodge and a Rebekah Lodge.

**Jurisdiction:** The right to exercise official authority. Alternatively, a body holding said authority or the geographical region over which that body has been assigned authority.

**Life Membership:** A program established in many Grand Lodges allowing members to pay a one-time fee which is invested to provide for the member's dues in lieu of making regular payments every term.

**Line:** See **progressive line**.

**Line Office:** A collective term referring to the offices of a lodge which constitute the **progressive line**. In an Odd Fellows lodge this includes the Outside Guardian, Inside Guardian, Left Scene Supporter, Right Scene Supporter, Conductor, Warden, Vice Grand, Noble Grand, and Junior Past Grand. At the Grand Lodge level, it only includes the Grand Warden, Deputy Grand Master, Grand Master, and Junior Past Grand Master.

**Local Lodge:** A lodge serving a local community which is subordinate to a Grand Lodge or directly to Sovereign Grand Lodge. Historically, these lodges were referred to as "subordinate lodges," but this term is less common today.

**Lodge Room:** The physical room in which a lodge meeting takes place. In a standard configuration it is entered through an **anteroom** through the **inner door**.

**Members' Register:** A book containing information about the members of a lodge, including name, address, occupation, and initiation dates.

**Minutes:** The official record of what transpired during a meeting. Minutes are usually written by the Secretary or equivalent officer.

**Motion:** A formal proposal for a parliamentary body to take a particular action. If "passed" it is to be enacted and if "failed" it is rejected.

**Non-Contributing Membership:** A membership status in which those who have at least 40 years of membership or are over the age of 75 and have at least 10 years of membership may be exempted from paying **dues**.

**Notice of Arrears:** An official notice **sealed** and sent by the Financial Secretary to indicate that a member is in **arrears**. It is required prior to **suspending** a member for nonpayment of **dues** or other indebtedness to the lodge.

**Official Card or Certificate:** See **dues card**.

**One-Day Class:** See **Degree Rally**.

**Open Installation:** See **public installation**.

**Opening Ode:** A song sung by the members of the lodge during the opening ceremony of a lodge.

**Opening Prayer:** A prayer recited by the Chaplain or similar officer during the opening ceremony of a lodge.

**Order of Business:** A prescribed set of tasks comprising the agenda for a meeting. In an Odd Fellows lodge, it is considered suggestive, and the presiding officer may utilize it or call for business in any other order desired.

**Parliamentarian:** An expert on the rules of order who is called upon to assist the presiding officer in their duty to enforce them.

**Patriarchal Degree:** The first degree conferred by an Encampment. It focuses on the lesson of hospitality to the stranger and to the brother and sister alike.

**Patriarchs Militant Degree:** The single degree conferred by a canton of the Patriarchs Militant. Also referred to as the "Chevalier

Degree." It retells the story of Abraham's triumph in the Battle of the Vale of Siddim.

**Per Capita:** The annual payment a lodge remits to its **charter-granting** body, such as a Grand Lodge, for every member. Also referred to as a "per capita tax" or "per capita fee."

**Pocket Jewel:** A smaller version of a **jewel** usually worn on a nameplate, which is slipped into a jacket pocket or hung from a chain around the neck.

**Primary Lodge:** See **home lodge**.

**Principal Chair:** The station from which a presiding officer governs a meeting. In a **lodge room**, this is typically the station along the wall furthest from the **inner door**.

**Progressive Line:** A predefined order of elected or appointed offices through which an individual progresses.

**Proposition:** In a parliamentary sense, refers to a proposal for the body to take a particular course of action. Propositions are generally offered via a **motion**.

**Public Installation:** An installation of officers held during a **recess** or when no meeting is open. Unlike a **closed installation**, it is open to the general public in addition to members of the unit. During a public installation, no signs, passwords, or other **secret work** are utilized. Also referred to as an "open installation."

**Quorum:** A sufficient number of members to hold a legal meeting. In most cases, at the **local lodge** level, this requires five members, one of whom must be qualified to preside.

**Rebekah Degree:** The single degree conferred by a Rebekah Lodge. It retells the stories of a variety of different biblical heroines.

**Recess:** A temporary pause in the proceedings of a parliamentary body. It may take the form of a "controlled recess" in which everyone remains in their seats or a "full recess" in which everyone is free to get up and walk around or exit the room until the meeting is called back to order.

**Regalia:** A **collar**, **jewel**, or other item denoting rank, station, or achievement within the Order.

**Reinstatement:** The process of returning to active membership after having been **suspended** for nonpayment of dues or having resigned.

**Resolution:** Legislation drafted for proposing a course of action to be taken by the body.

**Ritual:** A collection of the ceremonies used within a lodge. Also contains some of the primary laws of the Order.

**Roll Call Vote:** A vote conducted verbally by calling the roll of members and giving each the opportunity to respond "aye" or "nay" individually. The vote of each member is recorded in the **minutes.**

**Royal Purple Degree:** The third and highest degree conferred by an Encampment. It conveys the idea of the journey of life and rest from that journey.

**Seal:** An embossed emblem attesting that a document has been officially sanctioned by the body issuing it.

**Seating the Lodge:** Signaling the members of a lodge or other unit that they may be seated during a meeting. This is usually done by the Noble Grand or whomever is **chairing** the meeting.

**Second Degree:** See **Degree of Love.**

**Secondary Lodge:** A lodge in which a member holds **associate membership,** as opposed to their **primary** or **home lodge** where they pay **per capita.**

**Secret Work:** The passwords, **signs,** and other degree-specific materials which are not committed to writing except in the official albums issued by Sovereign Grand Lodge. Individual members are tested on these materials before they are advanced to the subsequent degree. Also referred to as the "Unwritten Work."

**Sick Benefit:** A form of pecuniary or financial assistance provided to a sick member to assist with lost wages, medical costs, or other needs arising as a result of their illness. These benefits were once commonplace among Odd Fellows lodges but are far less so today.

**Sign:** A physical gesture used when opening in a degree or addressing the **principal chair** when entering or leaving the **lodge room** while a meeting is open in that degree. Signs are part of the **Secret Work** of the Order.

**Special Deputy:** An officer appointed by an elected officer, such as a Noble Grand, Grand Master, or Sovereign Grand Master, to whom is delegated some of the authority of the elected officer. This is most common with Special Deputy Grand

Masters, who are dispatched by a Grand Master to perform an institution, observe or guide lodges experiencing difficulties, or **arrest a charter**.

**Special Meeting**: A meeting called for a specific, pre-defined purpose. This is in contrast to a regular meeting, which occurs at a fixed interval and may include any business that may properly come before the body.

**Sponsor**: An existing lodge member who vouches for an applicant for membership in a lodge.

**Standing Rules**: A collection of rules and procedures governing how an organization operates. In contrast to **by-laws**, they may be adopted, modified, or suspended by a simple majority vote.

**Subcommittee**: A subset of members of a committee charged with a more specific task than the committee as a whole.

**Suspension**: Temporary removal from the rights and privileges of membership, most frequently due to nonpayment of **dues**.

**Teller**: An individual assigned to assist in counting votes in an election. Often, tellers are selected by each of the candidates for office, to ensure a fair counting process.

**Term Password**: A password specific to a **jurisdiction**, selected each year by the jurisdictional head of that branch of the Order, such as the Grand Master for Odd Fellows lodges. This password is required for admittance to a meeting of the lodge.

**Third Degree**: See **Degree of Truth**.

**Three Degrees**: The three degrees of Odd Fellowship conferred subsequently to the **Initiatory Degree.** They are drawn from the Bible and must be completed prior to holding office in the lodge or joining appendant bodies under the authority of Sovereign Grand Lodge.

**Three Links**: The primary symbol and emblem of Odd Fellowship. The links represent the fundamental principles of Odd Fellowship: Friendship, Love, and Truth. The term may also be used to refer to the principles themselves.

**Transfer**: The process by which a member changes their **home lodge**.

**Transfer Certificate**: A document provided by the Secretary of the unit a member is **transferring** from to the unit they are transferring to, as a necessary step in enacting the transfer.

**Unanimous Consent:** A method of approving a non-controversial **proposition** by asking whether anyone objects. If there are no objections, the proposition is approved by unanimous consent.

**Valediction:** A brief statement of the values and beliefs held by Odd Fellowship. It is recited by the members when closing a lodge.

**Visitor's Book:** A book containing a record of all visitors to a lodge, including name, date visited, and **home lodge**.

**Voice Vote:** A vote conducted verbally by calling for "ayes" and "nays" in turn. All members voting respond in unison when their preferred voting option is called for.

**Warrant:** A document indicating that a lodge has voted to approve an expense, typically signed by the Noble Grand and the Secretary. It authorizes the Treasurer to pay the bill in question.

**Wicket:** A small opening in the **inner door** which can be opened to ascertain who is requesting admittance.

**Withdrawal Card:** A document indicating that a member has withdrawn from membership in their lodge. It may be deposited with another lodge that they wish to have as their new **home lodge**. It may also serve as proof of rank within the Order.

**Working into the Lodge:** The procedure by which a member gains admittance to a lodge after it is open.

# MICHAEL GREENZEIGER

Michael P.F. Greenzeiger is the Grand Master of the Jurisdiction of California (2021-2022), and presently holds a seat on the Board of Directors of the Historical Society for American Fraternalism.

He has been an Odd Fellow for nearly two decades, and during that time he has helped to build three successful lodges within the Order, and has brought in numerous younger members.

His Fraternal career began in High School with the Order of the Arrow, and he has been involved with multifarious other fraternal orders over the years.

Michael has made a historical study of the evolution of the symbolism in Odd Fellows ritual in particular. He brings a keen insight into the symbolism used by fraternal orders in their regalia and degree work.

By day, Michael works as a Data Scientist in the high tech field. He received a B.S. in Computer Science and a B.S. in Psychology from the University of Massachusetts Amherst as well as a M.S. in Neuroscience from Brandeis University. He is originally from the State of Massachusetts but presently resides in California with his wife and two children.

# AINSLIE HEILICH

Ainslie is an award-winning tattoo artist by trade and owner of Vintage Karma in Tuscola, IL.

Ainslie was always the kid in school who spent time drawing instead of taking notes. They weren't just random doodles, though; it was all part of what would become a 500-page comic book. This obsessive focus is now put into every tattoo he does. After earning an art degree from Virginia Commonwealth University, Ainslie began tattooing in 2004, and he founded Vintage Karma in 2007.

He is an Odd Fellow and founding member and Past Grand of Tuscola #316, which is right above the tattoo studio. Ainslie is also a member of Owl Creek Rebekah #91, Champaign Encampment #68, and Zonar Canton #18, all of Fisher, IL. He is also on the Grand Lodge of IL IOOF Web Committee and the Sovereign Grand Lodge Communications Committee and built and maintains their websites and social media, is a founder of the "Heart in Hand: The Modern Odd Fellow's Guide" blog, and is a co-host of "The Three Links Odd Cast" podcast.

When he is not tattooing or Odd Fellowing he maintains the official website and social media for his childhood hero, guitarist G.E. Smith.